Quantum Computing and Blockchain in Business

Exploring the applications, challenges, and collision of quantum computing and blockchain

Arunkumar Krishnakumar

BIRMINGHAM - MUMBAI

Quantum Computing and Blockchain in Business

Producers: Andrew Waldron, Jonathan Malysiak
Acquisition Editor – Peer Reviews: Suresh Jain
Project Editor: Tom Jacob
Content Development Editor: Dr. Ian Hough
Technical Editor: Karan Sonawane
Copy Editor: Safis Editing
Proofreader: Safis Editing
Indexer: Tejal Soni
Presentation Designer: Pranit Padwal

First published: March 2020

Production reference: 1310320

Published by Packt Publishing Ltd.
Livery Place
35 Livery Street
Birmingham B3 2PB, UK.

ISBN: 978-1-83864-776-6

www.packt.com

I would like to dedicate this book to the four wonderful ladies that rule my life.

My mother who inspires and supports me unconditionally. My two little princesses, Dhwani and Diya. They have been really patient, every time I got in to my little den to write this book.

Most of all, my dear wife Sumi, who has been the bedrock of my life and career!

`packt.com`

Subscribe to our online digital library for full access to over 7,000 books and videos, as well as industry leading tools to help you plan your personal development and advance your career. For more information, please visit our website.

Why subscribe?

- Spend less time learning and more time coding with practical eBooks and Videos from over 4,000 industry professionals

- Learn better with Skill Plans built especially for you

- Get a free eBook or video every month

- Fully searchable for easy access to vital information

- Copy and paste, print, and bookmark content

Did you know that Packt offers eBook versions of every book published, with PDF and ePub files available? You can upgrade to the eBook version at `www.Packt.com` and as a print book customer, you are entitled to a discount on the eBook copy. Get in touch with us at `customercare@packtpub.com` for more details.

At `www.Packt.com`, you can also read a collection of free technical articles, sign up for a range of free newsletters, and receive exclusive discounts and offers on Packt books and eBooks.

Contributors

About the author

Arunkumar Krishnakumar is an Investor at Green Shores Capital, a Venture Capital firm focusing on Deep Tech and Diversity. Arun and his team have made over 18 investments over the last four years. Arun sits on the board of four of his portfolio firms; the firms are either into AI, Data Science, or Blockchain. Arun is also on the board of trustees of Aram Foundation, an NGO in India focused on water conservation and environment initiatives.

Apart from his venture career, Arun is one of the top 100 Onalytica Fintech influencers. He is a podcast host and was a blogger on DailyFintech, which is the second most read Fintech blog in the world. Arun has contributed circa 150 blog posts over a period of 3 years at DailyFintech.

Prior to his career as a venture capital investor, Arun was working within capital markets data and technology at Barclays. He was also part of the leadership team within PwC's data analytics practice and was focused on banking and capital market clients.

> I would like to begin my acknowledgement with my beginning, my parents. I wouldn't be where I am in life and career if not for them.
>
> I would like to thank Packt and their amazing team for giving me this opportunity. It was a great experience working on this book. I would like to thank every single expert whom I have interviewed for this book. Their insights have been invaluable in getting the book to what it is.
>
> Most of all, I would like to thank all innovators. You keep me excited, yet grounded. You help me see the future, yet keep me mindful of present challenges. Most of all, you give me hope!

About the reviewer

David F. Beach is an American Technology Evangelist with over 15 years of experience in large-scale technology transformations for global enterprises and governments. With an undergraduate degree in Engineering, he finished his PhD in Physics with focus in Nano-Optics at the University of Basel, followed by Postdoctoral appointment at University of California, Los Angeles (UCLA). He has since been dedicated to helping global enterprises and governments through their technology transformation journey including IT, cloud, quantum computing, Data Science, security, and most recently artificial intelligence. He is also an advocate of other topics such as history and psychology.

In 2012 he launched QuantumBits.IT as a consulting platform on quantum computing, and in 2015 CentCom.Cloud delivering a single platform for a variety of tools used in global technology infrastructure. He is currently with Accenture Technology and previously worked at Oracle.

I would like to send my sincere gratitude to my mother as my true supporter in various stages of my life. Further thanks go to former teachers and colleagues whose ideas and feedback have helped shaping my ideals and goals.

Table of Contents

Preface

The book offers a glimpse of the future in the sense of how different industries could benefit from the new wave of computing. The book takes readers on a journey, starting by describing the limitations of today's computers, and laying out the possible solutions presented by quantum computing to go beyond those limits.

Who this book is for

This book is for professionals who would like to understand the potential applications of quantum computing in industrial scenarios. Readers who are looking for the "so what" of the technology, rather than get too deep into the technology itself, will find it an interesting read.

The book is also meant to address innovators across the world who are worried or curious about the potential collision course between today's cryptography algorithms and quantum computing. The book brings views from various industry experts in the fields of quantum computing, cryptography, and machine learning.

Readers will get a practical, realistic, and on-the-ground view of the potential of quantum computing. The book is not meant for readers who are looking to for a primer or textbook in the Math or Physics behind quantum computers, but rather those who wish to take a more business-focused perspective on the topic.

What this book covers

Chapter 1: Introduction to Quantum Computing and Blockchain

This is the first chapter of this book, where I touch upon the technological concepts that quantum computing and Blockchain are based on. This chapter also provides a brief history of the field of quantum physics over the last century, and how this led to the evolution of quantum computing.

Chapter 2: Quantum Computing – Key Discussion Points

This chapter discusses quantum computing terminology and key concepts in greater detail. The purpose of this chapter is to provide the readers an overview of the terms they will see through the rest of this book.

Chapter 3: The Data Economy

We live in a data era. Over the last 30 years the internet and the social media boom has helped create a lot of data. This has in turn helped fuel technologies like AI that are reliant on such data. We look at the role that data technologies like AI, Blockchain, IoT, and quantum computing could play in our everyday lives.

Chapter 4: The Impact on Financial Services

Financial services is a data-intensive industry. Most financial decisions around portfolio management and risk management are heavily reliant on simulations used by financial institutions. This chapter covers the potential applications of quantum computing on financial services.

Chapter 5: Interview with Dr. Dave Snelling, Fujitsu Fellow

An interview with Dave Snelling, the Program Director of AI at Fujitsu and one of the key stakeholders behind their Digital Annealer. Dave brings to life the applications of digital annealers that he is already working on, and the potential future he sees for quantum computers.

Chapter 6: The Impact on Healthcare and Pharma

This chapter brings to life applications of quantum computing in the field of healthcare and pharmaceuticals. Drug discovery is one of the key areas where the quantum computing could make a big difference. There are applications of Blockchain in the pharma industry that I discuss in this chapter too.

Chapter 7: Interview with Dr. B. Rajathilagam, Head of AI Research, Amrita Vishwa Vidyapeetham

The interview with Dr. B. Rajathilagam (BRT) gives us a view of the use cases for quantum computing and Blockchain in the emerging markets. BRT brings to fore her firsthand knowledge of the on-the-ground challenges for villages in India.

Chapter 8: The Impact on Governance

Elections are largely becoming testing grounds for AI and data science technologists. It could be a new future where election results could be accurately modeled using technologies such as quantum computing. This chapter explores the possibilities of the technology in future elections.

Chapter 9: Interview with Max Henderson, Senior Data Scientist, Rigetti and QxBranch

Max and his team at QxBranch modeled the 2016 American elections using quantum computing, and achieved a high degree of precision with their predictions. This interview covers Max's experience in doing so, his observations, and lessons learned from the process.

Chapter 10: The Impact on Smart Cities and Environment

We live in a world that is being affected by climate change and is in a climate emergency. This chapter looks at ways we could create smart cities using technology that can not only make our lives better, but can also help us to live more sustainably.

Chapter 11: Interview with Sam McArdle, Quantum Computing Researcher at the University of Oxford

One of the biggest challenges with quantum computers is the limited ability we have in correcting errors. In this chapter, I discuss these challenges with Sam McArdle, who is researching NISQ at Oxford University. Sam explains why error correction in quantum computers is such a hard task. He also touches upon the possibilities of using NISQ in fields like Chemistry.

Chapter 12: The Impact on Chemistry

Quantum computing is based on the principles of quantum mechanics that describes the behavior of sub-atomic particles. This is precisely why Chemistry is a very fitting application for quantum computers. In this chapter I discuss how quantum computers can be used to model the interactions between molecules during a chemical reaction.

Chapter 13: The Impact on Logistics

Logistics problems have been challenging for classical computers to solve. In this chapter I discuss how quantum computing can help solve some of the real-world problems in logistics. I also discuss the work firms like Airbus is doing to improve aerodynamics of their flights. On the Blockchain side, I explain the use of the technology within the supply chain and the efficiencies it can add to supply chains.

Chapter 14: Interview with Dinesh Nagarajan, Partner, IBM

Dinesh is a cyber security expert and a partner at IBM. In this chapter we discuss how technology innovation has helped enrich people's lives across the world and the cyber risks that it has brought to the table. We also discuss how firms and nation states can be more agile from a cryptographic perspective to face the threat posed by the new era in computing.

Chapter 15: Quantum-Safe Blockchain

In this chapter we talk about the elephant in the room. Is Blockchain under threat in a post quantum era? We take a step further to touch upon how data transmission on the internet could be at risk because of quantum computing. We also look at various cryptographic techniques that are quantum ready and how they can help us protect our data.

Chapter 16: Nation States and Cyberwars

What would a country do if it was equipped with a technology that can be used to take control of most encrypted data in the world? How close are we to getting to that reality? Is that even a possibility we should be prepared for? These are the questions I address in the chapter about nation states and their efforts to dominate the data technology world. Several billion dollars have been allocated for technologies such as AI, Blockchain, and quantum computing by countries that want to dominate this space.

Chapter 17: Conclusion – Blue Skies

A closure chapter summarizing the key takeaways from the book. I discuss the learning from the interviews and my thoughts on the comments from the experts I interviewed. I conclude with my views on the hype around quantum computing and how that could affect the direction of travel of the ecosystem. I note the efforts from top nations across the world to gain dominance in this space. I conclude by providing my views on the possibilities of this amazing technology – quantum computing.

Download the color images

We also provide a PDF file that has color images of the screenshots/diagrams used in this book. You can download it here: https://static.packt-cdn.com/downloads/9781838647766_ColorImages.pdf

Conventions used

Bold: Indicates a new term, an important word, or words that you see on the screen, for example, in menus or dialog boxes, also appear in the text like this. For example: "My professor Dr. B. Rajathilagam, who taught me about **Database Management Systems (DBMSes)** and **Object Oriented Programming** 20 years ago, is now leading AI and quantum machine learning research."

 Warnings or important notes appear like this.

Get in touch

Feedback from our readers is always welcome.

General feedback: If you have questions about any aspect of this book, mention the book title in the subject of your message and email us at customercare@packtpub.com.

Errata: Although we have taken every care to ensure the accuracy of our content, mistakes do happen. If you have found a mistake in this book we would be grateful if you would report this to us. Please visit, http://www.packt.com/submit-errata, selecting your book, clicking on the Errata Submission Form link, and entering the details.

Piracy: If you come across any illegal copies of our works in any form on the Internet, we would be grateful if you would provide us with the location address or website name. Please contact us at copyright@packt.com with a link to the material.

If you are interested in becoming an author: If there is a topic that you have expertise in and you are interested in either writing or contributing to a book, please visit http://authors.packtpub.com.

Reviews

Please leave a review. Once you have read and used this book, why not leave a review on the site that you purchased it from? Potential readers can then see and use your unbiased opinion to make purchase decisions, we at Packt can understand what you think about our products, and our authors can see your feedback on their book. Thank you!

For more information about Packt, please visit `packt.com`.

1
Introduction to Quantum Computing and Blockchain

It was the best of times, it was the worst of times,

it was the age of wisdom, it was the age of foolishness,

it was the epoch of belief, it was the epoch of incredulity,

it was the season of Light, it was the season of Darkness,

it was the spring of hope, it was the winter of despair.

I am sure Charles Dickens did not foresee quantum computing or Blockchain. His words from 160 years ago, however, still apply to the ebbs and flows we have seen with these two technologies. Quantum computing has been around for a good part of a century. In contrast, Blockchain was first introduced to the world in 2008.

Unlike the Blockchain wave that has hit us in recent years, quantum principles have been around for several decades. Quantum physics has been a very debated field and is fundamental to quantum computing. However, the field of quantum computing has gained momentum in recent times.

Despite the differences in the age of the two technologies, they have had interesting histories. For instance, most people who understand Blockchain agree that the framework is robust. However, the technology is still far from perfect, and that is true for quantum computing too.

The momentum behind quantum computing in the past decade has been largely due to advancements in algorithms and infrastructure. However, in my opinion, it is also because of the data age we live in, and some of the use cases for quantum computers are becoming clearer and relevant. In this chapter, I will cover the history of both these technologies that have had controversial pasts. Their place in modern society as transformational technologies is hard to dispute.

What this book does

The purpose of this book is to explore the overlaps between quantum computing and Blockchain. The two technologies are fundamentally based on cryptography. As a result, there is a possibility that they are on a collision course. However, when we look at the real-world applications of these technologies, they are quite complimentary to one another.

In this chapter, we will discuss technical concepts that are fundamental to quantum computing and Blockchain. We will delve into quantum computing and its history, and then touch upon some of the key concepts of Blockchain that are relevant to the thesis of the book.

One of the key themes that I would like to establish in this book is that *Technology is just a means to an end*. While it is important to understand it, and feel excited about the possibilities, a technology can only be special if it can make a difference to people's lives.

There is a lot of hype on social media that quantum computing would kill Blockchain. In a data age, both these technologies have a place. Quantum computing can vastly improve our problem-solving abilities. In a social media age, we will need our technologies to cope with big data volumes and understand the interdependencies between variables that we analyze. Quantum computing, when it goes mainstream, should address those areas.

On the other hand, a simple way to describe Blockchain's application is *Decentralized Data Integrity*. An immutable record of every transaction gets maintained and managed by the network. That is the fundamental advantage of Blockchain over data storage mechanisms we have used in the past.

Through industry-specific chapters and interviews with thought leaders in quantum computing, AI and machine learning, I will try to establish the business relevance of these two technologies. In doing so, I will establish that these two technologies have vertical synergies in a data centric world we live in.

In the next section, I will go through the history of quantum computing. In the process of doing that, I will also touch upon several key concepts of the technology.

An introduction to quantum computing

We are living through a data era, with several technologies sharing symbiotic relationships with each other. Of all the exciting technology paradigms, quantum computing has the potential to create disruption at scale. The principles of quantum physics, which are the bedrock of quantum computing, have been around for over a century.

An understanding of the evolution of quantum Physics is interesting because of the personalities involved and their contradicting philosophical views. However, the history of this field also gives us an insight into the counter intuitive nature of these concepts that challenged even the brightest minds. This chapter focuses on the story of quantum computing, and touches upon some of the basic principles of this technology.

The history of quantum mechanics

In a conversation between an investor and a professor in academia, the investor is often left thinking, "Wow, that is great, but so what?", and the academic is wondering, "Does the investor get it?". The exploration of quantum computing has been one such experience for me, where the nerd in me wanted to delve deep into the physics, math, and the technical aspects of the discipline. However, the investor in me kept on asking, "So what's of value? What's in it for the world? What's in it for businesses?".

As a result of this tug of war, I have come up with a simplified explanation of quantum principles that lays the foundations of quantum mechanics. For a better understanding of quantum computing, we need to first study the basics of quantum information processing with respect to the flow of (quantum) bits, and how they process data and interact with each other. Therefore, let us begin with the tenets of quantum physics as the basis of quantum information processing.

Quantum physics provides the foundational principles that explains the behavior of particles such as atoms, electrons, photons, and positrons. A microscopic particle is defined as a small piece of matter invisible to the naked human eye.

In the process of describing the history of quantum mechanics, I will touch upon several of its fundamental concepts. The discovery and the evolution in scientists' understanding of these concepts has helped shape more modern thinking around quantum computing. The relevance of these concepts to quantum computing will become clear as this chapter unravels. However, at this stage the focus is on how this complex field has continued to perplex great minds for almost 100 years.

Quantum mechanics deals with nature at the smallest scales; exploring interactions between atoms and subatomic particles. Throughout a good part of the 19th century and the early part of the 20th century, scientists were trying to solve the puzzling behavior of particles, matter, light, and color. An electron revolves around the nucleus of an atom, and when it absorbs a photon (a particle of light), it jumps into a different energy level. Ultraviolet rays could provide enough energy to *knock out* electrons from an atom, producing positive electrical charge due to the removal of the negatively charged electron. Source: `https://www.nobelprize.org/prizes/physics/1905/lenard/facts/`

Scientists observed that an electron absorbing a photon was often limited to specific frequencies. An electron absorbing a specific type of photon resulted in colors associated with heated gases. This behavior was explained in 1913 by Danish scientist Niels Bohr. Further research in this field led to the emergence of the basic principles of quantum mechanics. Source: `https://www.nobelprize.org/prizes/physics/1922/bohr/biographical/`

Bohr postulated that electrons were only allowed to revolve in certain orbits, and the colors that they absorbed depended on the difference between the orbits they revolved in. For this discovery, he was awarded the Nobel prize in 1922. More importantly, this helped to cement the idea that the behavior of electrons and atoms was different from that of objects that are visible to the human eye (macroscopic objects). Unlike classical physics, which defined the behavior of macroscopic objects, quantum mechanics involved instantaneous transitions based on probabilistic rules rather than exact mechanistic laws.

This formed the basis of further studies focused on the behavior and interaction of subatomic particles such as electrons. As research identified more differences between classical physics and quantum physics, it was broadly accepted that quantum principles could be used to define the idiosyncrasies of nature (for example: black holes). Two great minds, Albert Einstein and Stephen Hawkins, have contributed to this field through their work on relativity and quantum gravity. Let us now look into how Albert Einstein viewed quantum physics and its concepts. Source: `https://www.nobelprize.org/prizes/physics/1921/einstein/facts/`

Einstein's quantum troubles

We may have to go back some years in history to understand how Einstein got entangled (pun intended) in the world of quantum mechanics. For a layman, space is just vast emptiness, yet when combined with time, space becomes a four-dimensional puzzle that has proven to be a tremendous challenge to the greatest minds of the 19th and 20th centuries. There were principles of quantum mechanics that Einstein did not agree with, and he was vocal about it.

One of the key principles of quantum mechanics was *Copenhagen Interpretation*. This explains how the state of a particle is influenced by the fact that the state was observed; the observer thus influenced the state of the particle. Einstein did not agree with this indeterminate aspect of quantum mechanics that Niels Bohr postulated.

In 1927, Einstein began his debates with Bohr at the Solvay Conference in Brussels. He believed in objective reality that existed independent of observation. As per the principles of quantum theory, the experimenters' choice of methods affected whether certain parameters had definitive values or were fuzzy. Einstein couldn't accept that *the moon was not there when no one looked at it* and felt that the principles of quantum theory were incomplete. Source: `https://cp3.irmp.ucl.ac.be/~maltoni/PHY1222/mermin_moon.pdf`

One interesting aspect of this indeterministic nature of objects is that as babies, we tend to appreciate these principles better. This is illustrated in the peek-a-boo game that babies often love. They believe that the observer exists only when they observe them, and do not demonstrate the cognitive ability called *object permanence*. However, as we grow older, we base our actions on the assumption of object permanence.

Niels Bohr believed that it was meaningless to assign reality to the universe in the absence of observation. In the intervals between measurements, quantum systems existed as a fuzzy mixture of all possible properties – commonly known as *superposition states*. The mathematical function that described the states that particles took is called the *wave function*, which collapses to one state at the point of observation.

This philosophical battle between the two scientists (Einstein and Bohr) intensified in 1935 with the emergence of the property of *Entanglement*. It meant that the state of two entangled particles was dependent on each other (or had a correlation) irrespective of how far they were from each other. Einstein (mockingly) called it the *Spooky action at a distance*.

As a response to Bohr's findings, the infamous EPR (Einstein, Podolsky, Rosen) paper was written in 1935/36 by Albert Einstein, Boris Podolsky, and Nathan Rosen. The purpose of the paper was to argue that quantum mechanics fails to provide a complete description of physical reality. Podolsky was tasked with translating it to English, and Einstein was not happy with the translation. Apart from that, Podolsky also leaked an advance report of the EPR paper to the New York Times, and Einstein was so upset that he never spoke to Podolsky again. Source: `https://www.aps.org/publications/apsnews/200511/history.cfm`

The EPR paradox identified two possible explanations for the entanglement property. The state of one particle affecting another could potentially be due to shared, embedded properties within both particles, like a *gene*. Alternatively, the two particles could be making instantaneous communication with each other about their states. The second explanation was thought to be impossible, as this violated the theory of special relativity (if the particles were making instantaneous communication at faster than the speed of light) and the principle of locality.

> The principle of locality states that an object is influenced by only its immediate surroundings.
>
> The theory of special relativity states that the laws of physics are the same for all non-accelerating observers, and Einstein showed that the speed of light within a vacuum is the same no matter the speed at which an observer travels.

If entanglement existed, and if particles could influence *the state of each other* at a great distance, then the theory of locality was also considered to be breached. Hence, the EPR paper challenged the assumption that particles could communicate their states instantaneously and from a good distance.

Hence, the EPR concluded that the two entangled particles had hidden variables embedded in them, which gave them the information to choose correlated states when being observed. Albert Einstein continued to challenge the principles of quantum mechanics.

> *"Quantum mechanics is certainly imposing. But an inner voice tells me that it is not yet the real thing. The theory says a lot but does not really bring us any closer to the secret of the 'old one.' I, at any rate, am convinced that He does not throw dice."*
> *–Albert Einstein*

Einstein and Bohr could not come to an agreement, even in the presence of an arbitrator. This arbitrator came in the form of John Wheeler. In 1939, Bohr and Wheeler started working at Princeton University and shared a good working relationship. Wheeler was a pleasant persona and could speak German. Einstein – who was the professor in Exile at Princeton – became Wheeler's neighbor and there arose a possibility for these great minds to come together. Wheeler saw merits in Bohr's view on complementarity – where two particles could be entangled. He also agreed with Einstein's challenge to the theory that, *when we view particles, we unavoidably alter them*. Despite several attempts, John Wheeler did not manage to come up with a theory that convinced both Bohr and Einstein.

Bell's inequality

Following on from the likes of Einstein and Bohr, John Bell entered the arena of quantum in the latter half of the 20th century. He was born in Belfast in 1928, and after several years of flirting with theories of quantum mechanics, he finally chose to take the plunge in 1963 when he took a leave at Stanford University. He explained entanglement as the behavior of identical twins who were separated at the time of birth. If, after a lifetime, they were brought together, they would have surprising things in common. He had come across this in a study by the Institute for the Study of Twins. This led to the thought that perhaps electrons behaved like they had genes. At the minimum, it helped a layman understand what entanglement of quantum particles meant.

However, in 1964, Bell subsequently came up with Bell's inequality. Through a set of experiments on electrons and positron pairs, and probability theory, Bell proved that the conclusion of EPR was wrong. The assumption that particles had to have properties embedded in them to explain entanglement did not seem the right way forward after all. Bell's inequality was supported through several subsequent experiments. The probability explanation through Venn diagrams of Bell's inequality is simple. There is a simpler possible home experiment that can explain the spooky nature of quantum mechanics using a polarizing lens used on photons.

You can check out the YouTube video of the experiment here, `https://www.youtube.com/watch?v=zcqZHYo7ONs&t=887s`, and it does get quite counter-intuitive.

The video shows the following:

- Look at a white background through a polarized lens. It looks gray, indicating that a lot of light is being blocked from going through the lens.

- Add another polarized lens B, and you will observe less light coming through it – indicated by the background getting even darker.

- Now, by adding another polarized lens C on top of A and B, you would expect the white background to look even darker. But surprisingly, it looks brighter than with just A and B.

The results of the experiment can perhaps be explained by one possibility. What if the nature of the photon changes when it goes through one filter? This could mean the way the changed photon interacts with subsequent filters is different too.

I will explain another weird behavior of light particles (photons) using the Quantum Slit experiment later in this chapter. Currently, the behavior of subatomic particles is most clearly explained through the principles of quantum mechanics. If any new alternative is to be offered, it must be more convincing than the existing principles.

Quantum computers – a fancy idea

Whilst the theories underlying the behavior of particles in nature were being postulated, there were a few individuals who were starting to think about the implications of simulating these behaviors using classical computers. In 1965, the Nobel Prize in Physics was awarded jointly to Sin-Itiro Tomonaga, Julian Schwinger, and Richard P. Feynman *for their fundamental work in quantum electrodynamics, with deep-ploughing consequences for the physics of elementary particles.* It was in the 1980s that Richard Feynman first discussed the idea "*Can a classical computer simulate any physical system?*". He is considered to have laid the foundations of quantum computing through his lecture titled "*Simulating Physics with Computers.*"

In 1985, the British physicist David Deutsche highlighted the fact that Alan Turing's theoretical version of a universal computer could not be extended to quantum mechanics. You may ask what Turing's computer was.

In 1936, Alan Turing came up with a simple version of a computer called the Turing machine. It had a tape with several boxes, and bits coded into each one of them as "0"s and "1"s. His idea was that the machine would run above the tape, looking at one square at a time. The machine had a code book that had a set of rules, and, based on the rules, the states ("0"s and "1"s) of each of these boxes would be set. At the end of the process, the states of each of the boxes would provide the answer to the problem that the machine has solved. Many consider this to have laid the foundation for the computers we use today.

However, David Deutsche highlighted that Turing's theories were based on classical physics (0s and 1s), and a computer based on quantum physics would be more powerful than a classical computer.

Richard Feynman's idea started to see traction when Peter Shor of Bell Laboratories invented the algorithm to factor large numbers on the quantum computer. Using this algorithm, a quantum computer would be able to crack even recent cryptography techniques.

In 1996, this was followed by Grover's search algorithm. In a classical computer, when an item has to be searched in a list of N items, it needs, on average, N/2 checks to recover the item. However, with Grover's algorithm, the number of checks could be brought down to $\sqrt{N}$. In a database search, this offered a quadratic improvement to the search performance. This is considered a key milestone in the field of quantum computing.

Déjà vu

Grover's algorithm and subsequent work in this space have since accelerated the excitement and hype around quantum computing. More recently, tech giants IBM, Google, Intel, Microsoft, and a few others have ramped up their work in quantum computing. At CES 2019, IBM showed off their prowess through the launch of an integrated system for quantum computing for scientists and businesses. IBM also has a cloud-based quantum computing infrastructure that programmers could use. More on what the tech giants are up to will be revealed in *Chapter 16, Nation States and Cyberwars*.

When I first looked at the picture of IBM's quantum computer replica as revealed at CES 2019, my immediate thought was *Déjà vu*. The previous generation witnessed the rise of the classical computing revolution, with its far-reaching impacts upon all aspects of society. We stand on the brink of another revolution; we will be fortunate enough to see the evolution of quantum computing first-hand.

The weirdness of quantum

Before we explore quantum computing, it would be good to understand the behavior of particles as described by quantum mechanics. Below, I describe an experiment that helps us to understand the counter-intuitive nature of quantum theory.

A scary experiment

The famous Quantum Slit experiment describes the behavior of photons/particles and how they interact with each other and themselves. As we will see, this posed a challenge to physicists attempting to describe their behavior.

In the 19th century, a British scientist, Thomas Young, postulated that light particles traveled in waves, rather than as particles. He set up a simple experiment where he cut two slits on a piece of metal and placed it as a blocker between a light source and a screen. He knew that if light traveled in the same manner as particles, then the particles that passed through the slits would hit the screen. Those that were blocked by the metal would bounce off the surface and would not reach the screen. Effectively, if the light was made of particles, then the screen should look like a spray of paint on a stencil. *Figure 1* shows the experiment and the slit formation.

However, he assumed (before the experiment) that light was formed of waves, and the waves, when they passed through the slit, would interfere with one another and form patterns on the screen. The pattern would be defined based on how the waves passing through the slits interacted.

Where the waves interfered with each other (called constructive interference), the screen would display bright spots, and where peaks interfered with troughs (called destructive interference), they would form dark spots. Hence, the pattern would be slit shapes at the center followed by progressively darker slit shapes to the left and the right. Young successfully proved that light traveled in waves.

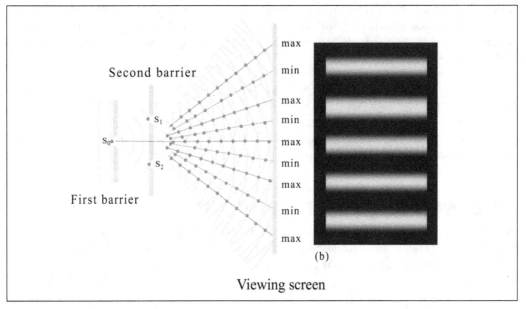

Figure 1: Young's double slit experiment

Einstein's photons – weirder now

Albert Einstein once more proved to be of great influence in the field of quantum mechanics. He proposed that light was made of photons – a discrete quantum of light that behaved like a particle. As a result, the experiment was repeated and this time, photons were passed through the slit one by one and the patterns still appeared. This could only happen if:

- Photons travelled in waveforms.
- All possible paths of these waveforms interfered with each other, even though only one of these paths could happen.

This supports the theory that all realities exist until the result is observed, and that subatomic particles can exist in superposition. As detectors were placed to observe photons passing through the slits, the patterns disappeared. This act of observation of particles collapses the realities into one.

We have discussed the three principles of quantum mechanics: superposition, entanglement, and interference. These principles are fundamental to the way in which particles are managed within a quantum computer.

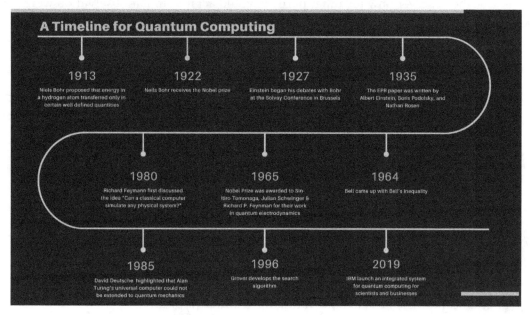

Figure 2: A quantum computing timeline

The history of quantum computing and the key milestones are captured in *Figure 2*. The key takeaway is the contributions made to the field that have brought this technology to the brink of achieving impact at scale.

Inside a quantum computer

Quantum computing has quantum bits called qubits (pronounced *cue-bit*) as their fundamental unit. In the classical computing world, bits take 0 and 1 states. Qubits exist in these two states, but also in a linear combination of both these states called superpositions.

Superpositions can solve some problems faster than the deterministic and probabilistic algorithms that we commonly use today. A key technical difference is that while probabilities must be positive (or zero), the weights in a superposition can be positive, negative, or even complex numbers.

The other important quantum mechanics principle that is fundamental to understanding quantum computers is **Entanglement**. Two particles are said to display entanglement if one of the two entangled particles behaves randomly and informs the observer how the other particle would act if a similar observation were made on it.

This property can be detected only when the two observers compare notes. The property of entanglement gives quantum computers extra processing powers and allows them to perform much faster than classical computers.

Quantum computers have similarities and differences compared to traditional transistors that classical computers use. Research in quantum computers is moving forward to find new forms of qubits and algorithms. For example, optical quantum computers using photons have seen significant progress in the research world since 2017. Optical quantum computers using photonic qubits work at room temperatures.

A quantum computer should satisfy the following requirements:

- Qubits need to be put into a superposition
- Qubits should be able to interact with each other
- Qubits should be able to store data and allow readout of the data

Quantum computers also demonstrate some features (typically):

- Tend to operate at low temperatures, and are very sensitive to environment/ noise
- Tend to have short lifetimes – the reasons are explained below

We encode qubit states into subatomic particles; electrons in the case of semiconductor quantum computers. There are several methods to create qubits and each method has advantages and disadvantages. The most common and stable type of qubits is created using a superconducting loop. A superconductor is different from a normal conductor because there is no energy dissipation (no resistance) as the current passes through the conductor. Superconductor circuits operate at close to absolute zero temperatures (that is, 0 Kelvin, or -273 degree Celsius) in order to maintain the states of their electrons.

Another qubit architecture where transistor-based classical circuits are used is called SQUIDs. SQUID stands for *Superconducting Quantum Interference Device*. They are used to track and measure weak signals. These signals need to only create changes in energy levels as much as 100 billion times weaker than the energy needed to move a compass needle. They are made of Josephson junctions. One of the key application areas for SQUIDs is in measuring magnetic fields for human brain imaging. Source: `https://whatis.techtarget.com/definition/superconducting-quantum-interference-device`

Superconducting qubits (in the form of SQUIDs) have pairs of electrons called Cooper pairs as their charge carriers. In this architecture, transistor-based classical circuits use voltage to manage electron behavior. In addition, a quantum electrical circuit is defined by a wave function. SQUIDs are termed artificial atoms, and in order to change the state of these atoms, lasers are used. As described earlier in this chapter, based on the principles of quantum mechanics, only light with specific frequency can change the state of subatomic particles. Therefore, lasers used to change the state of qubits will have to be tuned to the transition frequency of the qubits.

A superconducting qubit can be constructed from a simple circuit consisting of a capacitor, an inductor, and a microwave source to set the qubit in superposition. However, there are several improvements of this simple design, and the addition of a Josephson junction in the place of a common inductor is a major upgrade. Josephson junctions are non-linear inductors allowing the selection of the two lowest-energy levels from the non-equally spaced energy spectrum. These two levels form a qubit for quantum-information processing. This is an important criterion in the design of qubit circuits – a selection of the two lowest energy levels. Without the Josephson junction, the energy levels are equally spaced, and that is not practical for qubits. Source: `https://web.physics.ucsb.edu/~martinisgroup/classnotes/finland/LesHouchesJunctionPhysics.pdf`

Like the gate concept in classical computers, quantum computers also have gates. However, a quantum gate is reversible. A common quantum gate is the Hadamard (H) gate that acts on a single qubit and triggers the transition from its base state to a superposition.

Qubit types and properties

There are several variations of qubit circuits based on the properties here. The key properties that need consideration in the design of these circuits are:

- **Pulse time**: This is the time taken to put a qubit into superposition. The lower the pulse time, the better.

- **Dephasing time**: This is the time taken to decouple qubits from unwanted noise. The lower the dephasing time, the better. Higher dephasing times lead to a higher dissipation of information.

- **Error per gate**: As gates are used to create a transition in states of qubits when there is a faulty gate, the error can propagate onto qubits that were originally correct. Hence, error per gate needs to be measured regularly.

- **Decoherence time**: This is the time duration for which the state of the qubit can be maintained. Ionic qubits are the best for coherence times as they are known to hold state for several minutes.

- **Sensitivity to environment**: While semiconductor qubits operate in very low temperatures, the sensitivity of the particles involved in the construction of the circuit to the environment is important. If the circuit is sensitive to the environment, the information stored in the qubit is corrupted easily.

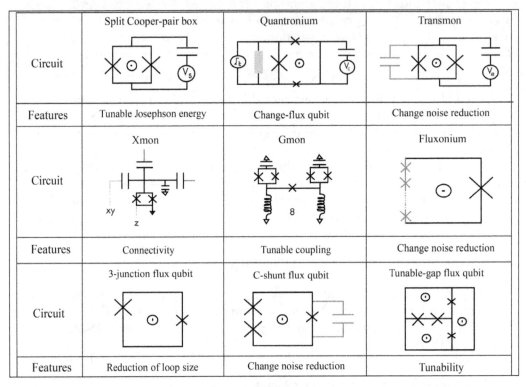

	Split Cooper-pair box	Quantronium	Transmon
Circuit			
Features	Tunable Josephson energy	Change-flux qubit	Change noise reduction
	Xmon	Gmon	Fluxonium
Circuit			
Features	Connectivity	Tunable coupling	Change noise reduction
	3-junction flux qubit	C-shunt flux qubit	Tunable-gap flux qubit
Circuit			
Features	Reduction of loop size	Change noise reduction	Tunability

Figure 3: Qubit circuits

IBM recently launched the 50-qubit machine, and also provides a cloud-hosted quantum infrastructure that programmers can go and code in. There are also several advances in quantum assembly language that will act as the interface between these machines and the code that developers write. *Figure 3* shows different qubit circuit types.

We've now covered the fundamentals of quantum computing, so let's move on to look at the other technology in focus for this book: Blockchain.

Blockchain and cryptography

Unlike quantum computing, Blockchain has had a relatively short history. If quantum computing is the Mo Farah of emerging technologies, Blockchain is the Usain Bolt. Several Blockchain properties have their roots in cryptography, and it is essential to understand some of the terminologies in order to be able to enjoy the rest of the chapter.

It is important to understand how Blockchain depends on cryptography. This would help us in subsequent chapters to understand how Blockchain and quantum computing could potentially collide in future. A detailed, yet simplified, description of some key terms of Blockchain and cryptography are as follows:

Hashing

Hashing is a process where a collection of data is input into a function to get a fixed length string as an output – called a hash value. We use them every day. When you create an email ID with a password, the password goes through a hash function, a unique string is created, and this is stored in the database of the email provider. When you try to log in again, the password entered is put through the hashing algorithm, and the resulting string is matched with the string stored in the data base of the email provider. If they match, you get to access your email.

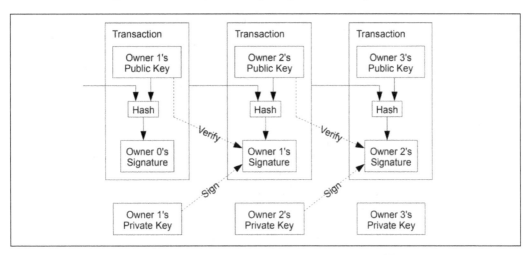

Figure 4: An illustration of the transaction process for Bitcoin. Source: https://bitcoin.org/bitcoin.pdf

The bitcoin hash

The bitcoin system uses a function called Hashcash. The Hashcash proof of work algorithm was invented in 1997 by Adam Back. The bitcoin hash uses two additional parameters – a nonce, and a counter. The nonce is just a random number that is added to the collection of data before it gets fed into the hashing function. So, the hash created is a combination of the previous hash, the new transaction, and a nonce. The bitcoin system requires the hash value to start with a certain number of zeros; the challenge of identifying the right hash value increases exponentially as the number of zeros increases. The counter parameter of the Hashcash function is used to record increments until the right hash value is arrived at.

Mining a bitcoin

The nodes in a bitcoin network work hard to find the hash value that has the correct number of zeros. They use different nonces to generate hashes, until the right hash is generated. This exercise takes a lot of computing power, and when the right hash value is found, the node that has achieved that will be rewarded bitcoins for identifying the right nonce.

Determining the nonce that, when put through the hash function, results in a specific hash value within a difficulty level is called mining. The difficulty level increases as the number of zeros increases. Mining bitcoins has become harder over the years as more computing power is required to determine the nonce. There are only 21 million bitcoins to ever be produced, and at the time of writing this book, about 17.5 million bitcoins have been mined. The reward to mine a block is at 12.50 bitcoins, and there are about 144 blocks mined per day. There are 65,000 more blocks to be mined before the mining reward halves again to 6.25 bitcoins.

A block

A block is just a group of transactions validated together. If a bunch of transactions are not able to make it into a block in time, they get moved into the next block. The number of bitcoins that are rewarded for mining a block started at 50 and is halved with every 210,000 blocks mined.

Proof of work

The term *proof of work* was coined by Markus Jakobsson and Ari Juels in a document published in 1999. *Proof of work* was used in the bitcoin system to ensure that transactions are validated through sheer computing power. After a chain of blocks has been established through this method, to hack through the block would require an immense amount of computing power too.

Also, in a *proof of work* system, the processing power that a node has decides the control the node has over the network. For example, in the bitcoin network, one CPU is equivalent to a vote, which can be exercised at the time of decision making.

Transactions

New transactions are broadcast to all nodes for validation. Transactions are collected into blocks and nodes are busy finding a proof of work for their blocks. When a node finds the proof of work, it broadcasts the block to all nodes that accept the block only if all transaction in it are valid. The acceptance of the block results in the network starting to work on new blocks.

Hacking a block means a new nonce needed to be identified that solved the work of not just one miner, but of all subsequent miners too. Also, when there are multiple chains of blocks, the longest chain of blocks, in terms of the amount of computing power required to create them, is accepted by the network.

Several of these concepts are quite fundamental to understanding how Blockchain networks work, and you should now be able to approach the topic of Blockchain with greater confidence. With that said, we'll now discuss another key concept of Blockchain: utility and security tokens. Understanding the differences between a security and a utility token has recently proven to be a conundrum for the global Blockchain community.

Utility versus security token

As solutions based on Blockchain started raising capital, they were broadly classified into two buckets – utility tokens or security tokens. A utility token is like loyalty points or digital coupons needed to use an application. Loosely, they are used for distributing profits (or dividends) when a firm makes money.

On the other hand, a security token derives its value from an underlying asset. For example, a real estate fund could be tokenized, and the token can be traded. The value of the token is derived from the value of the real estate fund. In the same way, firms raising capital can issue tokens and investors would get a share of the company. This is effectively owning equity in the company and is classified as a security token.

While I have made it sound like utility and security tokens are mutually exclusive concepts, they are often not. For instance, in the case of Ether (Ethereum's token), it is more of a utility than a security as the token is used across the ecosystem in applications and largely derives its value from Ether's demand. The SEC has developed a simple methodology to identify a token as a security, as security tokens fall under their regulatory umbrella. It's called the Howey test.

The Howey test gets its name from a Supreme court decision in 1946: SEC v W.J. Howey Co. Howey Co was offering service contracts for producing, harvesting, and marketing orange crops in Lake County, Florida. These contracts were sold to tourists who stayed at a hotel that was owned by Howey Co. The company sold land and service contracts to these visitors. The court was asked whether the land purchase plus the service contract created an investment contract. The court agreed, and the Howey test was born.

As per the Howey test, a transaction would be an investment contract (and therefore a security) if:

1. It is an investment of money
2. There is an expectation of profits from the investment
3. The investment of money is in a common enterprise
4. Any profit comes from the efforts of a promoter or third party

Let's take the Ethereum crowdsale in 2014 as an example. Money was invested (albeit in bitcoins) – and the investment was made by at least a few with a view that the tokens would increase in value over a period, and they could cash out at a profit. With the Ethereum crowdsale, the capital was pooled by investors in a scheme, and that is viewed as common enterprise by the SEC. And the value increase in Ether was expected to happen through the work of Vitalik and company. Therefore, Ether should be a security, as per the Howey test.

The way the Ethereum crowdsale happened in 2014, it is easy to categorize it as a security token. However, Ethereum is now the oxygen of a big community of applications. As a result, we can say that Ether is an example of a token, which initially raised capital like a security, but due to the way the firm and the technology have evolved, it is more of a utility today. Ethereum is decentralized due to the community it has and no longer just thrives on the initial founders of the firm.

Recently, I was part of a round table discussing the challenge in categorizing tokens as utility or security. I would describe it as a progress bar; at one end of it is the security token, and at the other end is the utility token. Depending on how the token derives it value and how it is used by the community, it would move closer to one end of the progress bar or another. Security vs utility shouldn't be seen as binary states of tokens.

We have discussed the background of quantum computers and touched upon some interesting Blockchain concepts too. The idea is to use these basic ideas as the building blocks before moving onto real-world applications across industries in future chapters. The cryptographic element is fundamental to these two technologies. Does that mean quantum computing makes Blockchain obsolete? We'll touch upon that question in future chapters.

Conclusion

The journey of Bohr, Einstein, Alan Turing, and several others almost a century back has now led to the invention of quantum computers. The hype and the headlines in this field are getting bigger every day. However, mass industry adoption of this technology is several years (if not decades) away. In this chapter, I wanted to take the reader through a journey and introduce key people, principles, events and technology components within quantum computing.

It is important to understand why qubits are different from bits that today's computing world largely relies on. This chapter provides quantum methods and real-world applications that we will touch upon in future chapters. Applications of optical quantum computers that use photons will also be discussed in a subsequent chapter.

We briefly touched upon Blockchain and the use of cryptography. This is also critical, so that we can see the technological overlap between the two technologies. It is essential that the Blockchain community views this overlap as an opportunity rather than a major roadblock. I firmly believe that both these technologies are here to stay, and definitely here to enrich our lives by complementing each other across industries.

There are several practical applications of quantum computers across industries, including healthcare, logistics, finance, and cybersecurity in general. We will cover these in detail in this book.

References

1. https://www.coinmama.com/guide/history-of-ethereum
2. https://medium.com/@aakash_13214/the-scalability-trilemma-in-blockchain-75fb57f646df
3. https://www.apriorit.com/dev-blog/578-blockchain-attack-vectors
4. https://www.investopedia.com/articles/personal-finance/050515/how-swift-system-works.asp
5. https://medium.com/altcoin-magazine/how-to-tell-if-cryptocurrencies-are-securities-using-the-howey-test-da18cffc0791
6. https://blog.advids.co/20-blockchain-use-case-examples-in-various-industries/

2
Quantum Computing – Key Discussion Points

At a recent event, I was asked a question on the kind of problems a quantum computer could solve that a classical computer cannot. The audience were also keen to understand why quantum computers were able to do things that classical computers have historically struggled with. A quantum computer could potentially model nature and the complexities that lie within. Classical computers are yet to scale to that extent as bits exist in two states. The ability of quantum systems to exist in superpositions allows them to deal with the problems of exponential. In order to understand how quantum computers can, in effect, leapfrog innovations in several industries, it is critical to understand the fundamental principles of quantum physics that underlie quantum computing.

Many of these principles of quantum physics have evolved over a century, and have a particular weirdness about them, as they are often counter-intuitive to minds that have dealt with behavior and the physics of macroscopic objects. I have tried to capture the core principles of quantum computing (as they are understood today) that can explain the behavior of subatomic elements that quantum physics deals with. The best way to understand them in detail would be to learn the physics and math underlying these concepts. However, the purpose of this book is to look at the practical applications of quantum computing. So, I have put together real-life examples, and relied upon very little math and physics to explain these concepts. The remainder of this chapter will discuss these concepts, starting with superposition.

Superposition

Superposition is one of the properties that differentiates a quantum computer from a classical computer. The qubits of a quantum computer can exist in 0s and 1s and linear combinations of both of these states. A quantum computer can achieve a special kind of superposition that allows for exponentially more logical states at once. This helps in solving problems such as factoring large numbers, which is typically hard for classical computers to solve. Classical computers are limited in terms of their ability to model the number of permutations and combinations that cryptography needs.

An example of the application of quantum computers in cryptography involves RSA encryption. RSA encryption involves two large prime numbers being multiplied to arrive at a larger number. The following examples should bring these challenges to life.

An exponential challenge

The story of the chessboard and rice brings to life the challenges in dealing with the exponential. When the game of chess was presented to a Sultan, he offered the inventor of the game any reward he pleased. The inventor proposed to get a grain of rice for the first square, two grains for the second, and four for the third and so on. With every square, the number of grains of rice would double. The Sultan failed to see what he was dealing with, and agreed to pay the rice grains.

A few days later, the inventor came back and checked with the Sultan. The Sultan's advisors realized that it would take a large quantity of rice to pay off the inventor. The 64th square of the chess board will need 2^{63} grains of rice, which is 9,223,372,036,854,775,808 grains.

Figure 1: Chess board and rice grains

The five coins puzzle

Linear regression is one of the statistical modeling techniques used to arrive at the value of a dependent variable x from independent variables a and b. A function $f(x)$ represents the relationship between x, a, and b.

Most real-world problems are often not as simple as arriving at the dependent variable from a few independent variables. Often, the independent variables a and b are correlated. Assume a and b interact with each other and their interactions affect the resultant variable x. All possible combinations of interactions of a and b need to be factored into calculating x. Assume, instead of just two variables, that x is dependent on a larger number of variables. The possible interactions between these variables make the problem hard to model for traditional computers.

Let's think about a game involving five coins. The aim of the game is to achieve either the smallest or the largest possible score after tossing them. Each coin has a value, which can be positive or negative, and can be heads or tails, which also translates to be positive or negative. The overall score in the game is calculated by each coin's *state* (heads or tails), multiplied by the coin's value, and adding the score of each coin together to derive a total.

Coin Identifier	State (Head = +1, Tail = -1)	Value	State* Value
coin1	1	4	4
coin2	-1	3	-3
coin3	1	3	3
coin4	1	5	5
coin5	-1	-1	1
		Total	10

Table 1: Detailing the five coins puzzle

If we wanted to get the lowest total possible total in this set up, we would need heads (+1) for all coins where the values are negative, and tails (-1) for all coins where the values are positive.

That would give us a total of -16, as shown in *Table 2*. Using the same logic, if I had to get the highest total, I would need heads for all coins where the values are positive, and tails where the values are negative, for a total of +16.

Coin Identifier	State (Head = +1, Tail = -1)	Value	State* Value
coin1	-1	4	-4
coin2	-1	3	-3
coin3	-1	3	-3
coin4	-1	5	-5
coin5	-1	1	-1
		Total	-16

Table 2: Getting the lowest possible score in the five coins puzzle

Now, let's add one more variable to the mix. Let us call it the correlation variable. The correlation between coin1 and coin2 can be represented by $C(1,2)$. We have to consider the coins as pairs as well as individual coins. We will have far more variables to deal with in this scenario.

For simplicity, if we have to find a total with just the first two coins:

Total = $S1W1 + S2W2 + (C(1,2)*S1*S2)$

However, if we wanted to identify the lowest total with just the two coins, we will need to trial it with both head and tail states for both the coins to get the minimal value for the total. That would be four states (HH, HT, TH, TT) for two coins. If we added yet another coin to the mix, the number of states would increase to eight states (HHH, HHT, HTH, THH, HTT, TTH, THT, TTT). The number of states to consider would be 2^N, where N will be the number of coins used to calculate the total. As we saw in the Chess example, this will quickly become a problem that is hard for conventional computers to solve. In a quantum computing world, the information of states could be stored more efficiently using superpositions. Qubits can be in both head and tail states at the same time.

A quantum computer addresses a quantum representation such as this and identifies the states of the coins to arrive at the lowest value. The process involves starting the system with the qubits in superposition, and adjusting the states to turn off the superposition effect. As the correlation variable is fed into the system simultaneously, the superposition states will be turned off, and classical states for each of the coins will be chosen (heads or tails).

Addressing the need for exponential computing power is a considerable difference that quantum computing brings to the world of problem solving. In real-world scenarios like simulating cancer cell behavior to radio therapy, modeling stock price actions to market risk factors, or finding the shortest and quickest flight route from source to destination, quantum computing can provide several answers with varying degrees of confidence.

As we discussed in *Chapter 14, Interview with Dinesh Nagarajan, Partner, IBM*, quantum gates act as operators that help qubits transition from one state to another. A quantum gate, in its basic form, is a 2 x 2 unitary matrix that is reversible, and preserves norms and probability amplitudes. Probability amplitude is a complex number that provides a relationship between the wave function of a quantum system and the results of observations of that system.

In simplistic terms, a qubit in a base state of 0 or 1 can be put into superposition or an excited state when it goes through a gate. An algorithm that uses quantum gates to interact with qubits and provide results is called a quantum algorithm. When a quantum computer is represented in a circuit diagram, the wires represent the flow of electrons through the circuit, and each gate represents a change in the pattern of movement of the electron. Therefore, quantum gates are effectively used to drive the system to produce a result. Unlike a classical computing algorithm, quantum algorithms often provide probabilistic results.

Takeaway: There are real-world problems that are currently unsolved, or are solved through approximations. Once quantum computers become mainstream, some of these complex problems can be addressed more effectively and with greater precision.

Let us now move on to the next quantum concept of entanglement.

Entanglement – spooky action at a distance

The quantum property of entanglement was referred to by Einstein as *Spooky action at a distance*. Two particles in a system are entangled if one particle in a system cannot be described without taking the other part into consideration. In a quantum computer, qubits demonstrate this property. So, the probability of observing the configuration of one qubit will depend on the probability of observing the configuration of its entangled other half. This property of qubits exists in a quantum system, even when the entangled pair are separated by a good distance. This means, if one qubit spins in a clockwise direction, its entangled pair could spin in a counter-clockwise direction, even when miles apart.

Recently, scientists in China have demonstrated entanglement at a distance of up to 1,200 kilometres. Source: `https://phys.org/news/2018-01-real-world-intercontinental-quantum-enabled-micius.html`

This experiment was conducted between a satellite and earth, where entangled particles were used to communicate instantaneously. The challenge in making entanglement happen over long distances is that the particles often get lost when transmitted through fiber optic networks. However, scientists have recently used laser beams on the world's first quantum-enabled satellite called Micius, to communicate using entangled photons across three different earth stations in China. Previous attempts at quantum communication were limited to a few hundred kilometres; this was primarily due to data channel losses that occurred in optical fibers.

Apart from long distance communication, quantum teleportation (which is based on entanglement) is an important concept in cryptography. Quantum teleportation is the process of transmitting information between two entangled qubits that could be separated by a long distance. In contrast to traditional means of secure data transmission, this method relies on entanglement of qubits and not on complex encryption functions. Quantum teleportation could be significant as it could soon be the foundational element of a secure internet or any communication network. In the next section, we discuss a Bloch sphere, which helps visualize the states of qubits.

Bloch sphere

A Bloch sphere, named after Felix Bloch, is a three dimensional, geometric representation of a qubit's states as points on the surface of the sphere. It also helps us understand how a qubit's state changes when put through a gate (operations). As it represents one qubit, it is not meant to demonstrate the entanglement property, where interactions between multiple qubits need to be considered. This section is mathematical by necessity, but it will be the only section in the book that uses math to this extent.

The poles of the Bloch sphere represent the classical states of a bit: $|0\rangle$ and $|1\rangle$.

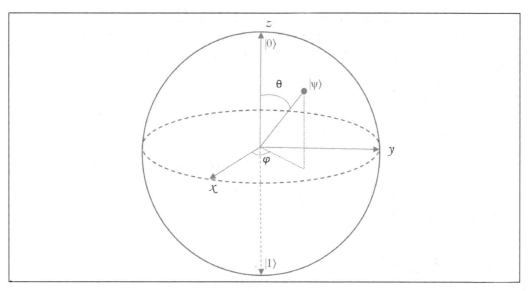

Figure 2: A Bloch sphere

The state of the qubit, $|\Psi\rangle$, diagrammatically represented by a Bloch sphere, can be given as:

$$|\Psi\rangle = \cos\frac{\theta}{2}|0\rangle + e^{j\varphi}\sin\frac{\theta}{2}|1\rangle$$

Equation 1: Quantum computing for computer scientists, N. Yanofsky and M. Mannucci, Cambridge Press, 2008.

In this representation, θ corresponds to the latitude and φ corresponds to the longitude of the qubit. Any point in the Bloch sphere can be represented by the range of values that θ and φ can take, given by $\theta \in [0, \pi]$ and $\varphi \in [0, 2\pi]$.

This means that:

- When $\theta = 0$, $|\Psi\rangle = 1|0\rangle + e^{j\varphi}\,0|1\rangle = |0\rangle$, and that represents the state of the classical bit.

- When $\theta = \pi$, $|\Psi\rangle = 0|0\rangle + e^{j\varphi}\,1|1\rangle = |1\rangle$, and that represents another state of the classical bit. This is because φ represents the longitude, and it is meaningless at the pole.

If θ took other values between 0 and π, this would lead to a superposition state of the qubit. So, while the poles of the Bloch sphere derived from the equation represent the states of a classical bit, the state of a qubit can be given by any point in the sphere.

How does the Bloch sphere represent the possible changes in states of a qubit, especially when they are observed? Continuing from the discussion in *Chapter 14, Interview with Dinesh Nagarajan, Partner, IBM*, we know that the state of the qubit collapses to the classical states under observation. The angle θ represents the probability with which the state of the qubit will collapse to either of the two states. If the arrow that represents the Bloch sphere is closer to the North Pole of the sphere, the state collapses to $|0\rangle$ and vice versa. In the next section, we look at one of the most impactful algorithms in the history of quantum computing.

Shor's algorithm

Peter Shor and his work have perhaps had the most impact on the evolution of quantum computing. In 1994, he proposed a polynomial time quantum algorithm for identifying prime factors. Richard Feynman [1982, 1986] had already proposed the idea of quantum computing to be more powerful than classical computers. However, Shor was the first to bring to light a practical application of quantum computers. Using his algorithm that demonstrates identification of prime factors of a large number, he inspired a generation of scientist to focus on the algorithmic acceleration possible using quantum computers.

Factoring has been a mathematical challenge for a long period of time. Think about the number 35. It has two prime factors: 5 and 7. Similarly, the number 142 has two prime factors: 11 and 13. If there was a large odd number N whose prime factors have to be identified, we will need to divide N by all prime numbers up to $\sqrt{N}$ to identify the factors. This is a brute force method and is computationally intensive. Modern-day RSA cryptography relies on prime factoring to encrypt all our data. Passwords for our logins, credit card details, and other sensitive information rely on the computational difficulties of factoring to be safe from hackers.

As it stands today, RSA 2048 has numbers going up to 617 decimal digits. While the factorization process has gone up through the RSA bit ranking, cracking an RSA 2048 number is a few years away. The Shor's algorithm provides a theoretical model to simplify factorization.

Factorization of a number can be simplified if the period of the modular exponential function is calculated. Let us take an example to understand the modular operation and the concept of period. That will help us go through the factoring algorithm.

The result of *a (mod b)* is the remainder when a is divided by b. A few examples are as follows:

$$12 \,(\text{mod } 5) = 2$$

$$21 \,(\text{mod } 7) = 0$$

$$18 \,(\text{mod } 7) = 4$$

The next step is to understand the concept of period. Say *N* is the number we need to find the factors of, and x is a co-prime to *N*. We use the following power function:

$$x^a \,\text{Mod } (N)$$

Now, to go through the factoring algorithm, let us take an example.

Say *N* = 91 and x = 3 (co-prime to *N*). When two numbers are co-primed, their **greatest common divisor (gcd)** is 1, applying the above power function to derive the period:

$$3^0 \,\text{Mod } (91) = 1$$

$$3^1 \,\text{Mod } (91) = 3$$

$$3^2 \,\text{Mod } (91) = 9$$

$$3^3 \,\text{Mod } (91) = 27$$

$$3^4 \,\text{Mod } (91) = 81$$

$$3^5 \,\text{Mod } (91) = 61$$

$$3^6 \,\text{Mod } (91) = 1$$

$$3^7 \,\text{Mod } (91) = 3$$

As you can see, the sequence starts repeating itself after six increments of a. This is the period, which in this case is "6". Identifying the period is a hard problem to solve in factorization. However, once that is done, the factors can be arrived at using the following methods:

$$\left(x^{\frac{r}{2}} + 1\right) + \left(x^{\frac{r}{2}} - 1\right) \equiv 0 (\text{mod } N)$$

As r = 6, N =91, and x = 3 in this example, we can arrive at:

$$28 * 26 \equiv 0 (\text{mod } 91)$$

According to the factoring algorithm:

gcd(28,91) or gcd(26,91) will be a non-trivial factor of 91, where gcd stands for *greatest common divisor*. And in this case, gcd(26,91) = 13. Once that has been identified, the other factor can be identified as 7.

That is a simple example of how the factoring algorithm works. Shor proposed that some of the steps in this factoring algorithm happen in a quantum computer, while the pre-processing and the post-processing took place in a classical computer. These are the steps that describe the algorithm:

Step 1: In the above example, pick 3 as the co-prime to 91 using a classical computer.

Step 2: Create two quantum registers. Register 1 will h store the increments of a, in x^a Mod (N). Register 2 will store the results of x^a Mod (N).

Step 3: Apply Quantum Fourier transforms to register 1 and compute the period r = 6 in parallel.

Step 4: Once the period is identified, find the gcd and arrive at the non-trivial factor of 91 using classical computers.

Shor's algorithm provided a way to do the modular exponentiation and identify the period using quantum computing. Every element in the sequence x^a Mod (N) contributes to the amplitude of the period of the sequence. For all periods calculated, other than the right one, the spin of these contributions is in different directions, and hence cancel one another out. The true period, the contribution from the sequence, points in the same direction and gets chosen as the right value with a high probability. We will now look at Grover's algorithm, which offers an increase in search performance on unstructured data.

Grover's algorithm

Lov Grover published a paper in 1996 describing Grover's algorithm. The application of Grover's algorithm to unstructured searches provides a quadratic speed up. If you want to find an item in a database and if the data is not sorted, using Grover's algorithm implemented using quantum computers can provide better performance than classical computers.

When a name had to be identified from *N* names within a database, and if the names were sorted, a classical computer could perform a binary search to find the name in logarithmic time. If the names were not sorted, then the search would involve scanning up to the *N*-1 name to find the right one.

If S_a is the element we are trying to find from the database of N elements, using Grover's algorithm can help solve the problem with $\sqrt{N}$ attempts. Qubits are prepared so that all numbers are in a uniform superposition using a Hadamard gate. Measuring the qubits at this stage would show that all results were equally likely:

Figure 3: Achieving uniform amplitudes

The following equation represents the uniform magnitude of all strings:

$$\sum_{s\in\{0,1\}^n} \frac{1}{\sqrt{N}} |s\rangle$$

Now, an oracle gate is applied to flip the amplitude of s_a and leaves the rest unchanged:

$$-\frac{1}{\sqrt{N}}|s_a\rangle + \sum_{\substack{s\in\{0,1\}^n \\ s\neq s_a}} \frac{1}{\sqrt{N}} |s\rangle$$

The graph can now be represented as:

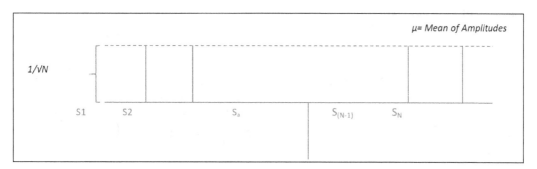

Figure 4: Flipping the amplitude string that matches

Now the amplitude of the desired element S_a has been flipped (to negative). Hence, the mean of the amplitudes μ would have been reduced. This is where the Grover diffusion operator is introduced to increase the amplitude of S_a absolutely.

All this operator does is to flip the amplitudes at the average. This results in the amplitude of S_a increasing to about $3/\sqrt{N}$ in magnitude. The amplitudes looks like the following diagram:

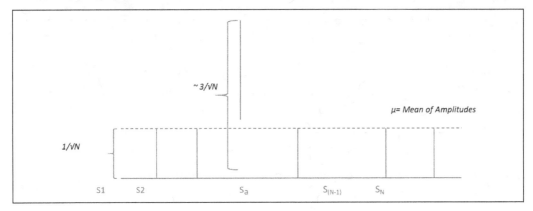

Figure 5: Flipping amplitudes at the mean

This process of applying the oracle gate and the Grover diffusion gate is repeated until the amplitude is significant enough. Care must also be taken that the amplitude of S_a is not too large that the mean amplitude turns negative, which in turn will start reducing the amplitude of S_a. At the point when the amplitude is almost one, the measurement of the qubits will provide the right answer. It can be demonstrated that this process, when repeated for about $\sqrt{N}$, provides accurate results.

Takeaway: The Shor and Grover algorithms laid the foundations for quantum computing and identified practical use cases that these algorithms can help solve.

We will now move on to quantum annealing, which is a technique used to address optimization problems.

Quantum annealing

We have seen how superposition of qubits achieved by operations using gates can solve real-world problems. There are other methods to arrive at an optimized solution. Quantum annealing is the process of arriving at global minima using quantum fluctuations. The quantum tunneling effect can help with transition between states in a quantum annealer.

During the quantum annealing process, the information required for optimization is modeled into a physical system. This process involves codifying an optimization problem of several correlated variables into a physical system (represented by qubits in superposition).

The solution to the problem is represented by the minimal energy state of the system, and the simplest function used to achieve this is called Hamiltonian. Quantum annealing powered by the quantum tunneling effect can address problems in logistics for example.

Quantum tunneling

Quantum tunneling is a quantum property where particles pass through high energy systems. In classical physics, when an electron encounters an electric field, it gets repelled if the electric field is stronger than that of the electron. Problems that are solved using quantum annealing rely on the quantum tunneling property of particles.

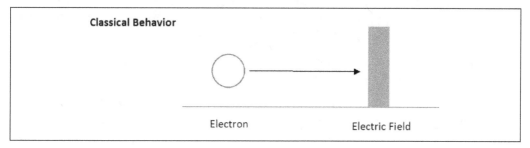

Figure 6: An electron approaching an electric field

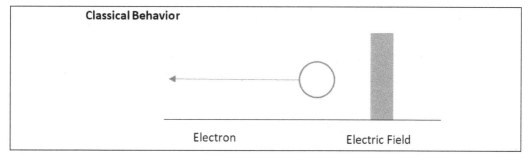

Figure 7: An electron repelled by the electric field

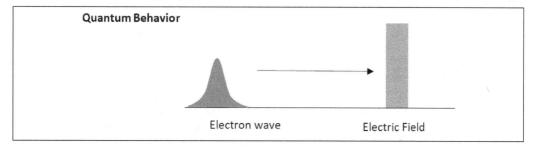

Figure 8: An electron wave moving toward an electric field

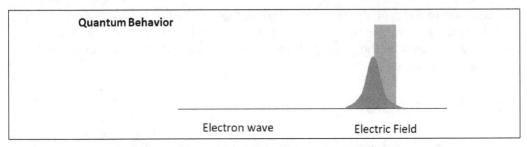

Figure 9: An electron wave tunneling through an electric field

Tunneling is a property that was observed by Friedrich Hund in 1927. If an electron, that is traveling as a wave encounters an electric field that repels it, there is still a probability that it will pass through the electric field and find itself on the other side of the field (*Figure 9*). subatomic particles display tunneling properties during a radioactive decay, when particles escape an unstable nuclei.

Quantum annealing is a process that depends on the tunneling properties of particles. Let us look at a practical example where quantum annealing can be used.

The traveling salesman

The traveling salesman problem is a well-documented application of quantum tunneling. Say we have a salesman selling goods across a country. The optimal route for him to go through the country would depend on the number of cities in the country. If the country has three cities (A, B, and C), the optimal route could be A -> B -> C or A -> C -> B or B -> A -> C or B -> C -> A or C -> A-> B or C -> B -> A. The number of possible routes (6) is dependent on the number of cities here (3). The number of possible routes can be given by the factorial of the number of cities as:

$$3! = 3 * 2 * 1 = 6$$

When the number of cities doubles to 6, the number of possible routes would be 6! = 720, which is a drastic increase. Apart from the increase in the number of cities, there could be other issues such as traffic jams at a point in time, or a road that is particularly bad. The optimal route, therefore, may not necessarily be the shortest route. We first need to set up the system to identify the optimal solution.

Let's prepare the system in a quantum superposition of many possible solutions of the problem. The system can be now viewed as a landscape of peaks and valleys. Peaks are high energy states and are expensive. Valleys, on the other hand, represent low energy states. As we transition between one valley and another, the probability of each solution evolves. The lower energy options become the more likely solution, until the highest probability solution is identified as the optimal solution.

In simulated annealing, heat is used to go over peaks and transition between valleys. With quantum annealers, the quantum tunneling effect allows us to *pass* the high energy *peaks* through tunnels instead of climbing them, as in simulated annealing.

Quantum annealing is driven by an external magnetic field that plays the role of the temperature in simulated annealing: the quantum annealing starts with a high magnetic field (high temperature) and ends up with a low magnetic field (low temperature).

Quantum annealing is the process of feeding the information required for optimization into a physical system. The solution to the problem will be defined by the ground state (lowest energy state) of the system. The function used for this process is called the Hamiltonian function, which manages information on the energy levels of the system.

We can use the Hamiltonian to manage the energy levels of the system based on a framework of constraints. In the traveling salesman problem, we can have higher energy levels assigned to longer distances, bad roads, traffic jams, and road closures. The optimal route would be the one with the lowest energy level. Considering this, how do we identify the lowest energy solution?

The Hamiltonian function, and the terms we add to it to increase the energy levels, would create peaks and troughs in the energy space. We need to find the troughs without having to climb the peak energy levels. This can be achieved by quantum tunneling, as described above. While this allows us to move from one trough to the other, how can we identify the lowest trough? A quantum technique called adiabatic quantum computation can be used for the purpose.

The term *adiabatic* comes from the theory of thermodynamics and means *without changing the amount of heat*. In this process, the system is initialized at the ground state, and then slowly evolved into more complex Hamiltonians whose ground states encode the solution.

Each Hamiltonian encodes the correct assignment of variables by assigning an *energy penalty* to all of the incorrect configurations. The peaks in the landscape have a higher penalty and the valleys have a lower penalty. The optimal solution with the lowest energy level generally has an eigenvalue of 0. We can time evolve the system to:

$$H(s) = (1 - s) H_0 + sH_1$$

At time $s = 1$, the Hamiltonian is $H(1) = H_s$, and the system will be in its ground state if the evolution has been slow. Eigenvalues and Eigenvectors are used across several real-world algorithms. They are used in modeling the physics of rotating bodies, oscillations of vibrating systems, and in risk modeling in investment banks.

Eigenvalues are defined below by Hoffman and Kunze (1971):

> *Eigenvalues are a special set of scalars associated with a linear system of equations (in other words, a matrix equation) that are sometimes also known as characteristic roots, characteristic values (Hoffman and Kunze 1971), proper values, or latent roots (Marcus and Minc 1988, p. 144).*

Reference: `http://mathworld.wolfram.com/Eigenvalue.html`

Quantum annealing can be used to solve optimization problems. However, we may not have to wait for quantum computers to use the principles of quantum annealing and quantum tunneling to achieve results. Fujitsu have already created a "*Quantum inspired digital annealer*" to solve challenging optimization problems in financial risk management and financial portfolio rebalancing.

Takeaway: Quantum annealing can be used in optimizing problems across several industries. Finance, logistics, healthcare, and smart cities are all areas where this technique can be used to optimize complex problems.

Despite all these amazing possibilities with Quantum techniques, decoherence is a major challenge. Let's look at that next.

Decoherence

We discussed the Quantum Slit experiment in *Chapter 1*, *Introduction to Quantum Computing and Blockchain*, where we saw that photons moved through the slits and behaved like waves (interfering with themselves), even though they were sent one at a time. When a particle exhibits properties of a wave, where it interferes with itself, it is said to be coherent. Decoherence is the loss or the suppression of coherence in a system.

The wave function that explains the behavior of the particle collapses when the state of the particle is observed. This process of decoherence, in which the particle that was in a superposition of states collapses to one of the two classical states when observed, is considered a bridge between quantum and classical physics. The experiment could be on an electron in superposition, and if the observer is measuring the z-component of the spin, the experiment will output a definite value of the z-component of the spin. The x-component could still remain in superposition. This aligns with Bohr's interpretation that properties in the quantum world come into existence when observed.

We know that macroscopic objects, such as human beings, do not exhibit this property – adopting a given state only when observed. Of course, we all exhibit virtuous characteristics when we know we are observed, and sometimes vice versa, but this is not the case with inherent attributes such as *alive* or *dead*! On a more serious note, how can things in the quantum world exist in multiple states at the same time until they are observed?

Erwin Schrodinger devised a thought experiment to illustrate the counter-intuitive nature, and seeming absurdity, of this concept:

A cat, radioactive material, and poison gas were placed in a box. If radioactivity is detected, the flask containing the poison gas would be broken and the cat would die. The radioactive material was small enough that radioactivity may not be detected for some time. Thus, at any given time, those outside of the box would be unable to determine whether the cat was alive or dead. Thus, by quantum logic, the cat could be considered to be both alive and dead!

Schrodinger questioned how this could possibly be the case within the quantum world, when it is clearly not the case in the macroscopic world. All quantum experiments thus far, however, have affirmed the theory that quantum objects do indeed appear capable of existing in two states until observed.

Quantum Error Correction

Quantum Error Correction (QEC) is a critical process that makes the results of the quantum system reliable. In the initial days of quantum computing, correcting a quantum computer efficiently without triggering decoherence of the computation was considered highly non-intuitive. A lack of reliable error correction in a quantum system was a major roadblock because quantum algorithms use interference, which is fragile. This interference made quantum algorithms sensitive to imprecision in the system and to the coupling between the system and the rest of the world.

Some of the common reasons for errors include:

1. Preparation of the initial state of the system
2. Decoherence of qubits can occur due to interactions with the environment
3. Inaccuracies in gates
4. Imperfections in the measurement process

Peter Shor and Andrew Steane developed the first set of quantum error correcting codes. While Peter Shor identified that 9 qubits could be put together to perform error correction on one qubit, Steane discovered a 7-qubit error correction methodology.

Loss in quantum information due to interference with the environment can be addressed using the distribution of information. If the information is distributed across several qubits instead of one qubit, the information is safer. In classical computing, error correction using repetition code uses three bits to store copies of information from one bit. So, unless two of the copies are error prone, the information is intact. While this is a simple process in classical computers, with quantum computers, copying information from one qubit to another is more complicated.

It was Shor who proposed a method to generalize the repetition code method for quantum computers. The solution he proposed was to encode a qubit with the repetition code on the basis states.

Post-selected quantum computation was developed by Emanuel Knill, and demonstrated that quantum computing at scale could be achieved through error detection rather than error correction. The quantum computer would have error detecting circuits and if errors (noise) are detected to have breached a threshold, the relevant subroutine of the algorithm is reset and re-run. This addresses high levels of error tolerance but has high resource requirements.

Another useful method for dealing with quantum errors is to use quantum error correcting codes called stabilizers. These are quite useful tools for developers of quantum systems. The stabilizer code specification has numerous applications, including the design of preparation circuits, correction circuits, and fault-tolerant logical gates. Using stabilizers to define quantum error correction codes helps apply logical operations on encoded data using correction circuits. The 7-qubit method developed by Andrew Steane, which constructs a logical qubit using seven physical qubits, has the ability to correct single X or Z errors.

Takeaway: The key takeaway is that error correction in quantum computing is a non-trivial exercise. The complexities in QEC and the various options available to address them are worthy of a whole book. It is a critical aspect of quantum computing that has helped transform quantum computing from theories to a practical possibility.

Conclusion

In order to understand the interviews in this book, and the key inferences from them, it is essential that this chapter is well understood by the reader. For the same reason, I have described the concepts of quantum computing using practical examples, with comparisons to classical computing equivalents. There are a few concepts of quantum computing that are hard to grasp without delving into the underlying physics (if not the math). In such cases, the simplification of the underlying concepts of physics in this chapter would help understand the weirdness in the behavior of microscopic elements that make up a quantum system. The simplified version may make a quantum scientist cringe, but I firmly believe that simplifying the narrative is critical for any technology to go mainstream.

References

1. https://www2.physics.ox.ac.uk/sites/default/files/ErrorCorrectionSteane06.pdf

2. https://journals.jps.jp/doi/full/10.7566/JPSJ.88.061009

3. https://arxiv.org/pdf/quant-ph/9508027.pdf

4. http://science.sciencemag.org/content/356/6343/1140

5. https://people.cs.umass.edu/~strubell/doc/quantum_tutorial.pdf

6. https://cs.uwaterloo.ca/~watrous/LectureNotes/CPSC519.Winter2006/05.pdf

7. https://grove-docs.readthedocs.io/en/latest/vqe.html

8. https://quantumexperience.ng.bluemix.net/qx/tutorial?sectionId=beginners-guide&page=004-The_Weird_and_Wonderful_World_of_the_Qubit~2F001-The_Weird_and_Wonderful_World_of_the_Qubit

9. https://medium.com/@jonathan_hui/qc-cracking-rsa-with-shors-algorithm-bc22cb7b7767

10. https://www.scottaaronson.com/blog/?p=208

11. https://quantumexperience.ng.bluemix.net/proxy/tutorial/full-user-guide/004-Quantum_Algorithms/070-Grover's_Algorithm.html

12. https://www.cs.cmu.edu/~odonnell/quantum15/lecture04.pdf

13. https://medium.com/@quantum_wa/quantum-annealing-cdb129e96601

3

The Data Economy

Recently, one of the chandeliers at my home got faulty and the electric circuit had some weird wiring issues. The bulbs attached to the chandelier started flickering, and within an hour or two all the bulbs had fused out following a few dangerous sparks. We had to get it fixed, but something else happened as well. My five-year-old, who saw it happen mentioned "Appa, this chandelier is losing internet connection, see, even the bulbs are not glowing anymore, can we please check the internet?"

I was surprised by the comment, and it made me realize the world we lived in. The next generation are so immersed in a world that is seamlessly connected, that they might not imagine it ever being otherwise. Such connectivity has its own challenges. Connectivity results in interactions, and interactions in turn result in data – really big data. Data resulting from these interactions is only valuable, however, if it can be sourced, managed, and analyzed efficiently. The connectivity that has resulted in the past few years via the internet as a data network has now seen a major upgrade. Thanks to Blockchain we now have value networks, where connectivity can result in peer-to-peer exchange of value.

This rise in peer-to-peer interactions (be it data or value) has some challenges and risks, including cybersecurity, data privacy, and self-sovereign identities. Over the years we have seen several firms that have lost or mis-managed customer data and have been exposed to reputational and regulatory risks as a result. On the same lines, we have seen capital markets prove inadequate in creating inclusive value frameworks, allowing the rich to become richer when the poor get poorer.

Emerging technologies such as artificial intelligence, Blockchain, and quantum computing can help in managing the new data economy. They can also help the world transition into a peer-to-peer value exchange network.

This chapter will take you through the advent of the internet, followed by the birth of technology firms that built their businesses on top of the internet. I describe how this subsequently led to social media and big data, which meant that we needed ways to manage the data explosion that followed. The rise of cloud and artificial intelligence on such huge volumes of data were logical next steps. Using Blockchain to manage data integrity, and quantum computing to better utilize data are currently in progress. Let us start with the internet.

The internet

The rise of the internet is well documented across the internet itself. However, I feel it would be a good start to understand some of the transitions technology has had over the last 50 years in order to get to the data-rich age we live in today. The internet was preceded by the invention and the spread of devices like transistors, the telephone, radio, and computers. An attempt to connect computers to share and broadcast information and collaborate was what led to the internet. It all began with the ARPANET.

The ARPANET

In 1962, J.C.R. Licklider of MIT wrote a series of memos describing the interactions that could happen on a network and termed it the **Galactic Network**. The other breakthrough in thinking happened when Leonard Kleinrock at MIT, came up with the theory that communication using packets instead of circuits was the way forward. This inspired the work of Lawrence G. Roberts, who developed the plan for ARPANET and published it in 1967. As a result, in 1969, Kleinrock's Network Measurement Center at UCLA hosted the first node on ARPANET. **Stanford Research Institute (SRI)**, UC Santa Barbara and the University of Utah joined the network as subsequent nodes. The first message between the hosts happened between Kleinrock's laboratory and SRI.

ARPANET expanded very quickly as more and more hosts were added to it. However, it was only after **Network Control Protocol (NCP)** was implemented in 1971-72 that ARPANET users could develop applications. Using NCP, users could access computers remotely and send files. It acted as a transport layer and defined the process to connect two computers. Further reading: `https://www.internet-guide.co.uk/NetworkControlProgram.html`

The year 1972 was significant as the first email program was launched where users could read, forward, and respond to messages. In the micro-messaging world we have today, emails are primarily used in formal communications. In the history of the internet, however, email was a critical step.

TCP/IP

ARPANET paved the way for communication within a network using packet switching. However, interoperability and connecting to other networks using different technologies happened when the **Transmission Control Protocol/Internet Protocol (TCP/IP)** was developed by Bob Kahn. TCP/IP as it was called later, has become the bedrock protocol for the internet that we use today. TCP/IP is a specification for how data interactions happen over the internet and how data should be broken into packets, transmitted from the source, and received at the destination. TCP defines how application channels can be created over a network (in this case the internet) and IP provides an identifier or an address for the packets' destination. The following figure describes the architecture of the internet using TCP/IP:

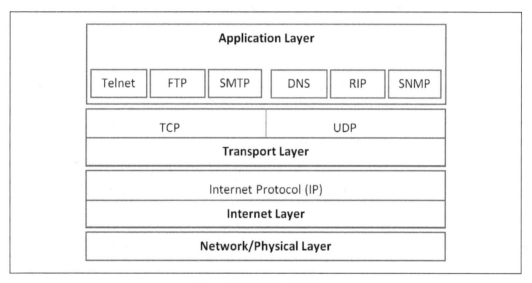

Figure 1: TCP/IP architecture

The Network Layer is where data gets moved in packets across physical wires, cables, or fiber optics. The Internet Layer identifies the host using what we call the IP address, and spots the router closest to the destination. The Transport Layer is responsible for the end-to-end transfer of data irrespective of the underlying network. It also takes care of error handling, flow control, and congestion control to avoid a lot of data being sent through the same router. The Application Layer covers the protocols that we use for applications like emails, file transfers, and websites.

The development and evangelizing of the TCP/IP protocol was a significant phase in the evolution of the internet. ARPANET subsequently moved from NCP to TCP/IP after a few years of planning, and the transition was surprisingly smooth.

In 1989, a British scientist called Tim Berners-Lee came up with the concept of the **World Wide Web**. This meant **Uniform Resource Locators** (**URL**) could be a space to hold information. These URLs could be interlinked and accessed using the internet. By 1990, Tim also came up with **HyperText Markup Language** (**HTML**), the language that was the bedrock of the web.

The boom, the bust, and the boom

Several firms incorporated the TCP/IP protocol through the 1980s. However, it was only in the 1990s that the mainstream adoption of the internet took place. Several internet-based businesses started to shape up through the 1990s, and personal computers started to become common place. As the convergence of these two innovations (the internet and PCs) happened through the mid-90s, there was a boom in the internet market. Several firms saw a growth of about 500% in two years' time. For example, **AOL** (**America Online**) grew from $70 million at IPO in 1992 to over $150 billion in early 2000.

Thanks to the irrational exuberance of the late 90s, the **Venture Capital** (**VC**) industry splurged money into start-ups at will. Valuation models used by these VCs to assess investment opportunities were fundamentally flawed, and in many cases there were no valuation exercises performed. Several firms without sound business models got funding at crazy valuations, resulting in a bubble and a bust (described as follows). This is a classic example of how history repeated itself, as the dot net bubble repeated itself, though at a smaller scale, with the Blockchain/cryptocurrency industry in late 2017/2018. Key events through this boom and bust can be timelined as follows:

The Boom

- Aug 1995: Netscape began trading, marking the launch of the internet era
- Apr 1996: Yahoo went public and saw a doubling up of share price on day 1
- May 1997: Amazon went public and saw a 30% increase in share price on day 1
- Jan 1998: NASDAQ opened the year at 1574.10, registering a two-year gain of 50%
- Sep 1998: Google was founded by Larry Page and Sergey Brin
- Sep 1998: eBay went public and its share price closed at 163% on the opening day
- Mar 2000: NASDAQ hit a peak of 5132.52

The Bust

- Mar 2000: Three days after its peak, NASDAQ lost 4.5%
- Apr 2000: NASDAQ lost 25% of its value in a week and the bubble had burst
- Dec 2000: eBay shares traded at a low of $2.81 (the first day close was at $47.35)
- Dec 2000: NASDAQ ended the year at 2470.52, a 52% loss from its peak in March
- Mar 2001: eToys shares were worthless. The firm exhausted $800 Million in three years and filed for bankruptcy.
- April 2001: TheGlobe.com shares slipped below $1.00, and got delisted from NASDAQ
- Nov 2001: Amazon shares hit a low of $5.51

The Recovery

- Q1 2003: Amazon reported its first annual profits of $35 Million
- Aug 2004: Google went public and its shares rose 18% on the opening day

As the sun set on the internet empire in the early 2000s, most firms lost value within weeks. Many firms went bankrupt and investors lost their capital. However, after a painful few years the dust settled. Several of the other internet/technology companies recovered from the dot com bubble burst. However, it was a slow process. Microsoft shares didn't get back to their highs of December 1999 until October 2016. The popping of the dot com bubble identified firms that went on to define the future of computers and the internet. The survivors of the dot come bubble went on to build the framework for what we know today as social media.

Social media

The internet revolution was followed by yet another technology paradigm – social media. While the internet was about connecting people and sharing information, the information that was available to be utilized was still limited (relatively).

Social media created interactions, blogging, and micro-blogging opportunities, leading to a data explosion.

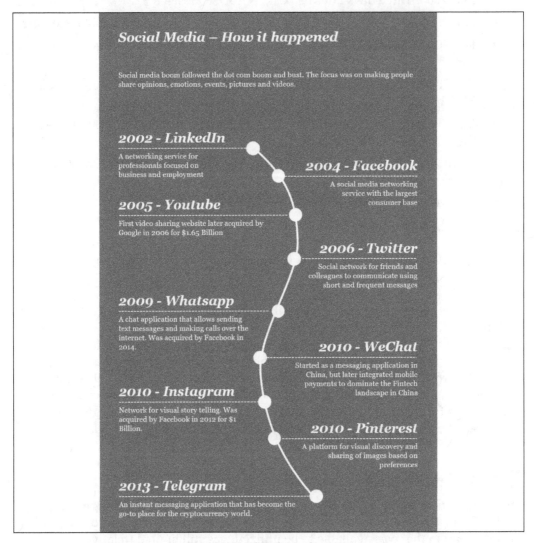

Figure 2: Social media applications

As social media took the world by storm, there were a few key developments with big technology firms. Facebook spotted early winners in Instagram and WhatsApp. While Instagram was a steal at $1 billion, the acquisition of WhatsApp at $19 billion did raise some eyebrows. The size of the market that these applications were addressing, however, justified the cost. Also, by the time WhatsApp was acquired in 2014, Facebook's revenue in advertisements alone was about $12 billion, and the user base was at 1.3 billion people.

Despite the success of Facebook's revenue model, they were clear that they had to expand their user base globally. Their ambition was to have every internet user as a customer, and where internet penetration was poor, they even strategized ways to provide the internet. The race for user data was on, and as they offered their services free, their users were their commodity.

Let us touch upon the size of the market and the amount of data created using these social media applications. This will help us understand why the emerging technologies that are covered in this chapter are relevant now more than ever before. These numbers will shed light on why the big technology firms were focusing on growing their customer base.

Some numbers to note are (as of January 2019):

- 4.2 billion people use the internet
- 3.4 billion people actively use social media
- Facebook and WhatsApp create 60 billion messages a day
- 45 billion WeChat messages were sent in 2018
- 46 TB of data is consumed on WeChat during 1 minute of the morning rush hour
- Google has answered 450 billion unique queries since 2003
- 300 hours of video are uploaded to YouTube every minute

You can clearly see the monstrous growth of data in the world based on the preceding statistics. Much of this growth has been driven by the widespread adoption of social media by users across the world.

> *"There were 5 exabytes of information created by the entire world between the dawn of civilization and 2003. Now that same amount is created every two days."*

> *– Eric Schmidt, Ex-CEO and Chairman of Google in 2010*

This data has been used by the tech-giants over the years for various commercial purposes. This has also led to a backlash from governments, regulators, and even customers on data privacy rights. The scandal where Facebook shared data on 87 Million people with Cambridge Analytica created a lot of reputational issues for the firm and highlighted the need for better data controls and regulations. The tag **#FacebookIsDead** started trending, and many millennials and Generation Z users moved away from the social media giant due to their treatment of user data. It was clear that data regulations, governance, and controls were mandatory. But before moving on to that, let us first look at how firms managed this big explosion of data using big data technologies.

Big data

The term **Big data** was coined by Roger Mougalas in 2005, a year after Web 2.0 was coined. Web 2.0 was used to indicate the data era where traditional business intelligence tools were ineffective due to the size of the data they had to deal with. The same year, Yahoo developed Hadoop on Google's MapReduce with an ambition to index the **World Wide Web**. Hadoop is an open source framework that can handle both structured and unstructured data.

Structured data is identified by well-defined data types, data rules, and controls that they would adhere to. Structured data typically sits in databases where the exact parameters of data are predefined. Oracle, Microsoft SQL Server, and several other database management systems were very focused on dealing with structured data.

Unstructured data does not have the same level of structural discipline, primarily because of the way it is generated. Unstructured data comes in all shapes and forms most of the data that exists in the world today. It could be data generated from social media, emails, chats, voice recordings, and videos. Social media necessitated the efficient management of unstructured data and several technologies started to emerge to address this opportunity.

Another classification of databases is relational and non-relational. Relational databases like MySQL, Microsoft SQL Server, and Oracle store data in a structured format within tables. These tables can be linked to each other through relationships. These relationships make sure the integrity of data is intact.

However, the downside of this model is that, it takes a lot of time to transform data into a relational schema. Therefore, it may not be the best option when data volumes are huge, and processing is often expected to be in a fraction of a second. Extracting data from a relational database is typically done using **Structured Query Language (SQL)**.

Non-relational databases like MongoDB, Neo4J, and Cassandra store data in formats such as JSON or XML. They come in handy when data consistency is less important, and availability and query response times need to be more important. These databases also allow for horizontal scaling more seamlessly. This is important when large data volumes are involved.

Before getting into the depths of how big data management happens, it would first be useful to understand how structured data is sourced, managed, and analyzed.

Structured data processing

In a traditional environment where data sticks to well-defined data types, the process of sourcing, preparing, managing, and delivering them in a format suitable for reporting and analytics involves a process called **ETL – Extract**, **Transform**, and **Load**. The system where all these processes happen in an organization is called a **data warehouse**. We'll briefly discuss each of these processes, as follows:

Extract

Data is sourced from across the organization in various forms and stored in tables in a database called the staging database. The sources could be flat files, a messaging bus, or a transaction database that is highly normalized for quick transaction writes. Source to target mappings are pre-defined to ensure that the source data was delivered to the staging area in a compatible structure (data type). The tables in the staging database act as the landing area for this data.

Transform

Data in staging tables goes through transformations that are predefined. These transformations are identified well ahead of time and coded into the system. Where data is identified as incompatible with these transformations and the rules set within the system (data types, logical criteria), the data is logged into an error-handling queue.

Load

Transformed data is then loaded into the data warehouse, and by this time it is generally high quality. This final database could also be a data mart, which is often a miniature data warehouse satisfying a specific purpose or part of an organization. In any case, there are several hops that data needs to take before getting to a shape where it is ready for analysis and reporting.

This process used to work in a conventional setup. However, it may not be practically possible to find a place to store 2.5 quintillion bytes of data (the data created per day) that do not stick to the semantic limitations of a structured database. Hence the need for a shift in approach using big data platforms. Let us now look at how unstructured data management has addressed some of the challenges posed by the data era.

Unstructured data processing

Conventional database management systems are not designed to deal with the volume of data and lack of structure often associated with the internet. The key components of a big data system include:

Data sources

Data sources in a big data system can be text files, messages from social media, web pages, emails, audio files, and video files. With the rise of the **Internet of Things (IoT)**, data generated by the interactions of machines would also be a source that big data systems need to deal with.

Data storage/Data lake

Data from these sources are stored in a distributed file store system like the **Hadoop Distributed File System (HDFS)**. The distributed nature of the store allows it to deal with high volumes and big data sizes. Data lakes can also deal with structured data, but do not need data to be in a structure.

> *Firms that successfully implemented a data lake have outperformed competition by 9% in organic revenue growth (as per research by Aberdeen)*

Source: `https://s3-ap-southeast-1.amazonaws.com/mktg-apac/Big+Data+Refresh+Q4+Campaign/Aberdeen+Research+-+Angling+for+Insights+in+Today's+Data+Lake.pdf`

Unlike a traditional data warehouse, data lakes get a schema at read time.

Data processing

Data processing in a big data infrastructure could happen in different ways depending on the nature of data fed into the system:

- Batch processing is typically used to process large files. These batch jobs process incoming files and store the processed data in another file. Tools like Hive, Pig, or MapReduce jobs can address this type of processing.

- Real-time data processing happens in a system where data is from social media or IoT devices as a continuous flow of data needs to be handled. This data flow is captured in real time, and this could also involve using a message buffer to deal with the real-time volumes.

- This data can then be transformed using conventional techniques and moved into an analytics database/data warehouse.

- Alternatively, where the conventional process is not preferred, a low-latency NoSQL layer can be built on top of the data files for analytics and reporting purposes.

Let us now look at different architectures that have been explored to manage big data.

Big data architecture

There are big data architectures that address both the handling of high-volume data and accurate analytics requirements. For instance, the Lambda architecture has a hot path and a cold path. The hot path handles high volumes of data coming in from sources like social media, however, for read operations, the hot path provides quick access with lower data accuracy. On the other hand, the cold path involves a batch process that is time-intensive, but processes data to provide highly accurate analytics capabilities.

The hot path typically holds data only for a short period of time, after which, better quality data processed from the cold path replaces this data. The Kappa architecture took inspiration from the Lambda architecture and simplified it by using a stream processing mechanism and just using one path against the Lambda architecture's two. This takes away the complexity of duplication and ensuring the convergence of data. Frameworks like Apache Spark Streaming, Flink, and Beam are able to provide both real-time and batch processing abilities.

The third architecture used by big data systems is the Zeta architecture. It uses seven pluggable components to increase resource utilization and efficiency. The components are as follows:

- Distributed file system
- Real-time data storage
- Pluggable compute model / Execution engine
- Deployment / Container management system
- Solution architecture
- Enterprise applications
- Dynamic and Global resource management

The benefits of this architecture include:

- Reducing complexity
- Avoiding data duplication
- Reducing deployment and maintenance costs
- Improving resource utilization

Breaking down the solution into reusable components adds efficiencies across several aspects of developing and managing a big data platform.

While the architectures are interesting to understand the maturity of the technology, the outcomes are perhaps more important. For instance, big data systems have allowed for better use of data captured in the form of social media interactions. The maturity of infrastructure to handle big volumes of data has helped clever customer-specific services provided across several industries. Some of the common use cases we have seen using social media analytics for example are:

- Sentiment analysis for brands

  - Brands can use social media analytics to understand sentiments about their brands or recent launches and tweak their offerings accordingly.

- Customer segmentation and targeted advertisements

  - Several social media platforms provide details on exactly where organizations were getting the biggest bang for their buck on marketing. Firms can fine-tune their marketing strategies based on this information and reduce cost of acquisition of customers.

- Proactive customer services

  - Gone are the days when customers had to go through a cumbersome complaints process. There are several instances where customers have logged their complaints about a particular experience on Twitter or Facebook, and the brands have acted immediately.

- Political campaigns

  - Even political campaigns before elections are managed proactively using social media insights. The West is perhaps more used to such activities, but in India for example, Prime Minister Narendra Modi has managed to capture the attention of his followers using clever social media tactics.

  - Several Asian political organizations have been accused of releasing fake news during a political campaign to mislead voters. For instance, WhatsApp was used as a platform to spread fake news about the India-Pakistan air battles just before the 2019 Indian elections. The Brexit referendum in 2016 is another example where parties were accused of voter manipulation. Source: `https://www.bbc.com/news/world-asia-india-47797151`

There are several other ways in which organizations use social media data for continuous consumer engagement. For instance, understanding sentiments of users, proactively managing complaints, and creating campaigns to increase brand awareness can all be done on social media.

As an investor, when I assess firms, one of the key dimensions I take into consideration is their awareness and ability to drive brand awareness, customer acquisition, and continuous engagement through social media channels. Understanding the advantages of using social media effectively has become a basic attribute to running a business. It is no longer just an option. The rise of social media saw firms move from on-premise servers to cloud-based infrastructure. There may not be a causation, but there definitely is a correlation between social media and the cloud.

The cloud

Big data frameworks that architecturally catalyzed the big data revolution were also supported by the evolution of cloud computing in parallel. Without these technology paradigms going mainstream, it would not have been possible to capture, store, and manage large volumes of data. It all started in 2002, when Amazon launched its online retail services. They had to procure massive servers to manage the Christmas season peak in traffic. At other times, the utilization of their servers was about 10%, and that was commonplace in those days.

The team at Amazon identified the underutilization patterns of their servers and felt that they could create a model to improve utilization during non-peak times. Sharing their server infrastructure with others who needed server resources could add efficiencies for everyone. The concept of cloud infrastructure was born.

Jeff Bezos and his team of executives eventually decided to make the most of the unused server capacity during non-peak times. Within a year, the team at Amazon had put together a service that offered computer storage, processing power, and a database. This business model transformed the innovation landscape as server infrastructure became more affordable for startups.

Amazon Web Service (AWS) went live in 2006 and by 2018 it was a $26 billion revenue-generating machine. Google, Microsoft, IBM, and others followed suit; however, Amazon have clearly got their nose ahead. 80% of enterprises were both running apps on or experimenting with AWS as their preferred cloud platform by 2018 (as per Statista). The cost of starting a business has plummeted since the mainstream adoption of cloud services.

Procuring infrastructure on a need basis has also made it cost-efficient to run and scale businesses.

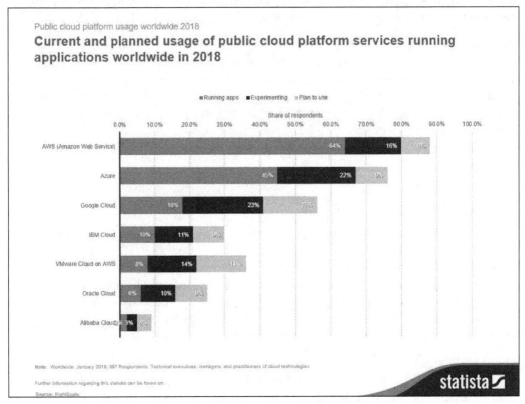

Figure 3: Planned and current use of public cloud platform services worldwide, 2018.
Source: https://www.statista.com/statistics/511467/worldwide-survey-public-coud-services-running-application/

As cloud services matured and scaled, several new models emerged, namely, **Software as a service (SaaS)**, **Platform as a service (PaaS)**, and **Infrastructure as a service (IaaS)**.

SaaS is a model in which a software application is virtually managed on a server by a vendor and accessed by users over the internet. Google Docs was one of the early examples of this model. Today, we use cloud-hosted SaaS for several day to day applications for the simplest of tasks, from document management to conducting teleconferences. Thanks to this model, our laptops do not cry out for software updates on applications every other minute. However, we have also become increasingly reliant on the internet and feel dysfunctional without it.

PaaS is a model where instead of providing an application over the internet, the vendor provides a platform for developers to create an application. For instance, many vendors offer Blockchain in a PaaS model, where developers can use cloud-managed software development services to create Blockchain applications. IBM offers a similar service for quantum computing too, however, that can also be bucketed into the IaaS model.

IaaS is a model where computer resources are offered as a service. This would include server storage, computing and networking capacity, disaster recovery, and many others. This has helped large organizations to reduce their infrastructure footprint by moving to the cloud. Data centers were migrated to the cloud, hence achieving efficiencies across computer resources, but also reducing their carbon footprint.

With these advances in architectural, software, and infrastructure technology paradigms, the data age had well and truly taken off. We had figured out ways of creating and managing data at scale. However, what we weren't very good at was exploiting data volumes to develop intelligence at scale – intelligence that could challenge humans. Enter AI.

Artificial intelligence

I mentioned AI as if it was actually developed for the first time after the social media explosion. Nothing could be further from the truth; AI has been conceptually around for a long time. The concept of robots behaving like humans was introduced in science fiction in the early 20th century. Yet, it only started to become a serious field of research from 1950, when Alan Turing posed the question,

"Can Machines Think?"

Origins of AI

As Alan Turing started exploring that question, he came against not only mathematical challenges, but also theological objections. He refuted the argument that God had given an immortal soul to humans, but not to any other animal or to machines, hence no animal or machines could think.

He made it clear that, in attempting to make machines think, we (the society and humans) were not standing against God's will. He argued that it wasn't the first time theology and science would take seemingly contradicting positions.

He pointed out that the Copernican theory disagreed with the biblical verse below. Copernicus had proposed that the sun was the center of the universe and the earth and the other planets revolved around it.

> *"He laid the foundations of the earth, that it should not move at any time"*
> *(Psalm 104:5)*

Alan Turing also laid out his views of the future for thinking machines.

> *"I believe that in about fifty years' time it will be possible, to program computers, with a storage capacity of about 10^9, to make them play the imitation game so well that an average interrogator will not have more than 70 per cent chance of making the right identification after five minutes of questioning. The original question, "Can machines think?" I believe to be too meaningless to deserve discussion. Nevertheless, I believe that at the end of the century the use of words and general educated opinion will have altered so much that one will be able to speak of machines thinking without expecting to be contradicted.*
>
> *I believe further that no useful purpose is served by concealing these beliefs. The popular view that scientists proceed inexorably from well-established fact to well-established fact, never being influenced by any improved conjecture, is quite mistaken. Provided it is made clear which are proved facts, and which are conjectures, no harm can result. Conjectures are of great importance since they suggest useful lines of research."*

The practical challenges of even attempting AI experiments were huge in those days. Computational power and data storage capacity (or lack the thereof) were the largest bottlenecks. Computers not only had to store words, but also needed to understand the relationships between them in order to conduct meaningful communication.

There were scientists and researchers who were bullish that machines would have the general intelligence of a human being. They came up with different timelines for "**AI Singularity**." Despite AI winters when the technology was viewed as hype, the research community made consistent progress; in the 1980s the concepts of deep learning were introduced by John Hopfield and David Rumelhart, and the field of AI started to get a new boost through a surge in research funding.

The first practical breakthrough perhaps happened in 1996 when grandmaster Gary Kasparov was defeated by IBM's Deep Blue in a game of chess. Deep Blue was a computer program, and the result of the game was hugely publicized and was considered a big breakthrough in the field at that time. Around the same time, Microsoft integrated a speech recognition software developed by Dragon Systems into its Windows operating system.

The scientific community had realized that AI was not just a program that miraculously behaved like a human. It was an approach that used algorithms built using high volumes of good-quality data. This allowed algorithms to get a better understanding of the context in which the machine was operating in, and provide relevant answers as outputs.

The imitation game

Another contribution from Turing was the Turing test. The test was called *The Imitation Game*. The game was constructed as follows:

- There were three rooms, each connected through computer screens and keyboards to the others.

- In the first room sat a human, in the second a computer, and in the third a "judge."

- The judge's job was to identify (through five minutes of interaction) the human and the machine based on their responses.

- Turing proposed that if the judge were less than 50% accurate in identifying the human or the machine, it meant that the judge was as likely to pick either the human or the computer. That made the computer a passable simulation of a human being and intelligent.

Over the years, there were several simplifications of this experiment that programmers used as a litmus test for the intelligence of their solutions. Some subsequent researchers have criticized the ability of the Turing test in identifying genuinely intelligent systems, whilst other papers have been written in defense of the test. Irrespective of that, the contribution of Alan Turing to the field of Artificial Intelligence is no doubt immense. He was the visionary who sowed seeds for future generations to reap the benefits.

Avatars of AI

I often find people using AI interchangeably across many of the more detailed branches of AI listed out in *Figure 4*. Oftentimes, using **AI** to refer to a machine learning solution gets challenged. The way I see it is that these sub-clusters of AI focus on leveraging data to make better decisions. In some scenarios this intelligence augments humans, and sometimes machines make the decisions themselves and learn from them.

The algorithmic details of AI, like Neural Networks, clustering, and Bayesian networks are all covered as techniques under branches of AI:

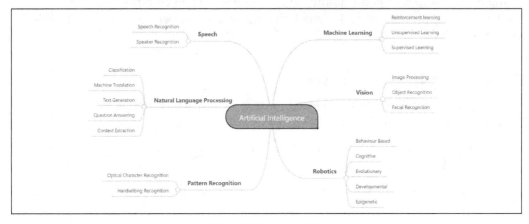

Figure 4: Branches of AI

Machine learning is perhaps the most common form, where patterns are recognized in data and predictions are made using these patterns. The pattern recognition process involves feeding a lot of data to algorithms, and developing the solution to learn with this training data. After the machine has learned from the training data, it is used to apply the learning to a new set of data. If the new set of data exhibits similar patterns to the training data, then the machine highlights them. Therefore, the breadth and the quality of the training data is very critical in the learning process. Let me explain this with an example I was involved in.

I had the privilege of sitting on the IBM Watson evaluation board, when I was at PwC in 2014. We were evaluating the feasibility of using IBM Watson for regulatory solutions. Since 2008, the financial regulators of the UK and EU had come up with several complex regulations, and banks were expected to understand volumes of regulatory text and ensure compliance. Thousands of lines of complex regulatory text to cover, with complementary and conflicting regulatory rules and frequently changing regulations all made it very hard for the banks to stay on top of their regulatory obligations.

The IBM Watson solution that we were evaluating would take all the regulatory texts (in legal language) as inputs. We would also provide as inputs natural language versions of those regulatory texts (where available). Two regulatory experts would work with IBM Watson, and in what they called the *Watson going to School* process, the AI engine would get trained in the regulations. The experts would ask the AI a question regarding a regulation, and when the answer was provided, the experts would give a thumbs up or thumbs down, depending on the quality of the answer. This helped the AI engine learn over time and get better at answering simple, mundane questions on a huge pile of regulatory texts.

In this case, the problem is pretty clear – we are asking the machine to look into the regulatory text and provide relevant answers. However, there are instances where despite a lot of data being available, analysts don't know what they are looking for in the data. We use a method called unsupervised learning to identify the issues and anomalies that the data has. Using that, we get to the process of understanding the underlying variables that influence the anomalies.

Robotics is another area where there have been significant strides over the last 10 years or so. Countries like South Korea have taken robotics to a whole new level by deploying about 700 robots per 10000 employees in the manufacturing industries. The numbers on the following chart represent 2016 figures. The latest figures show that the numbers for South Korea have increased to 710 robots for every 10000 employees.

Robotics is used in conducting surgeries, conducting rescue operations that are potentially harmful to humans, customer services in banks, logistics, construction and even agriculture. Several of these uses are in prototype/pilot stages, but are showing promising signs. Industrial applications for robots are starting to gain clarity, especially in areas where there are repetitive and mechanical tasks.

As a result, low-skill, high-frequency, mundane jobs will be taken over by machines. In the asset management industry, AI is used to make portfolio management decisions as the machine can go through millions of data points to arrive at a decision much better than a human brain can.

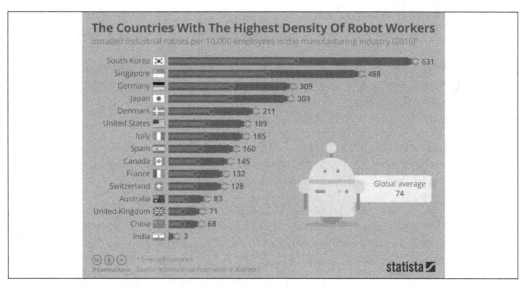

Figure 5: Countries with the highest density of robot workers in 2016

Applications of AI in today's world are unlimited. Every day new avenues and real-world opportunities open up for AI. The availability of data has made the AI boom possible but has also opened up a whole new can of worms around data privacy, data ownership, and data security. With centralized monopoly of consumer data, it is often unclear how our data is being used, shared, and monetized. This is where a technology like Blockchain could help.

Blockchain

As we briefly touched upon earlier, the Blockchain framework has several properties that make it apt to solve some of the data ownership, security, and privacy challenges. In today's mostly non-quantum technology landscape, Blockchain also provides data security better than centralized data management systems. At the same time, Blockchain has limitations that might affect mainstream adoption if not addressed. The history and the technology architecture of Blockchain (the Bitcoin Blockchain) was discussed in *Chapter 1, Introduction to Quantum Computing and Blockchain*.

There are several properties of Blockchain that allow its application across multiple industries. However, keeping our focus upon the topic of the data economy, let us see how Blockchain and its capabilities joined the party at the perfect time.

Decentralization

Decentralization has been the magic mantra of millions of Blockchain believers across the world as the technology has gained in popularity over the years. Thanks to the scalability trilemma that we discussed earlier in this book, decentralization often seems to be an obstacle to achieving commercial scale. Where scalability has been achieved by Blockchain, decentralization has often been traded off, making it an elusive utopian idea that we all want the world to move towards.

However, decentralization does have its advantages. Over the years, we have all gotten used to client-servers systems, where most of the data is stored on the server. The challenges with this architecture are that:

- The server that holds most of the data is an easy target for cyber criminals. Hacking a centralized system to get hold of critical information is easy. There have been several instances where banks have been hacked and millions of clients' data was lost.

- If the centralized entity ceases to exist, data owned by customers is often lost. If Facebook filed for bankruptcy and ceased operations, the entire dataset of 2.3 billion users worldwide could be lost.

In a decentralized system, a version of data where consensus has been achieved is stored across all nodes on the Blockchain. So, bringing down a node in the Blockchain will not mean data loss.

While decentralization protects against data loss, it can also ensure that data ownership is not centralized. It is starting to become increasingly important for every consumer to manage their data, economic and social identity. Management of identity cannot be centralized with one firm for the reasons mentioned before as disadvantages of client-server systems. The mechanism of managing identities within a decentralized network is called self-sovereign identity management.

Thanks to the Blockchain framework, the idea of self-sovereign identity is starting to look less elusive than it once was. In a day and age where data is considered the new oil, and attention (in the media and social media) is considered the new gold, identity must be owned and managed by every individual. If I had a profile on Facebook for 10 years, I would need to have complete transparency on how Facebook was using my data and monetizing it. Any unapproved usage or selling of customer's data can no longer be tolerated.

Before delving further into decentralized traceability that helped with managing self-sovereign identity, let us look at the features that prevent cyber-attacks on the Blockchain system itself.

Immutability

In a system where every block generated uses the hash of the previous block, anyone looking to create a false transaction on the Blockchain needs to brute-force through the entire chain of blocks. Another logical way of achieving consensus on a counterfeit transaction in a Blockchain is to gain control of 51% of the nodes. This happens in a Blockchain that has lost popularity. In such a network, someone could take over the network to get to 51% control of the network.

There are other ways in which Blockchains can be hacked, like the DAO hack that resulted in the hard fork of Ethereum and the birth of Ethereum Classic. However, those issues occur when the framework's logic is fundamentally vulnerable.

If such vulnerabilities are forgotten for a minute, Blockchain as it stands today acts as an immutable network. Once a transaction is created, it becomes very hard for someone to hack and change. While immutability is certainly a desirable Blockchain property, it is used in contexts where traceability is needed too.

Traceability

It is not hard to build traceability and auditability in traditional database management systems. However, when traceability is clubbed with other features of Blockchain it makes it decentralized-immutable-traceability, and that is special. There are several applications of this property of Blockchain in managing intellectual property in a data-intensive world. It also allows you to keep track of how your data is being used by third parties, and where relevant, for you to be paid for that as a customer.

A few weeks ago, I was talking to a Blockchain architect, and we were discussing the user journeys many sites offer, where we had to enter a username and password to use their services. He was insistent that the world needed to move on to solutions where a customer's digital identity was not stored at an application level. Rather, it should be stored at a protocol level. And every time a customer's identity needed to be checked, applications could tap into this protocol.

This means that applications like Facebook and Twitter wouldn't necessarily be the central holders of an individual's digital identity. Identities would have to be ideally managed by a decentralized network of governments. However, when the network is managed by a few governments, it is considered centralized and as the antithesis of Blockchain. The point here, however, is not the degree of decentralization. It is more the fact that identities will have to be managed at a more fundamental level.

As identities are managed, so will data owned by individuals be managed. And more, users' data will be attributed to them, and they will be informed of any money a firm made by using their data. It is the user's decision to choose providers who can use their data to make money. For example, an individual may be happy for their data to be used (anonymously at an aggregated level) to help make lending decisions in banks, but they may not be OK with a big Wall Street bank using it to cross-sell products to more customers.

For instance, a user may be OK with their data being used by firms who have a low carbon footprint, but when a mining, oil, or gas company wants to use their data to make any strategic/commercial decisions, they would want them to pay a slice of their earnings from the decision into an environmental charity.

It is not just enough to create an ecosystem that allows data creation, sharing, and monetization. It is essential to build the governance and controls around it to enable careful use of data. In a world where cyber-attacks will soon be used by nation states to wage war against each other, these controls will decide the winners from the losers. Countries could stop spending time and money on nuclear warheads and start spending more time and energy on protecting the data of their citizens using technologies such as Blockchain.

As we go through technologies that are fundamental to the data era, one that has stood out is quantum computing. It is still early days for the field, but the possibilities are promising.

Quantum computing

In a sequence of technology innovations that have made the data economy possible, quantum computing is perhaps the cherry on top. We have touched upon various aspects of quantum computing that made it such a revolutionary technology paradigm. On a practical basis quantum helps us solve some key problems that weren't possible before. Many of these practical problems are covered through interviews in this book. With quantum computing, AI gets to run on steroids, Blockchain gets a new facelift (perhaps after a painful surgery), and big data management and utilization could go through a major rethink.

Cybersecurity would look very different when inherent quantum properties like entanglement is used to transfer information over large distances. Businesses would be able to make real-time data-driven decisions, with higher degrees of confidence. In essence, thanks to emerging technologies, we should be able to make the most of the data we have created.

Conclusion

Every few years, we see new technology trends emerge. No major technology since the rise of the internet has managed to thrive without enriching the data economy. Be it AI, Big data, Cloud computing, Blockchain, the IoT, 5G, or quantum computing, they all interact with the data economy and contribute to it. Some of them have more use cases at the Application Layer, some of them at the Protocol Layer, and some of them at the Physical/infrastructure Layer. Irrespective of that, they have all been disruptive at scale.

The internet laid the foundations of these exciting few years of data innovation. Social media built on them. Once we had data created through social media, it was all about making the most of it using emerging technologies. Some of these technology paradigms had been around even before the advent of the internet and social media. But the availability of rich, contextual user data helped innovators refine their approach in using and further developing these technologies.

The connectivity offered by the internet allowed for new economic models to be created. A connected user base, the network effect, and the engagement that was created offered rich data. Businesses thrived in making the most of this data, while offering their services free of cost. Value was created digitally using Blockchain.

A small network grew into an ecosystem, and a digital economy was created. All this happened over the last 15 years at a staggering pace. The question that comes up is, can quantum computing enrich this wave of innovation?

In the next few chapters, we will study the potential applications of quantum computing and Blockchain across several industries.

References

1. http://sitn.hms.harvard.edu/flash/2017/history-artificial-intelligence/
2. http://jmc.stanford.edu/artificial-intelligence/what-is-ai/branches-of-ai.html
3. https://medium.com/@chethankumargn/artificial-intelligence-definition-types-examples-technologies-962ea75c7b9b

4

The Impact on Financial Services

The financial services industry has historically been slow in embracing innovation and cutting-edge technology. It is partly because banks, asset management, and insurance firms have seen themselves as being in the business of providing financial products. They have considered technology as cost centers and non-core to their business. However, that approach has been challenged by two key changes in the business landscape.

The recession in 2008 saw several key shifts in how financial services firms interacted with innovative technologies. Banks had huge regulatory pressures after the recession. This meant they had to be careful about how creative they got with financial products they were offering to their customers. Banks had to report more details to the regulators about their product and service offerings. As a result, innovative products became scarce. There were large overheads related to back office technology and processes. In the UK alone, £5 billion is spent by banks every year on regulatory compliance. With the increase in regulatory pressures came a surge in risk management processes and technology.

The other shift in the landscape was the rise of financial technology firms termed as *FinTechs*. FinTechs were innovative young companies that were using digital methods to offer financial services in a more customer-centric fashion. They were young and didn't have the burden of legacy technologies. This helped them create new business models, technology solutions, and operating models in a very short time span.

As banks and financial service firms were grappling with regulatory pressures, the nimble FinTechs blindsided them. Before they realized it, banks saw their top line challenged by FinTechs that were growing fast and increasing their customer base. On the other hand, regulatory processes were creating bottom-line pressures. The solution was for financial services firms to turn technology into a competitive advantage.

The last 5 years have seen financial services firms embracing new technologies such as AI and Blockchain with varying degrees of success. In this chapter, I discuss the potential applications of quantum computing in financial services, and touch upon some of the industry applications that are the right fit for this technology.

As banks were grappling with the FinTech force, they wanted a silver bullet to solve the problem. Blockchain was introduced just after the FinTech hype took off, and banks latched on to the technology for several reasons. One was to create a perception that they could embrace innovation and lead with technology. They also felt Blockchain could bring them massive operational efficiencies across several banking processes. Blockchains are being experimented with in banks for processes from the onboarding of a customer, where **Know Your Customer** (**KYC**) checks would be made for the real-time settlement of a transaction. This would eventually be their competitive advantage.

As banks explored ways of combating the FinTech challenge with emerging technologies, there were ecosystems created on Blockchain across the world. These ecosystems had the potential to challenge the very fundamentals of the traditional capital markets. The Blockchain ecosystems wave rode on the principles of decentralizing financial services. The capital markets that we have today are highly centralized, disintermediated, and are often inaccessible to people that need them the most. Blockchain was going to change all that and provide financial inclusion at scale. At least, that was the vision. This posed another major challenge to banks.

In this chapter, I touch upon different areas and applications that Blockchain was trialed in and areas where there were success stories. Financial services are an industry that is inherently complex due to the business models and interactions across the globe. The data complexities involved within several banking functions require technologies that can help make the most of the data. Hence, it is also important to discuss the impact that quantum computing could have on financial services.

Quantum computing applications

I have spent the last 10 years of my career heavily involved in risk management and fund management. When I first moved into risk management in 2010 from front-office technology at Barclays Capital, I noticed two key opportunities.

One, risk management was a data-hungry field, and two, technology had not penetrated the field well enough (in comparison to front office). Over the last decade, I have witnessed risk technology across different banks mature into what it is today.

Risk management and reporting in an investment bank involves a lot of data processing. The role of the field is to look at the financial positions that the firm has taken in the market and assess the risks around these. After the recession of 2008, banks were mandated to hold reserve capital that is calculated based on risks associated with a portfolio. The **Value-at-Risk (VaR)** methodology is used to calculate the worst possible loss a firm could make with a confidence level defined by the risk appetite of the firm.

There are several sub clusters of risk management, such as market risk, credit risk, operational risk, and conduct risk. However, we will focus on how market risk and credit risk work, primarily because they are very data and computation intensive. This makes them an ideal candidate for quantum computing solutions.

Market risk

Market risk is the factor that models the effect of market movements on a firm's trading positions. A bank can take positions in various products traded in the market. Every product has a pricing mechanism. The role of the risk management function is to identify the market risk factors that affect the variables involved in pricing the product.

Let's take an example of a financial bond. It is a simple debt product that is priced by discounting future cash flows using an interest rate. The cash flow is generally fixed in the form of a coupon payment, and the variable used to discount the cash flow is an interest rate. The price of the bond can be calculated by using the interest rate data that is sourced from firms like Bloomberg. As the interest rate is used to discount cashflows, if the value of the interest rate goes up, the bond price comes down, and vice versa.

When a bank takes a long position (buys) in a bond, and if the interest rates go up, the price of the bond falls. Therefore, the market risk of a bond position is calculated by modelling the price of the bond, when market risk factors affect the interest rates used. This is a simple example.

There are often several variables used to compute the price of a financial product. When there are multiple risk factors affecting these variables, it makes it computationally intensive to calculate the risk. We also find that some of these variables are correlated with each other; when one variable changes, it causes another variable to change. These interactions need to be modelled to price the product and the risks associated with positions.

If a position increases the risk of a portfolio, risk managers identify that, and ensure that the front office takes a hedging position to reduce the overall risk of the portfolio. All this data is used to calculate the VaR and the capital requirements of the firm. The process involves large volumes of data, complex computations and simulations, and cutting-edge data analytics.

In a tier 1 bank, there are millions of positions that are fed into the risk engines every day. These positions are re-priced on a daily basis using market data, and risks are calculated by applying the risk factors to these re-priced positions. The correlation between these variables makes it harder for classical simulation techniques to assess the risks. As a result, banks sometime choose to approximate prices and hence the risk is also an approximation.

The approximation calculated every morning works in a normal scenario in banks. However, in a crisis situation, when a bank finds itself dealing with an intra-day market disaster, existing systems and processes are severely lacking. They need to be able to price their risks quicker and at a higher level of accuracy, so that they can take necessary market actions. Understanding risks in a market stress scenario helps banks either hedge existing positions more efficiently, or to liquidate positions that are creating big exposures.

Existing technologies used in banks offer ways to approximate their risks. Using quantum computing to model market risk can offer two key advantages:

- Risks can be calculated more accurately as correlation across different variables can be modelled in.
- Risks can be calculated in near real time to address intra-day stress scenarios.

Measuring risks more accurately using correlation modelling is important. As a simple example, Let's assume that a bank has big positions in British Airways. Banks would typically model the direct impact of Brexit on the FTSE 100, and therefore British Airways. However, Brexit has an impact on the global economic outlook. On the day of the Brexit referendum, the price of oil along with several other commodities fell. A fall in oil prices is good news for airlines. Therefore, it is important to model the direct implication of a market risk on stock positions. But it is also critical to understand the correlation between the market movement and other factors that could affect the banks' market positions.

I touch upon the technical limitations that banks face in greater detail later in the chapter. That should also help you understand how exactly quantum computing techniques can help with market risk calculations.

Market risk is not the only place where quantum computing can be used. Credit risk is perhaps a more mature and computationally intensive field that can benefit from this technology too.

Credit risk

Credit risk is the risk that the counterparty that a firm is transacting with will default on its obligation to the firm. There are several variables that go into modelling whether a firm or a person will default. This is typically captured by credit ratings and modelled using the *probability of default*. As different credit information about a counterparty is captured, the credit rating migrates to better or worse.

There are different levels of credit ratings, AAA being the best and CCC being the worst. These credit ratings are more relevant with institutional transactions. Credit scores are more common in a retail banking context. Based on several variables, the credit rating of a counterparty (institutional or retail) could move up or down, and that could decide whether a bank would make or lose money. Let's take a retail banking example. Bond rating reference: `https://www.investopedia.com/terms/b/bondrating.asp`

John and Mary are two customers of a bank with different credit profiles. Both are applying to the bank for a mortgage. During the mortgage application process, the bank checks their credit files and credit scores. Let's assume John has several credit lines, like a credit card and a personal loan and he also has defaulted on one of his obligations 3 years back. Mary has a cleaner credit file with no defaults and a controlled set of well managed credit lines. They are both requesting a mortgage for an apartment costing £200,000. Every other aspect of the mortgage is the same for both applicants.

The bank will typically price John's mortgage at a higher interest rate, and Mary will get a better deal. This is exactly what happens in an institutional space as well. Based on the credit rating of a counterparty the products are priced. When the probability of default of the counterparty is higher, the credit rating is lower, and the product is priced higher.

However, banks need to evaluate this information every day. If the product for a counterparty is priced at X, and if the counterparty's credit rating has suddenly been downgraded, the bank's exposure has increased. That needs to be reflected in the capital that the bank sets aside, which is captured in the **Credit VaR (CVAR)** and economic capital calculations. Many banks use Monte Carlo simulations to calculate the CVAR and economic capital.

Very similar to market risk technology limitations, Credit risk algorithms also have limitations that could potentially be resolved by quantum computing. Faster computing is critical during a market crash scenario. Accurate computing helps assess risks at a more granular level.

Let's assume that bank A has an active position with bank B. It could mean that at some point in time bank A expects a settlement from bank B. Therefore, the credit risk of bank B needs to be calculated on a regular basis. But bank B could perhaps have big exposure to the UK where most of its business lies. If Brexit hits hard, bank B could struggle to make its payment to bank A. Instead of Brexit in this case, it could also be bank C to whom bank B has huge exposure. So, understanding the network of money and being able to calculate the credit risk of bank B accurately is important.

Before getting into how quantum computing can help these fields, let's first look into the technology and process limitations in greater detail.

Technology limitations

Now that we have understood the data processing challenges involved in modelling product prices, risks, and VaR, let's look at the limitations of existing technologies in dealing with them. We briefly touched upon the limitations in previous sections. It is important to understand them in greater detail before delving into how quantum computing can help.

There are several real-world scenarios where some of these risk management processes need to be performed during the day. They are called intra-day reporting processes. When there is a market crash or a stress event during the day, intra-day VaR needs to be calculated to make sure the banks are capitalized for the stress scenario. However, some of these processing engines are so slow that they take hours to perform the "*re-calcs*" as they are called.

Monte Carlo simulations have been able to provide an accurate estimation of the expected returns. However, they have often been less accurate when timescales are short. They need a lot of computing power, and when there is an increase in data volumes, this problem is magnified.

The other challenge is the limited ability of existing computing methods to deal with correlated variables. This comes back to the discussion in *Chapter 2, Quantum Computing - Key Discussion Points*. We touched upon the limitations of classical computing frameworks to deal with modelling a dependent variable Y, from several variables $X1, X2, X3,..Xn$. If the calculation of Y involves capturing correlations between $X1, X2, Xn.$, that makes it harder for classical computers. These are two scenarios where quantum computing can make a difference.

As quantum computing algorithms gain popularity, there are several firms that are looking at ways of bridging the gap between classical and quantum computing. Quantum-inspired techniques offer a good leap in performance.

Some of these solutions are ready to be used in an industrial environment, One of the key solutions that has seen the light of day is Fujitsu's quantum inspired annealing algorithm. Using the algorithm, they have been able to reduce latency with risk models. Let's now look into the details of how quantum computing could help with risk management.

Quantum-Inspired Digital Annealing

We discussed the method of adiabatic quantum annealing in *Chapter 2, Quantum Computing - Key Discussion Points*, and its applications in solving combinatorial probability problems. Quantum annealing is a method to handle the real-world problems that classical computers have struggled to solve. Technology service providers such as Fujitsu and Hitachi are working on digital annealing that uses classical computers and takes inspiration from quantum computing principles. These digital annealing solutions are already being applied in real-world scenarios within the financial services industry.

For example, Fujitsu have developed a Digital Annealer using "Ising." The Ising model was proposed by Wilhelm Lenz in 1920. The model describes how a large collection of atoms that can exist in two different states interact with each other. These atoms are arranged in a multi-dimensional lattice, and the state of one atom affects that of neighboring atoms. The cloud implementation of the solution went live in May 2018. They call it the "*FUJITSU Quantum-Inspired Computing Digital Annealer Cloud Service.*"

In Fujitsu's Digital Annealer, atoms within magnets are used to model a problem that the annealer will solve. The state of the atoms represents the states of the variables. The energy associated with each individual atom and the spin correlations can be calculated accurately. The interactions between the atoms and their influence on each other's spins decide the solution to the problem. The ability to identify the solution to the problem using a low-energy state is similar to quantum annealing, as explained in detail in the next section.

Fujitsu has co-created the quantum-inspired algorithm for this new architecture, working with Toronto University, and **1QB Information Technologies (1QBit)**, based in Vancouver, Canada.

Quantum annealing

This setup is like the quantum annealing system where states of particles represent the variables involved in the problem. Using the Ising model in a classical computing setup has helped Fujitsu to achieve quantum-like efficiencies in complex calculations. This methodology can also be extended to portfolio rebalancing in asset management and ATM replenishment in retail banking.

Figure 1 describes the principles behind the annealing method to identify the right fit across several variables:

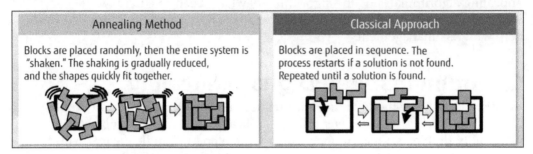

Figure 1: The Annealing Method versus Classical Approach.

The Digital Annealer operates at room temperature unlike quantum computers, and therefore can maintain states for longer.

This can also be achieved by several quantum computing algorithms. The **Quantum Approximate Optimization Algorithm (QAOA)** can arrive at a solution to optimization problems in polynomial time, where classical methods take exponential time.

Algorithms that have exponential time complexity grow much faster than polynomial time algorithms. The variable that expresses the runtime is in the base in polynomial time and in the exponent in exponential time. A quick example could be the following. If n represents the runtime variable:

$$Polynomial: n^2$$

$$Exponential: 2^n$$

If n is 1000, the polynomial equation delivers 1000^2, which is 1,000,000 and exponential delivers 2^{1000}, which is 1.071509e+301 (practically huge).

So the speed at which quantum algorithms can calculate is much higher than classical techniques. Quantum annealing can also be used to deal with combinatorial optimization problems that are designed to identify a local minimum.

As described in *Chapter 2, Quantum Computing – Key Discussion Points*, annealing (digital and quantum) is a process where thermal fluctuations allow the system to jump between different local minima. In quantum annealing, these jumps are possible due to the quantum tunneling property. Quantum tunneling allows more efficient ways of exploring the energy landscape, when the energy barriers are high. The process of using qubits to achieve a quantum annealing - based optimization solution is as follows:

1. Using gates (like Hamiltonian), model the input data into the state of a set of qubits.

2. Set the qubits into superposition.

3. Apply an algorithm to arrive at a system state that holds the correct answer.

4. Using quantum interference, increase the probability of measuring the correct state.

5. Measure the qubits for the results.

The following image shows how the adiabatic evolution combined with quantum tunneling helps identify a low-energy solution state:

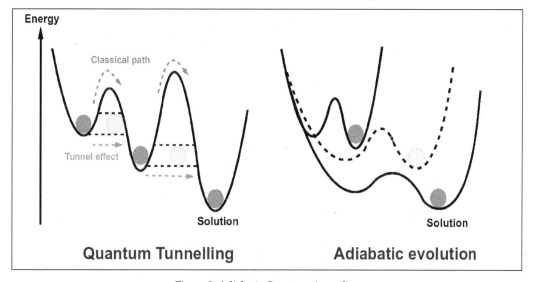

Figure 2: Adiabatic Quantum Annealing

Quantum annealing offers a great deal of efficiency to the risk modelling processes within banks. However, quantum computers are still in their infancy and decoherence make them impractical for enterprise use at this stage. As discussed in *Chapter 2*, *Quantum Computing - Key Discussion Points*, decoherence leads to the loss of information due to the environment of the quantum computer.

D-Wave Systems and IBM have tried to solve some of the financial services modelling challenges using their quantum computers. They ran limited instances of financial data through their quantum annealers and found comparable performance to classical computers. Fujitsu's testing of the Digital Annealer has provided answers to financial services problems in seconds. These problems used to take several hours to days in the past. One such example is within portfolio management, as we discuss in the next section.

Dynamic portfolio selection

Before discussing the impact of quantum computing on financial portfolio management, let's try and understand the problem statement. In the asset management industry, portfolio managers make investment decisions and build portfolios of stocks, bonds, commodities, and other asset classes. Dynamic portfolio selection is a process where the allocation of the portfolio across different asset classes represents investors' risk appetite. Portfolio rebalancing is performed to ensure the allocation is managed on a regular basis.

Some investors prefer a high-risk portfolio with a view to getting higher returns. They would typically have a higher allocation of volatile securities. If the risk appetite is lower, there would be a larger allocation of high-grade, low-volatility assets. Asset management firms typically have risk/investment committees that periodically ensure that portfolio allocation is in alignment with investor preferences.

Many asset management firms take days for this process, and it is typically performed once a quarter. However, this is insufficient during periods of high market stress and volatility. The portfolio could yield stable returns if rebalancing is performed more regularly.

A simple example would be an imaginary portfolio where we have 50% equity (stocks) and 50% debt. Let's assume that stocks were performing well due to, say, many technology **Initial Public Offerings** (**IPOs**), and irrational exuberance from market participants. In that scenario, the allocation of stocks in the portfolio will increase due to market movement in the price of technology stocks. A portfolio manager, who wants to keep the allocation of stocks at 50%, might need to sell some stocks and rebalance the portfolio. It is a simple enough solution.

Let's add one more asset class to our imaginary portfolio. The portfolio now has a 40% allocation of equity, 40% of debt and 20% of commodities. Assume, due to geopolitical tensions in the Middle East, the price of oil (held in the portfolio) went up. The portfolio manager would have to rebalance the allocation. However, an oil market spike often results in the fall of airline stocks (also held in our imaginary portfolio). Therefore, movement in one cluster of the portfolio has caused the movement in another. This is termed as **correlation**.

In a real-world scenario, instead of three such clusters, there are more granular industry allocations across asset classes with correlation between them. It is a difficult task to model the effect of increasing the allocation of one cluster of the portfolio on another. Much like the credit risk and market risk problem, arriving at an optimal solution by modelling a set of correlated variables into a computer needs quantum algorithms.

Apart from the mathematical challenges, portfolio managers need to take into consideration real-world frictions such as transaction costs. It typically takes about 30 stocks in a portfolio to achieve optimal diversification. Rebalancing such a portfolio on a regular basis will be expensive if transactional costs are high.

After rebalancing, the portfolio's performance will need to be measured for optimal returns. This is typically done using performance indicators such as the Sharpe Ratio. The Sharpe Ratio is defined as the average return earned in excess of the risk-free rate per unit of volatility or total risk. Source: `https://www.investopedia.com/terms/s/sharperatio.asp`

There are several methods to perform portfolio rebalancing. The **Hierarchical Risk Parity (HRP)** method has been a recent development in the asset management industry. HRP is a risk-based portfolio optimization algorithm. It uses machine learning techniques to identify the underlying hierarchical correlation structure of the portfolio. Groups of similar assets compete for capital, resulting in a diversified portfolio.

The quantum-inspired Digital Annealer developed by Fujitsu is used to create a hierarchical correlation structure from an asset price change variance matrix. Clustering of the correlation of over 500 stocks can happen instantly, where it was performed quarterly (typically) in a traditional asset management setup.

Fujitsu's Digital Annealer has also demonstrated its capability in returning a 60% higher Sharpe ratio for its optimized portfolio. While frequent portfolio rebalancing will have transaction cost implications, it is essential to perform the task during times of high volatility.

The example discussed is that of a Digital Annealer, however, the same level of optimization could be achieved using quantum annealers. As explained in the previous section, quantum computers are yet to achieve mainstream capabilities due to decoherence. If the loss of data to noisy environments can be managed, quantum annealers can solve several optimization problems.

The process of portfolio optimization also uses a machine learning algorithm called **Principal Component Analysis (PCA)**. What does that mean? As described before, portfolio optimization involves modelling the ideal allocation using several correlated variables. However, wouldn't it be easier if we were able to reduce the number of variables and have no correlations between them? That is exactly what PCA helps us with.

PCA is a technique that uses a principle called feature extraction. Using PCA for optimization, we can drop the least important variables in a portfolio. Each of the remaining variables used are independent of each other, which means correlations need not be explicitly modelled in. Describing PCA in more specific detail is beyond the scope of this book, but those who are interested can read more at `https://towardsdatascience.com/a-one-stop-shop-for-principal-component-analysis-5582fb7e0a9c`

The cost of performing PCA using eigenvalues and eigenvectors is highly prohibitive. The computational cost is $O(N^2)$ for an $N \times N$ matrix. Banks can have millions of stocks, which means N could be in the millions. However, using a quantum PCA algorithm, it has been demonstrated that the cost of performing the same computation is $O(Log N)^2$. This should help PCA go mainstream within financial services, as it massively simplifies portfolio optimization. Reference: S. Lloyd, M. Mohseni, and P. Rebentrost, *Quantum principal component analysis*, Nature Physics 10, 631 (2014). Source: `https://www.nature.com/articles/nphys3029?platform=oscar&draft=journal`

We discussed the use of quantum computing in a capital markets business within risk management and portfolio management. Quantum-inspired digital annealers are currently being tested at Natwest Bank in the UK for managing their network of ATMs. Let's discuss that in the next section.

ATM replenishment

Let's look at a retail banking scenario where quantum computing could help. Replenishing the cash in an ATM accounts for about 35-60% of the total cost of operating an ATM. In this day and age, where high street banks are challenged by cashless, branchless banking business models, operating efficiently is fundamental to staying ahead of competition. According to the Bank of England, there are just over 65,000 ATMs in the UK, delivering over 2.5 billion withdrawals per year. Reference: `https://www.statista.com/statistics/445117/cash-machines-in-the-united-kingdom-by-bank/`

It is very essential that banks can model the amount of cash that is kept in ATMs, while minimizing movement of cash within the network. The largest ATM network in the UK has about 6,000 ATMs in it, and classical computers haven't been able to calculate a replenishment model in real time.

The cost of computation required to model the replenishment has been so prohibitive that a real-time solution to the problem hasn't been achieved using classical computers.

The model needs to come up with an optimized distribution plan, considering any abnormality or sudden increase in demand for cash in a neighborhood. This has several properties that are like the travelling salesman problem that we discussed in *Chapter 2, Quantum Computing - Key Discussion Points.*

This is another combinatorial optimization problem that is a good fit for quantum annealing. Some of the UK banks are already in conversations with Fujitsu (as per the following recent announcement) to use their Digital Annealer for real-time ATM replenishment modelling. Source: `https://www.fujitsu.com/global/digitalannealer/pdf/wp-da-financialsector-ww-en.pdf`

Banks like Natwest and BBVA are already exploring quantum computing to solve some of their computationally and data-intensive problems. It is interesting to see the approach that firms like Hitachi and Fujitsu have taken to develop quantum-inspired technology using classical computing infrastructure. This can help with the transition in the algorithmic, computational, and even philosophical thought processes of the industry. As the industry prepares to be disrupted by quantum computers, this transition process will be necessary. Now that we have discussed applications of quantum computing in financial services, Let's look at Blockchain and its use cases as well.

Blockchain applications

In a recent conversation with a technology-expert-converted-CEO, I asked the question, "Why do you use Blockchain in your application?". He said, "I don't have to. I can use a traditional database and provide a version of it to each one of my clients. When one of them creates a transaction, I can write code to identify it, and trigger a copy to be written into all other databases. I would then build a mechanism where if one of these clients changed the records, I triggered an alert to the entire network about it and hope it all would somehow work as a framework. Alternatively, I could let Blockchain do it all for me."

I loved the answer. Typically, others would go on to defend Blockchain technology and its merits over traditional data management systems. That response should give you a simple view of Blockchain's abilities as a data register, or as it is famously called, the ledger. As far as the financial services industry is concerned, there are very few areas where Blockchain hasn't been tried. I will go through areas where the technology has seen good traction, and then go on to touch areas where Blockchain could be used to create financial ecosystems in a futuristic sense.

Anti-money-laundering (AML) and Know Your Customer (KYC)

AML and KYC processes have been critical within financial services, especially since regulatory pressures have increased over the past 10 years. The investment within compliance functions within banks skyrocketed as they incurred punitive damages from the regulators due to a lack of governance and controls. In 2012 HSBC were fined $1.9 billion in penalties, in a settlement over money laundering. They were proven guilty of being a conduit for drug kingpins and rogue nations. Their network was being used by clients whose identities or transactions had not been verified by the bank's systems and processes. Source: https://www.reuters.com/article/us-hsbc-probe/hsbc-to-pay-1-9-billion-u-s-fine-in-money-laundering-case-idUSBRE8BA05M20121211

As described in *Chapter 1, Introduction to Quantum Computing and Blockchain,* Blockchain could act as an identity ledger and provide self-sovereign identity services across the world. This has implications across social media, access to online services like emails, banking, government (elections), tax planning, refugee management, and several other areas where identity is critical. In the context of this chapter, Blockchain is currently gaining traction as a KYC and AML tool. As a customer, when I go to a bank to open a current account, the bank gets several documents from me to make sure I am who I say I am. All these documents are verified and stored in the bank's systems and files. Now, if I wanted to go for a mortgage with another bank, I must go through the same KYC processes. Sometimes, these processes take weeks as resources are spent to verify the identity of the customer. This would change with Blockchain-based KYC and AML.

As Blockchain can be an immutable transaction ledger in an ecosystem, several banks and firms in India have come together to trial the technology for KYC and AML purposes. In this model, several banks and financial services firms join a Blockchain network. As they check the identity of the customer, they register the customer's details on the network secured using cryptography.

> *"One way to leverage this technology is to help create an ecosystem. As a step towards that, we informally set up the India Trade Connect along with Infosys"*
>
> *–Abhijit Singh, Head of Technology, ICICI Bank.*

This customer information can be shared across the network, when another firm requires the customer's details for KYC. The firm will take the customer's permission and save several days of repeating the KYC process.

Singapore has also been spearheading prototyping across several Blockchain use cases. The **Monetary Authority of Singapore (MAS)**, the regulator in the country, has created a collaborative environment for innovation to thrive. HSBC, Bank of Tokyo-Mitsubishi UFJ, and the OCBC bank have trialed a KYC Blockchain.

Some central banks have driven initiatives that are looking into a digital national identity platform and the banking e-KYC and AML systems together. Client Onboarding is an interesting use case of Blockchain we discussed. But the current industry does a fair job of it, and it is not broken at scale. If there is one area where Blockchain could digitize a largely paper-based value chain, it is Trade finance. The next section expands on the use of Blockchain for trade finance.

Trade finance

In June 2018, I planned to launch my Rhetoriq podcast, with the first season focused on Blockchain and financial inclusion. One of the areas we wanted to focus on was trade finance, primarily because we knew the value chain was yet to be digitized. Trade finance covers the products used by firms across the world to conduct their trade and commerce. Global trade value chains have largely been paper-based, brick and mortar, and haven't benefitted from the digital era. The other big opportunity in trade finance is that most trade routes across the world involve several stakeholders' counterparties and intermediaries.

Regulators, agents, logistics providers, bankers, exporters, importers, and customs officers are all involved in making a global trade route work. Most of these stakeholders in the value chain check and verify and pass the trade to the next stage. Every step of the process involves successful validation of the previous step.

However, most trade value chains typically involve one-to-one interactions and handshakes. There is no visibility of the interactions between two parties. This results in duplication of efforts across the trade route, and often there is a lack of transparency about the status of the trade.

Banks and financial services firms across the world provide letters of credit and financing for trade and commerce to thrive. Therefore, it is in their interest to ensure that the trade value chain across the world becomes operationally more efficient. Several firms and consortiums have come together to solve this problem.

One of the guests of my Rhetoriq podcast was David Henderson from Sweetbridge. He discussed the challenges of solving key issues with trade finance and stressed the need to have a narrow problem area to solve to get the product working in a commercial environment successfully.

we.trade, Marco Polo, and Batavia are notable Blockchain players in the trade finance world. we.trade is a consortium of banks that focus on trade across **small and medium-sized businesses (SMEs)** within Europe. The consortium includes KBC, Société Générale, Deutsche Bank, HSBC, Natixis, Rabobank, UniCredit, Santander, and Nordea.

In March 2019, Marco Polo conducted their first live trade finance transaction on their platform. The platform runs on R3's Corda Blockchain and was used by Commerzbank and LBBW for two transactions between technology company Voith and pump and valve manufacturer KSB.

Batavia was led by IBM and three banks had participated in the network. However, in Q4 2018, three of the banks moved to we.trade network, referring to it as the merger of we.trade and Batavia. As more interledger protocols go mainstream, some of the smaller Blockchains should be able to co-exist with the bigger ones.

The trade finance industry is a low-hanging fruit for Blockchain as it doesn't suffer from legacy systems. This is unlike some of the other banking functions that Blockchain consortiums have tried to exploit. As the value chain offers a greenfield opportunity for the technology, it is more likely to be a success story for Blockchain than other financial services use cases.

The introduction of Blockchain into trade finance would make it more efficient. Tracking of goods in near real time can keep trade finance providers well informed. It can reduce corruption at scale across several trade corridors of the world. By bringing in immutable transaction registering capability, it can also bring financial inclusion for individuals involved in trade.

Most firms working on this use case are doing so in a limited and safe environment. The real benefit will be realized only when this is opened up to a larger community and several world trade routes. As the ecosystem on the Blockchain grows, the benefits of the trade ledger will grow too.

We have discussed international trade and Blockchain's role in that particular space. Let's now look at how Blockchain can help with international money transfers.

Remittance

Remittance in the banking context is defined as the process in which a foreign worker sends money back to their home country. The remittance market has been growing steadily over the years. 2018 saw a record volume of $529 billion sent to middle- and low-income countries. This was a 9.6% increase from the 2017 remittance volumes.

Most developing countries see remittance as their largest source of external funding. In 2017, India topped the beneficiary countries list with $69 billion of remittance flowing in. China had $64 billion in remittances in 2017, and Asia Pacific had a 53% share of Global remittance inflow volumes. More details about this market can be gathered from the World Bank's website. Reference: `https://www.worldbank.org/en/news/press-release/2019/04/08/record-high-remittances-sent-globally-in-2018`

It is important to understand the impact remittance has on the GDP of some middle- and low-income countries. *Figure 3* highlights the dependency that many emerging economies have on remittance. Some of these countries have 30% or more of their GDP relying on remittance inflows.

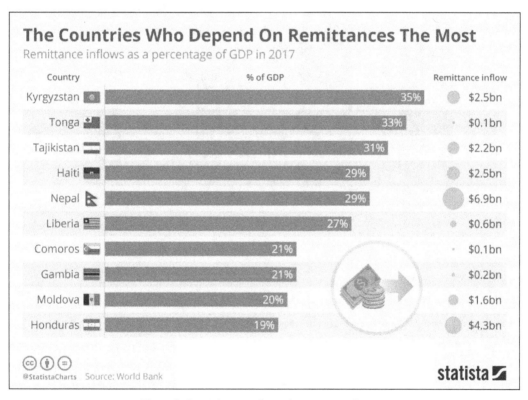

Figure 3: Countries most dependent upon remittances

With the sheer size of the remittance market and reliance on this source of cash by several countries in the world, many firms have turned their attention to this market. The traditional money transfer firms like Western Union and MoneyGram have approached the market using an agency model. Western Union is present in over 200 countries with 500,000 agents and MoneyGram has over 350,000 agents.

The intermediaries make the value chain inefficient and expensive. The costs of remittance are still very high and that creates opportunities for disruptive firms using Blockchain. *Figure 4* shows the trends in the costs of transactions between 2016 and 2018. Several remittance-focused firms like TransferWise have made this value chain more efficient and user-friendly. However, there are still efficiencies to be had in this market.

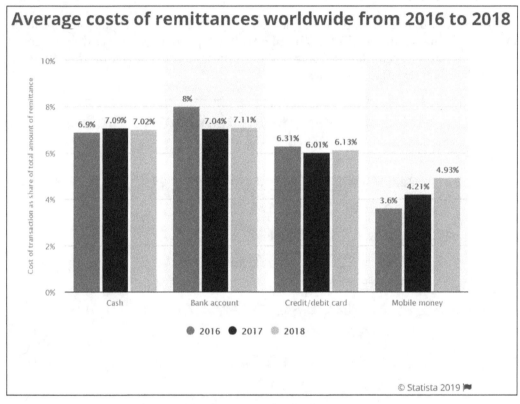

Figure 4: Worldwide average costs of remittances, 2016-2018

We have had a brief look at the remittance market through a retail lens. In today's international money transfer process, banks have relationships with correspondent banks to make the payment to a party overseas. As a result, inefficiencies exist when firms want to transfer money from one part of the world to another.

For example, let's take firm A who wants to transfer funds from their Citibank account in the US to their supplier firm B's IDBI bank account in India. Citibank may not have a direct relationship with IDBI bank, and ICICI may be the correspondent bank in India. This means, the money will have to be routed through ICICI before it reaches the supplier's IDBI bank account.

This process has several drawbacks:

- Correspondent banks take a commission to facilitate the payment
- Every hop of the money adds time to the process
- There is often very little transparency on where the money is at any point in time

As a result of these inefficiencies, using Blockchain to disintermediate the value chain, reduce transaction costs, and bring near real-time transparency to the state of the money transfer is extremely useful. As we know, bits have no boundaries. Therefore, when a Blockchain is used for remittance, the two parties involved will make a peer-to-peer transaction between their wallets.

This process doesn't require a middleman to facilitate the transaction. It only requires that the sender and the receiver of the money is on the Blockchain, and every transaction is registered on the Blockchain. Tracking the transaction is critical in an institutional context, as it can help banks and other institutions involved in a transaction to manage cashflows.

At the start of 2019, Ripple had extended its partnerships to over 200 banks worldwide to enable cross-border transactions. IBM have launched a cross-border payment infrastructure called IBM World Wire that uses the Stellar Blockchain. Another notable name is JP Morgan who have announced their work on JPM Coin using their proprietary Quorum Blockchain. Amongst several institutional experiments in the Blockchain space, I have followed SWIFT's pilot closely. The pilot is quite significant in the context of Blockchain and remittance, largely because of the role of SWIFT in cross-border payments.

A SWIFT experiment

The SWIFT experiment is a key initiative to create a prototype of a cross-border payment messaging infrastructure on a permissioned Blockchain. SWIFT is the acronym for "**The Society for Worldwide Interbank Financial Telecommunication.**" SWIFT's messaging infrastructure is used by banks to communicate quickly and accurately about money transfers.

SWIFT is one of the key mechanisms behind international money transfers between institutions. There are over 10,000 member institutions on the SWIFT network who send over 25 million messages every day. Between 2017 and 2018, SWIFT conducted a Blockchain pilot to understand the feasibility of using Blockchain for their infrastructure.

After almost a year of the feasibility study on **Distributed Ledger Technology (DLT)**, the takeaways were as follows:

- Cross-border payments could work on a DLT-based infrastructure.

- Intra-day and real-time liquidity management could be performed using DLT.

- About 34% of the cost of an international payment is due to the correspondent bank's trapped liquidity. DLT could add efficiencies here.

- Further progress is required with infrastructures within banks to use DLT more effectively.

- 528 channels were used in the SWIFT pilot. In the real world, more than 100,000 channels would need to be defined and DLT should handle the volumes.

- Banks' back offices rely on legacy technology and operations that aren't yet suited to interoperate with DLT.

The result of the SWIFT experiment was a stark warning to the banking industry who were looking at Blockchain as their silver bullet. It demonstrated that no technology could fix broken processes and legacy systems that lacked standards.

We have looked at efforts to tackle the institutional cross border payments space. Let's now look at the activity within the retail remittance world.

Retail remittance

Retail remittance is a $500 billion market to exploit. However, the challenge with retail remittance is that, there are very few firms who have a broad enough customer base to have global relevance. That is why Facebook's experiment to add cryptocurrency-based payments to WhatsApp is very exciting. With over 1.5 billion users across the world, this could be an effective retail remittance platform. WhatsApp payments (non-cryptocurrency) are already being piloted in India, which is its largest market, with 200 million users.

In several African economies, Blockchain is being used to accelerate financial inclusion initiatives. Financial inclusion is the process of offering financial services like lending money to people who historically haven't had access to them. There are firms like the Wala Foundation, Humaniq, and Sela Technology Solutions who are using Blockchain to provide financial inclusion in the region. They typically perform a KYC check on their customers and provide them with a Blockchain wallet. This has helped unbanked people to find a means of holding and transferring funds digitally. In the process of doing so, they also create an economic identity for themselves as all their transactions are held on the Blockchain.

Remittance using Blockchain for retail customers is a more compelling use case in emerging markets than in the developed part of the world. In the developed world, Blockchain can be used to save transaction costs. In Africa and Latin America, remittance can be used as a means to move money out of an unstable economy to preserve the value created.

For example, a customer in Zimbabwe or Venezuela fearing that his bank balance would lose 50% of its value in a day due to the local economic landscape could immediately transfer the funds to Bitcoins. This is a known trend in Venezuela, who adopted a central bank-backed digital currency to steer clear of sanctions and negative sentiments from global stock markets. The effectiveness of their move is debatable, but it remains an application of Blockchain. Let us now look at the central bank digital currency initiatives across the world.

Central bank-backed digital currency

Central bank-backed digital currency has been a topic of interest across the world, especially through late 2017 and the whole of 2018. The initial narrative for Blockchain was about decentralization and disintermediation. However, the Blockchain community started to appreciate that the purpose of the middleman in a value network was establishing trust. The middleman sometimes took a slice of the pie for fulfilling that purpose. In the case of a central bank-backed digital currency, the middleman could help establish governance and order.

Many central banks across the world have been toying with the digital currency idea for some time. The MAS have been testing the waters through its pilots and prototypes. Despite the cryptocurrency ban, the **Reserve Bank of India (RBI)** has been exploring this idea too. The most sensational announcement came in 2018, however, when Venezuela launched their digital currency.

The president of Venezuela, Nicolas Maduro's video went viral when he announced that they were using Petro as their digital currency, which was backed by real-world assets. The Petro pre-sale was launched in March 2018, and raised about $735 million on its first day. The key aspects of Petro were as follows:

- Hugo Chavez had foreseen a "strong currency backed by raw materials."
- It was announced in December 2017 that the Petro would supplement Venezuela's Bolivar and help overcome US sanctions.
- The government would produce and control the supply of Petro.

- The value of Petro would be tied to the cost of a barrel of Venezuelan oil, and they had committed 5 billion barrels of oil to the currency.

- At the price of oil at the time of the pre-sale, 100 million Petros could help raise around $6 billion. That would help Venezuela pay a portion of their debt.

With all these features, Petro still didn't succeed. There were two major objectives of Petro. One was to curb the devaluation of the Bolivar (Venezuelan currency), by pegging the value of Petro to the country's oil wealth. The other key objective was to circumvent sanctions in the international markets.

Petro failed to achieve both these objectives. There were several reasons for that:

- The government had planned several measures to enrich the Petro ecosystem, by allowing mining, and backing it up with further reserves. However, none of those measures were executed.

- The international community's sentiments towards the Venezuelan economy were low. Therefore, a cryptocurrency backed by the country's assets was viewed as a risky option.

- In 2018, Donald Trump issued sanctions against the Petro.

- The crypto community didn't get involved, as it saw Petro as a very centralized ecosystem.

In the end, the very aspect that was projected as the strength of the Petro (backing by the country's oil reserves) worked against it. It is a lesson to future central banks and regulators that plan a digital currency. The currency is only as good as the assets underlying it.

The digital currency story in India, however, is slightly different. While it was about resolving the debt solution and evading issues with sanctions in Venezuela, it was more about accountability, transparency, and efficiencies in India. The RBI is exploring digital currency due to the unsustainable costs of printing and managing paper currency. 7 billion Indian Rupees (~$100 million) is spent every year on creating and managing the Rupee.

That is part of the motivation to move to a digital currency. The larger motivation is that the infrastructure to identify every single citizen in the country is already in place in the form of Aadhaar. If the Rupee went digital, anyone holding the Aadhaar card could create a digital wallet and get on the banking system. It would create financial inclusion at scale and be a leap-frog moment for the world to draw inspiration from.

In May 2019, the MAS completed their digital currency proof of concept with the Bank of Canada. Accenture and JP Morgan were involved in the experiment involving exchanging the **Canadian Dollar (CAD)** for the **Singapore Dollar (SGD)**. The principle of **Hash Time Locked Contracts (HTLC)** was used to ensure an all-or-nothing guarantee. HTLC uses smart contracts to synchronize all the actions making up a transaction so that either they all happen, or none happens.

A few takeaways of the approach are as follows:

- The MAS network was built on the Quorum Blockchain and the Bank of Canada network was built on Corda.
- Interledger payments were used to send the funds between the two Blockchains.
- The HTLC method could be used for multi-party transactions in a trustless network. However, in a permissioned Blockchain, typically used by institutions, if one leg of a transaction fails, there could be different models to roll back the successful legs of the transaction.
- They also explored models where intermediaries (correspondent banks) were involved in conducting the transaction.

Clearly this space is in its infancy. However, the potential is huge if the infrastructure can handle high transaction volumes. This can be clearly seen with China's CBDC initiative. As a response to Facebook's Libra initiative, several Chinese leaders urged the nation to launch its digital currency. The trade war with the US accelerated the thinking and as a result, at the point of writing this chapter, the date for the launch of China's CBDC has been set to November 11. If China successfully launches its CBDC, many Asian economies will follow.

Even with China's CBDC, they have used Blockchain only in a limited fashion due to the technology limitations. There is still a lot of work to be done to ensure the technology scales. The regulatory framework around this and the exception handling of broken or unfulfilled transactions will have to be modelled, understood, and agreed globally. Another exciting development of Blockchain is in security tokens, which digitize real-world assets and help democratize the exchange of these assets. Let's look at them in the next section.

Security tokens

I touched upon the utility versus security tokens conundrum in *Chapter 1, Introduction to Quantum Computing and Blockchain*. Here, we'll discuss what a security means in the eyes of a financial regulator like the **Security Exchange Commission (SEC)**. The SEC uses the "Howey's Test" to assess whether something is a security or not. It was a test used by the Supreme Court in 1946 to rule a judgement on a real estate case and has since been used to identify securities.

The Howey test typically asks three questions:

1. Is there an investment of money?

2. Is the investment in a common enterprise?

3. Is there an expectation of profit from the work of the promoters or the third party?

In the first question, the term "money" is used explicitly. However, the question was later extended to include other assets as well. As a result of this framework of thinking, several ICOs based out of the US had to deal with punitive damages in the hands of the SEC.

Many of them felt they were utility tokens, as they helped build an ecosystem, but in the eyes of the regulator they were security tokens with the mask of a utility token. As this argument continues, the rise of security tokens and the ecosystem around it in 2018 and 2019 has been remarkable to watch.

As a **Venture Capital** (**VC**) investor, I often encounter questions about the liquidity of this asset class. When I pitch to my investors for capital for my fund, I get asked "When can I exit my investment in your fund?". Or "Can you return my money by the end of next year as I plan to buy a property at that time?". My answer is, please do not plan your liquidity based on your investment into a VC fund.

Liquidity is a critical issue in some asset classes like venture capital, private equity, and real estate. Security tokens bring the much-needed liquidity to these asset classes. The ICO boom in 2016-2017 really focused on early-stage venture capital. I felt quite excited at that time about the possibilities because it democratized fundraising to an extent not seen before. It globalized fundraising and challenged the VC community in doing so. However, it failed because it lacked in two key aspects:

- It focused on an asset class, where the inherent value of the underlying (early-stage private equity) was hard to assess. Therefore, when the bubble eventually burst, people lost all their money. If the underlying had inherent value, the losses would have been limited.

- It didn't have the governance and controls to support the funding ecosystem and ended up becoming prey to human greed.

I believe the model still has merit, however, there needs to be a robust framework to support it. However, with more regulatory controls being thought through, more ecosystem maturity, and with underlying assets with better inherent value, security tokens have a much better chance of going mainstream.

At the start of 2019, DX Exchange announced the launch of their Blockchain platform to tokenize NASDAQ stocks. There have been several projects across the world that were focused on tokenizing real estate assets. This allowed people to invest smaller amounts into real estate, but more importantly, provided liquidity if the investor wanted to sell their stake.

In one of my recent panel discussions, I jokingly mentioned that there would be a time in my life when I could trade the tokenized mangoes from my mangrove in India for tokens of Buckingham Palace. It is already theoretically possible using security tokens.

One other key development with Blockchain in financial services is the "*Death of decentralization.*" As the Blockchain narrative unfolded over the years, one of the key "*Pitches*" for the technology was that Blockchain would decentralize and disintermediate Wall Street. It was expected to be highly disruptive in that sense, and several big names from Wall Street jumped ship to Blockchain firms to make it happen.

However, through 2018 and 2019, most events pointed to one key trend for me: that decentralization is a myth. Value networks cannot be decentralized as easily as it was initially portrayed. As the Blockchain ecosystem has evolved, we have seen centralized exchanges grow faster than decentralized ones. We have now started seeing firms like Flovtech, based out of Switzerland, who provide liquidity to these exchanges.

I am extremely delighted for start-ups like Flovtech, as they bring liquidity to small and new Altcoins listed on exchanges. However, that just goes to show that the decentralization drive has failed. Blockchain-driven value networks were once hailed as the new capital markets, however, they are just a more digitized and liquid version of the old capital markets. Permissioned blockchains, central bank digital currencies, centralized exchanges, and liquidity providers all point to a centralized Blockchain economy.

Conclusion

The financial services industry is confronting disruption at scale from two key forces: regulation and technology innovation. As banks wake up to the fact that technology is no longer non-core to their business, they start to explore new ways of gaining competitive advantage. One of the key areas to achieve operational excellence in financial services is by using the right technologies for middle-office and back-office processes.

In the past, banks and financial services firms have relied upon cost-effective ways of reaching optimal solutions. Be it in risk management, portfolio management, or any other data and computation-intensive problem, they have often traded off accuracy in the interest of achieving a time-sensitive, cost-effective solution. Where accuracy was needed, it meant that more computational power or more time would be required to arrive at a solution.

As the race for technology adoption was led by Fintech firms, banks have now shunned the legacy approach to innovation. Banks across the world, like BBVA, Barclays, and DBS have all taken a digital-friendly approach to please their customers. While that may help them with their top line, the bottom line must be preserved using cutting-edge technology, at viable costs.

Quantum computing has highlighted the use of new-age methods to solve computationally-intensive problems. They can provide results in a short span of time, which is critical in several banking scenarios. Be it for optimizing interest rate swaps by netting agreements or calculating **High-Quality Liquid Assets (HQLA)** in a treasury scenario, quantum computers offer real-time solutions.

Combining principles of machine learning with quantum computing algorithms can yield disruptive results for banks. The usage of quantum PCA in portfolio optimization can help simplify the process of dealing with thousands of correlated variables to arrive at a final model.

The focus for FinTechs over the past few years has been customer-facing use cases, and I firmly believe that is a missed opportunity for these technology-intensive financial services providers. This is because, if they do not focus on achieving operational excellence through cutting-edge technologies such as artificial intelligence, Blockchain, and quantum computing, they will soon be overtaken by the banks.

It is critical for banks to focus on what the FinTechs are yet to achieve – scale. With the data volumes that they command and with their huge customer base, banks should be able to leverage these technologies to regain lost ground.

In this chapter, we have looked at the applications of emerging technologies such as quantum computing and Blockchain in financial services. Health and wealth are often the core industries that technology should focus on to create leapfrog moments. In the next chapter, let us focus on the use of these technologies in healthcare and pharmaceuticals.

5

Interview with Dr. Dave Snelling, Fujitsu Fellow

In the previous chapters of the book I provided a view on the technological details around quantum computing and Blockchain. I discussed use cases of these two technologies across different industries. I discussed how the technologies had several aspects in common, and there were technical reasons why I felt they were on a collision course. However, when we look at things from a business benefit perspective, we see that they are largely synergetic to each other.

The book's first objective was to establish the technological concepts behind these two groundbreaking technologies. Once we discussed that, the focus of the book moved on to the *so what* of these technologies. I wanted to establish that these technologies will have an increasingly large place in our lives over time. However, that is still an incomplete picture when we lack the views of those who are working firsthand with these technologies in order to make that happen.

In this chapter and the subsequent ones, I publish the contents of my interviews with quantum computing experts. These interviews were eye-opening for me, especially where we discussed possibilities of changing people's lives at scale. In this chapter I have captured the discussion between me and Dave Snelling from Fujitsu.

Dave has had several roles within Fujitsu. He is a Fujitsu fellow and distinguished engineer, Program Director of Artificial Intelligence, and part of the CTO EMEA office at Fujitsu. He began his career after studying high-performance computing during his university days. After a few brief career hops, including one within academia, he joined Fujitsu 22 years ago.

The first time I met Dave was at a Fujitsu-hosted event at their offices in Baker Street in London. Dave presented the impact of digital annealers in finance and logistics. After his presentation, when I was introduced to Dave, he was mentioned as the brains behind Fujitsu's Digital Annealer. For a minute, I thought it might be a long technical chat with a scientist. It turned out to be a chat where Dave was very eloquent about the practical applications of the Digital Annealer.

I knew straightaway that I had to interview Dave for my book. We met again a few weeks later, and this time, I briefed Dave about my plan for the book. We met at the Fujitsu offices, and Dave was kind enough to provide his views on quantum computing in a much more comprehensive manner. The best part of the chat was when Dave picked up my tablet and drew a graph representing how quantum computers, classical computers, and digital annealers would evolve over the next two decades.

We then scheduled a session for the interview, and Dave provided his thoughts on how he saw quantum technology being used across different industries. The interview is captured below:

Arun: Dave, thank you very much for agreeing to do this interview. Let's start with a brief overview of how you got into quantum computing, and your explorations in the field of quantum computing.

Dave: Short of sending you my CV, I started out when I left graduate school for the first time. I did high-performance computing at graduate school and came over to Europe with a start-up working in the same space. The start-up then went bankrupt, as a lot of them did over the years. That was back in 1983-84. I did a little bit of consulting after that and then I taught at the Universities of Leicester and Manchester until about 1997, mostly teaching novel computing and object-oriented design.

I then joined Fujitsu to support their supercomputing project at the European Centre for Medium Range Weather Forecasting (ECMWF). I've been at Fujitsu ever since. My initial days at Fujitsu were mainly spent in the laboratory. I spent a lot of time looking at a variety of different things, starting with high-performance computing.

I started to work on grid computing, the predecessors to cloud computing. Towards the end of my time at the labs and in my transition over to the business unit, I was working around artificial intelligence. About 2 years ago Fujitsu announced its Digital Annealer. I had to school up on quantum computing very quickly, and my past experiences helped. So, I push quantum computing research at Fujitsu, but initially I came at it from the commercial side.

My technical background was necessary to really understand what the challenges are for what I call *true quantum computing*. I was also able to address the use cases that the Digital Annealer could address from both a technical and a business strategy point of view. So, that's sort of where I've gotten to now. For the past year, I've been the go-to person for technical aspects across international business around the Digital Annealer within Fujitsu.

A major part of my role is, of course, keeping my marketing people and our own salespeople from selling a product as something that it isn't (he laughs). I also make sure that in all our internal and external communication we are clear that what we are selling is not a quantum computer. This is a Digital Annealer, but it's quite good at solving some problems.

What are those problems? How do we then map them and so forth? That's where I am.

Arun: Thank you so much for that. That leads us nicely into the next question. Can you please tell us about the Digital Annealer and how it came to be?

Dave: I can tell you the background of the Digital Annealer. It was developed by a team in Fujitsu laboratories in Japan. We have a team there with a history in custom technology design. The team identified the *combinational optimization* problem as a key target to resolve, which may have been inspired by some of the developments in the early days of D-Wave. That gave Fujitsu the indication that the market for tailored solutions to combinational optimization problems was about to emerge.

As early as 2011, D-Wave developed quantum computers (128-qubit) that were focused on optimization problems using quantum annealing techniques.

Combinatorial optimization problems are those where mathematical techniques are applied to find optimal solutions within a finite set of possible solutions. The set of possible solutions is generally defined by a set of restrictions, and the set is too large for exhaustive search. An example is the traveling salesman problem, where the total traveling distance must be minimized while each client is visited exactly once. Source: `https://www.sciencedirect.com/topics/computer-science/combinatorial-optimization-problem`

In fact, it is now emerging. So, the timing was just about right. We then set about it with a pure scientific technical approach. How do we make this happen? The Digital Annealer is the result of that undertaking to develop technology that will address the combinational optimization subset of quantum applications.

That has then become a piece of technology with a complete service wrapped around it. Fujitsu now provides these services across multiple stages, beginning with identifying whether the problem is suitable for combinational optimization. We then make sure that the problem in hand is big enough to warrant a seriously high-performance solution to it. Small combinational optimization problems don't need the Digital Annealer. There are also some problems that are too big. We're working on addressing these problems in time, of course. Therefore, the process starts with identifying an industrial problem and then the real challenge is mapping the business problem within the industry to a *quadratic unconstrained binary optimization problem*.

The Quadratic Unconstrained Binary Optimization problem QUBO has become a unifying model for representing a wide range of combinatorial optimization problems, and for linking a variety of disciplines that face these problems. A new class of quantum annealing computer that maps QUBO onto a physical qubit network structure with specific size and edge density restrictions is generating a growing interest in ways to transform the underlying QUBO structure into an equivalent graph having fewer nodes and edges. Source: https://dl.acm.org/citation.cfm?id=3160134

Arun: Interesting. Just building on top of that, why did we need this Digital Annealer. Why couldn't we have solved these combinatorial optimization problems using traditional machine learning techniques?

Dave: The nature of combinational optimization problems is that they do not lend themselves to exact solutions. My favorite example is the typical knapsack problem. I probably told you this in a previous conversation, but here for your readers, I will give it to you again.

The *knapsack problem*: We have got 27 items (that's a carefully picked number!). Twenty-seven items to pick up and put in my backpack, and I can only carry a certain amount of weight. I want to get the most value in there. Some of the items just come with their own intrinsic value, but there's also the possibility of interaction between items. For example, the gold ring and the diamond have individual value, but as a diamond ring they have even more value. That kind of interaction is positive.

There's also negative interaction. Among our list of items, we also have a chicken and a fox. Negative interaction is true of these – they're not likely to get along. You know you don't want to put both of them in your backpack, because then you have a dead chicken and a messy fox: less value than if you take just one or the other.

The complexity of interactions in this kind of problem are simply not solvable in any tractable manner using modern technology that we have today. In fact, if you could weigh 1,000 backpacks every second, to try all the possible combinations, it would take you 500 trillion millennia to find the optimum combination.

I've always liked that because 1,000 packs per second and 500 trillion millennia are numbers that people are going to stop and understand. So that kind of a problem is a combinational optimization problem. Beyond a certain scale, you cannot feasibly identify exact solutions – even with the Digital Annealer. So, what you're looking for is one of the heuristic approaches.

A **heuristic** technique, often called simply a **heuristic**, is any **approach** to problem solving, learning, or discovery that employs a practical **method** not guaranteed to be optimal or perfect, but sufficient for the immediate goals. Source: `https://www.101computing.net/heuristic-approaches-to-problem-solving/`

The approach used by the Digital Annealer is simulated annealing, which is a very effective way of finding the local minima and then finding a deeper minimum.

A **graphics processing unit** (**GPU**) is a specialized electronic circuit designed to rapidly manipulate and alter memory to accelerate the creation of images in a frame buffer intended for output to a display device. Source: `https://en.wikipedia.org/wiki/Graphics_processing_unit`

So, for that kind of problem we can use a heuristic approach on a conventional machine or on GPUs. We have an emulator for the Digital Annealer that runs on GPUs. It is many thousands of times slower on the GPU than on the Digital Annealer, but it does a good job of solving small problems because it can emulate the way in which the Digital Annealer evaluates all the possible changes from one state to the next. As you know, each state is described as a string of bits. The Digital Annealer evaluates what would happen if you changed each one of those individual bits and evaluates all of those simultaneously. Now, that's about 130,000-way parallelism – and all on the same chip.

If you tried to do that with a CPU cluster to get 130,000 cores talking to each other, you'd have a huge machine. Of the many problems you might associate with such a machine, one of the biggest issues is that you can't have the cores all talk to each other every cycle, whereas in the Digital Annealer these 130,000 different cases can be evaluated and compared with each other simultaneously.

When you try to do the same thing on a GPU you do a little better than you do on a CPU, but you still don't have the connectivity. That's what you have on the Digital Annealer - very tight coupling for a particular class problem. It only does the simulated annealing across a binary field of 8,192 bits.

In addition, there's a cooling cycle, which slowly varies the sensitivity as a simulated annealer moves from one possible solution to another. That automatic cooling is built into the hardware.

> A simulated annealer needs a cooling schedule. If the temperature is too low, the annealer will not be able to escape the local minima. When the temperature is too high, it will struggle to converge to a local minima. The cooling cycle needs to be planned based on what the sensitivity of the annealer needs to be.

In addition to that, there is some hardware built in to detect when you've fallen into a local minima. You can then encode how sensitive you are to that detection and then the hardware will automatically, temporarily raise the temperature and start searching again. You get up to a higher temperature to get out of that local minimum and then start cooling down again, remembering of course where you were.

There are some cases where you can get the actual minima if you know your problem has a number that's going to be the minimum. For example, in pure constraint optimization problems the annealer can just find any solution that matches all the constraints.

Arun: Have you tried the knapsack problem with your Digital Annealers?

Dave: Oh yes, we have. We have run the classical set of combinatorial optimization problems such as graph coloring, max cut, knapsack, and the travelling salesperson. The knapsack problem for me is like portfolio optimization in finance. Therefore, if I could solve the knapsack problem, I believe, we can solve portfolio optimization in finance. What (*stocks, bonds, derivatives, cash, commodities and in what proportion*) am I putting into my portfolio?

The weight is the maximum budget I'm allowed to carry on the portfolio, the volatility is the way in which the different assets (like *stocks* and *bonds*) behave against each other. Some of these assets work together, some of them work against each other. In the case where they work against each other, that's a good thing because you want them to create the diversification needed. So, there is optimizing in that context.

The travelling salesperson problem itself should be avoided because the pure travelling salesperson problem has so many decades of research and mathematics against it that it's easy to solve. If you take variants on it, they are more interesting. One of the projects we've worked on with BMW is welding the bottom of a chassis on a car. You have several seams that you have to weld. What is the fastest way to do all these welds?

A couple of things are different between the classical travelling salesperson and the welding problem. When you visit a *city* (point of welding), you must stay there for however long it takes you to do that weld. Therefore, there's a time associated with being in the city. In the case of the welding example, because the seam is in two dimensions you come out somewhere else in your map so it's kind of like a wormhole.

It is a time delayed wormhole where you can go in either end and come out the other end. Now when you have those variations (from the classical travelling salesman problem), and you put those kinds of constraints into your problem, you no longer have a classic travelling salesperson problem that you can solve on your laptop, because it's just gotten way more complicated.

Such a problem is well within the scope of the Digital Annealer to address, however. The DA can process up to about 90 seams, and it can even operate with multiple welding robots sharing each other's workspace. So, it is like two robots working together telling each other, "While you're over there, let me just do a couple of these for you." Working in this manner, the robots can work much more rapidly. We've had some big success with that in terms of adding efficiencies to the manufacturing process.

 BMW and Fujitsu are working on a Digital Annealer-powered solution to add efficiencies to BMW's manufacturing processes. The explanation above from David refers to the initiative, where the Digital Annealer worked on a problem that is similar to the travelling salesperson's problem. BMW factories have several robots attending to several tasks on a car. The Digital Annealer is being used to make the robots more efficient in assembling cars.

Arun: Would you be able to reveal any statistics in terms of the efficiencies you've managed to achieve for that particular use case?

Dave: For that particular use case BMW have published a press release about it.

And the press release reveals the following:

> *"Currently, prototype quantum computing solutions addressing this challenge can compute optimized routes for seven welded seams. Working with FUJITSU Quantum-Inspired Computing Digital Annealer, a major automotive OEM has already tested and optimized 22 seams, cost effectively increasing the number of cars produced using the same resources, and this is about to be raised to 64 seams (with 8,192-bit scale) making a disruptive change."*

Arun: Great. I had a question on the applications of the Digital Annealer. Over the last six months, since we've started talking about this, I've met some people working on tough problems using quantum computing. The problems range from modelling elections, traffic management, climate modelling, and even recession modelling. With all these different applications possible, what are the low-hanging fruits? What are the other exciting areas you are focusing on?

Dave: As mentioned before, we are looking into manufacturing – like the work with BMW, where we're optimizing the manufacturing processes. And that's a low-hanging fruit in the sense that we know how to solve the problem, and it has a big impact if you can increase production to keep up with demand, i.e. without having to build a new factory. Portfolio optimization is another big impact area in the finance sector that we're looking into.

The second area is for something like Solvency Capital Requirement (SCR). It is important to be able to find a portfolio that gives you a sufficiently safe SCR. I think it is probably the most complicated computation we've tried to put through the Digital Annealer.

Arun: I've been more of a capital markets person and less of an insurance expert. I understand SCR is an equivalent of value at risk (VaR), is that right?

Dave: It is similar, but it is from the insurance sector driven by regulatory requirements. With SCR, we balance an approximation and then compute the actual SCR on the balanced portfolio (of assets). The Digital Annealer is not actually solving for the SCR, but rather a proxy for it. We've tested that the proxy behaves exactly the way that the actual SCR does. We're happy with that kind of process.

We would be looking at VaR, but we haven't got to that yet. We are helping one of our customers to assess the value to the business of more frequent rebalancing, or better-quality rebalancing, or being able to use a larger asset pool to generate their portfolios from inception. However, I can't give you any performance numbers on that yet.

Arun: I had a question on the frequent rebalancing solution. The technology (Digital Annealer) could allow for instantaneous rebalancing if you wanted it to happen. But the transaction costs of doing that will make it financially unviable. In your process of rebalancing and providing recommendations to rebalance, do you also take that transaction cost into account?

Dave: What we do with our approach on the rebalancing cost is this: you can do the assessment and make a separate decision on making the change. So, you can assess every day and when it becomes financially viable you can execute the portfolio rebalancing. We have done some explorations into limiting the percentage of the portfolio that changes at any point, too.

We can rebalance in such a way that only about 10% of the assets change, and they only change by 2 or 3% each. It may be that the rebalancing is a smooth process rather than totally chaotic. Otherwise, you're basically creating a new portfolio every time. But we can also encode constraints to say, *give me a new balanced portfolio where only 5% of my assets change by less than 10%*. That kind of flexibility and constraint management gives us an ability to deal with transaction costs.

Arun: That's interesting. What are the problems you are working on within logistics?

Dave: We've done traffic management using digital annealers in Japan where, rather than a point-to-point journey, you have several point-to-point journeys all at once. You think about a network of taxicabs, taking frequently taken routes and all of them going through the same part of town. If you could tell some of your taxis to take the slightly longer route to reduce congestion, overall, everybody has a quicker journey by about 40%. This would work in Tokyo where they did the study, because the taxicab drivers will do what they're told. This probably wouldn't work in London.

Arun: The Digital Annealer won't work for Indian roads either. As you may know, in India people use intuition to drive rather than the rules of the road, so there is more chaos that the annealer may struggle to cope with. The number of vehicles and people on the road is several times higher (than London), so it would be computationally intensive too.

Dave: Yeah, but this approach would work in military operations and in autonomous vehicle networks. It is not a market today, but something that can happen. In terms of actual transport, one of the bigger problems is not so much which way does the van drive. It's what do we put on the van? This is relevant in a scenario where a van carries something on it to distribute across cities, and digital annealers are used to optimize the route of the van.

That's a much more interesting and challenging problem than just what's the shortest route for the van. One of the examples of that is ATM replenishment. Now this is obviously a disappearing market, but there is at least one bank in every country that will be required to have cash available in almost every town. So, there's at least one customer for this kind of application. But the question there is not so much how you deliver the cash to the stations most efficiently. It's how much cash do you put in which ATM?

Based on how much cash gets distributed, you may now want to visit that place less frequently for topping up the ATM. Because what you're really trying to do is keep the minimum amount of cash in ATMs overnight.

There is also a whole class of problems around job shift scheduling, which at its base is graph coloring. A potential customer I've got has a network of engineers. If these engineers must go out and fix things, which engineer do you send? Which engineer do you put on the shifts? Which day of the week do you send them so that you get all the constraints met, like they all must work 37 hours a week?

We also have constraints such as these engineers needing 2 days off each week. All of them must work some late shifts. When I modelled it, my first version of that problem went way beyond the number of bits I had in the Digital Annealer. So, that problem required partitioning. That's part of our [Fujitsu's] service that wraps around these solutions.

Even as we go to our million-bit target machine, we may have to partition the problems. The larger solutions around partitioning are going to be a part of our business offering. I know that the folks at D-Wave have good software for partitioning for poorly connected or weakly connected annealers. The D-Wave second generation has only 15 nearest neighbors for each bit.

On our chip we've got an 8K-way connectivity to every bit at 64-bit precision. But when we go between chips, we're going to have similar kinds of challenges. It's the same kind of challenges that mechanical engineering CAD (Computer Aided Design), CAM (Computer Aided Manufacture) faced when we try to do simulations, say for energy fields around the components of a mobile phone. You must do 3D modelling to build your mesh and then partition the mesh to put it onto your clustered supercomputer. Partitioning for multiple digital annealers is the same kind of problems.

Arun: Is it [the partitioning solution] already live or are you planning or working on it?

Dave: The clustered machines are not live yet, it's in the lab. The clustering software is still under development. It's targeted for release in 2020. So, it's not that far off.

Arun: I look forward to that. We've touched upon logistics, we've touched upon financial services, we've touched upon traffic management as well and labor management. Are you doing anything in healthcare?

Dave: Yes. Pharmaceuticals is the best way to describe it. The way you use an annealer for that is not to identify the final solution. It is to look for a proxy for the solution, like we did with the SCR in the insurance example. Let's say it's a cancerous cell and you know you want to lock into it with your radioactive drug. To do that, you need to figure out how to design your drug in such a way that it can target that cell only. It turns out that the number of molecular simulations required to solve that problem is enormous.

It takes several hours (hundreds of hours depending on many factors) of computer time to do each one of these simulations, and there are huge costs associated with that. The strategy with the Digital Annealer is we start with a basic molecular structure that we can add things to. For example, we could start with a Benzene ring (C_6H_6). In a Benzene molecule, you've got a ring of six Carbons, with each Carbon bonded to a Hydrogen. You can swap out Hydrogen, so you have 6 different places to put 50 different things. That translates to six to the fiftieth power kind of combinations.

We solve that problem by narrowing things down, using the molecular bond energies to determine the best candidates for producing a feasible molecule. It's not perfect, but it's a lot better than nothing. The possible interactions between the neighboring molecules also need to be factored in. The bond between them is also important because that's a constraint.

This modelling is particularly valuable in the design of drugs. That's an area we're looking at. From a market perspective that's going to take a little bit longer [for the digital annealer to get into]. The pharmaceuticals industry is happy with running great big suites of chemical tests and are slow in adopting new technologies, so it is going to be a penetration challenge. Now, that's healthcare for you.

Arun: Protein folding is a major modelling challenge, and if we got it right we could expedite the drug discovery process. Thanks for touching upon that Dave. What areas of quantum computing do you think will deliver first?

Dave: In my view, there are three broad classifications of the quantum computing world. There is the gate computer, then we have the annealers – both digital and quantum. Also, there's what I call the *analog* quantum devices that can be used to solve a problem in quantum physics. In the *analog* category, you wire up your quantum device to describe a problem in nature.

It's just programming nature into the computer and that's going to produce some results way before gate computers do. Annealers are going to produce results first because we're doing that now with the digital annealer, quantum annealers won't be far behind. But these analog quantum devices will come somewhere in between. They're going to start before we get gate computers cracking RSA algorithms. That will have some important discoveries coming out of physics. This is primarily because they've made a quantum device that when it's doing what it's doing, it's answering a bigger question.

Arun: Interesting. So, when we met last time you drew me a graph. I am not sure if you remember that? [The somewhat rough-around-the-edges drawing is shown below:]

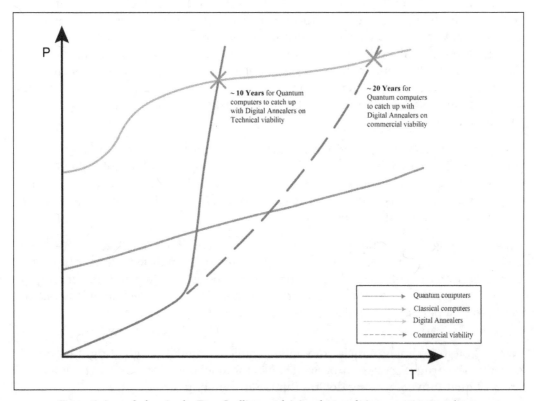

Figure 1: A rough drawing by Dave Snelling, explaining the trends in computing paradigms

Dave: Yes, I do. There's this point on the graph where the digital solution and the quantum solution cross over. One is where they cross over in terms of solvability and then they cross over in terms of pricing. The digital annealers will eventually be commoditized and that will bring their price down progressively, which will push your commercial viability curve farther to the right.

Arun: So why do you feel this trend is beneficial? I think you've spoken about that. Can we briefly discuss the differences between applications of gate-based computers and quantum annealers?

Dave: The biggest one with gate-based is that it's quite simple. A gate-based quantum computer, in theory, will be Turing complete. So, anything that you can describe with a Turing machine, you could put on a quantum gate. You could probably encode a Turing machine onto a quantum gate machine, and you'd be done.

 A Turing machine is a hypothetical machine thought of by the mathematician Alan Turing in 1936. Despite its simplicity, the machine can simulate ANY computer algorithm, no matter how complicated it is. Source: `https://www.cl.cam.ac.uk/projects/raspberrypi/tutorials/turing-machine/one.html`. A Turing complete programming language, or a computing device is equivalent to a Turing machine, in the sense that it can implement any algorithm.

The following is just my opinion. In some ways, I think that gate-based computers have distracted the market from the development of quantum-based solutions, particularly in the analog space that I talked about. There is probably the lower-hanging fruit in that analog space that we could get to by building special-purpose machines.

Now one special-purpose machine is the quantum annealer. They're encoding a direct Hamiltonian operator and then minimizing the energy so you can code your problem up that way. Combinatorial optimization happens to be amenable to annealing. In that sense the digital and quantum annealers solve a very specific problem.

We have an algorithm for factoring integers on the annealer. It doesn't scale to RSA levels, but it does work. If somebody were to actually build a closely coupled million-bit digital annealer, you would probably be getting close. But we're not going to build a closely coupled one. We're going to build a clustered one and then the clustering makes it real hard to use it as a cracker (of RSA).

Arun: With so many opportunities to solve unsolved problems, what are your main challenges when you go to the industry to sell the annealer?

Dave: The go-to-market strategy when we're talking to customers is to be very precise that the Digital Annealer solves exactly one kind of problem. The biggest challenge we face is getting people to step away from what they've heard about Quantum Artificial Intelligence and Quantum Machine Learning.

Arun: Interesting. So, this is something I hear often. It is that we seem to have got distracted with gate-based machines.

But what they don't realize is that quantum computing has given us a way to model nature into a computer. Instead of translating Physics into Math and bending that into computer science operations, you just get to model Physics into machines. During the translation (Physics to Math to computers), we lose a lot of quality information, but in the quantum world it [the loss of information] doesn't happen.

Dave: Well, I agree with that entirely because that's this *analog* quantum computer I keep talking about. Now we almost need to put quotation marks around *analog* because otherwise people may not necessarily understand the context in which I call them analog. The quantum annealers are in the middle ground as they are a kind of general-purpose analog device. But if you could build an analog device that would match your protein (in the healthcare example) and then just let it reach its final low energy state, you have everything.

Arun: Something you mentioned when we met earlier was that logistics was perhaps the biggest market for some of the combinatorial optimization problems. I have seen several complex financial services problems firsthand. We have risk management in financial services, for example, that is quite data-intensive. We deal with millions and millions of data points in this space. If we could solve risk management challenges using annealers, why would optimization be harder in logistics? Is it the dimensionality of data that makes logistics harder?

Dave: From a practical point of view, coding it up in logistics is constraint-driven. Whereas the portfolio optimization space, for example, is mostly driven by the objective function. Typically, when you're describing an annealing problem you have the objective function. Which is what you're trying to optimize. So, when you're trying to optimize for portfolio balancing, you're trying to minimize your risks. Then you put two constraints against that, one is a maximum return and the other is a minimum spend.

You can also code it up as a dual objective function, in terms of a risk parameter that does the balance between risk and return. After this, you can constrain it based on the total budget. So that's one side of the picture.

In the logistics space, it's basically all about constraints. Constraints in the encoding process tend to explode the complexity of the problem. This is because you typically encode the constraint by building the quadratic terms as part of the problem solution. You're using part of the information space to give the code your constraints and so it does make it a little more challenging to also then use this information space to encode your objective function. In addition, sometimes your constraints in logistics will lead to higher order polynomials instead of quadratic.

Arun: Moving on to another topic, I was looking at the semiconductors industry. There are a lot more options for qubit circuitry than just a silicon-based semiconductor model that is used for classical computers. There are different types of materials being used, different models being used. So how do you think that is going to affect the industry? Would it kill the semiconductor monopolies if different types of Qubit circuitry were coming into the picture for it?

Dave: There's a lot of exotic technology coming out around the quantum space in Josephson junctions that have done their own hype cycles followed by periods of quiet. You know, as I remember, Josephson junctions were around decades ago. They then just vanished and now they're coming back under this quantum umbrella. You also have the high-temperature superconductors. They're probably going in and out of popularity.

 A Josephson junction is made by sandwiching a thin layer of a non-superconducting material between two layers of superconducting material. The devices are named after Brian Josephson, who predicted in 1962 that pairs of superconducting electrons could "tunnel" right through the non-superconducting barrier from one superconductor to another. Source: `https://www.scientificamerican.com/article/what-are-josephson-juncti/`

Arun: One final question, Dave. Quantum supremacy – do you think anyone is close to it?

Dave: No, they are not, based on the classical definition. There are other definitions of quantum supremacy that say *can you solve a problem faster on a quantum computer than you can on a computer?* In that sense, yes many of them are close to quantum supremacy.

The fact is that, solving a problem in half a millisecond is very impressive. But if you can solve it in 2 seconds on a laptop, then does it actually change your business model? No. So is it quantum supremacy? Yes, but no.

If it's solving a problem that needs to be solved every month and can take 6 hours on a regular cluster, do you need a Digital Annealer or a quantum device? It's just a straight economic thing. It's not driven by the time window. So, quantum supremacy is a buzz word for sure, at least when discussed at a business level. As soon as somebody wants to say that they've done something with a quantum computer that no one has ever been able to do before – they can claim *quantum supremacy* and you know it will become just a marketing flag.

There is a little cynicism coming out here (from me) that you cannot attribute to Fujitsu. A lot of the hype around quantum supremacy is to secure funding for this kind of research. Firms and research teams use this as a hammer to drive attention and receive research funding. I am particularly keen to see some supremacy in the *analog* space we discussed earlier.

Other areas where I would like to see some meaningful breakthroughs are quantum communication, quantum sensing (for example: gravity sensing), and quantum imaging. These are awesome use cases of quantum computing that use entanglement. The gravity sensor for instance, is very sensitive to gravity. You can sense someone walking behind a wall and can see their gravity signatures on quantum devices. The UK quantum research organization is currently doing a lot of work in this space [1].

Arun: I have been speaking mostly with practitioners and will be talking to UK research organizations soon. Most of them are into academia. This book is focused largely on the practical implications of these technologies; however, it would be good to capture where the research world is heading to.

Dave: Absolutely. Personally, I'm not following the research space right now. I'm busy trying to do a practitioner's role and solving industrial problems.

Arun: Thank you, Dave, I have taken so much of your time. Thank you very much for your insights.

Dave: You are most welcome. I look forward to seeing the finished book.

Conclusion

My conversation with Dave Snelling was very insightful, and there were several takeaways from it. The primary takeaway is how digital annealers can smoothen the entry for quantum computers and annealers in a few years' time. This transition is interesting from both a technical capability perspective and a commercial viability angle.

The other key point that I would like to stress is David's focus on the *so what* of technology. Gate-based computers, so what? Quantum supremacy, so what? And the list goes on. This is an important lesson for technologists: it is very important to identify a problem to solve, and then deploy technological resources towards the solution. I often find technologists creating solutions that are looking for problems, and that is never a good place to innovate from.

It is pretty evident that Dave is enthusiastic about the possibilities of quantum computers. We discussed use cases across several industries in this chapter. However, David also warned us about the possibility of getting too excited about the hype around quantum supremacy.

I personally am inspired by Dave's ability to simplify the narrative. For someone with so many years of laboratory experience, with a long technical background, his storytelling capabilities are amazing. Last but in no way least, I am genuinely touched by how grounded and open he was in sharing his views and thoughts on this industry.

References

1. `http://uknqt.epsrc.ac.uk/about/uknqt-hubs/`

6
The Impact on Healthcare and Pharma

I was born and brought up in a village about 75 miles from the southernmost tip of India. My parents were reasonably well placed in the society and we didn't face any financial challenges growing up. As a result, I personally didn't have to struggle for quality healthcare as I grew up. However, I have seen the medical infrastructure, or the lack of it, on offer to the less fortunate. As a result, I feel a sense of purpose when it comes to innovation in healthcare.

Over the years, several breakthroughs have been achieved in healthcare due to advancements in vaccines, diagnostics, medicines, and surgical procedures. It's hard to ignore these achievements. Source: `https://www.medpagetoday.com/infectiousdisease/publichealth/17594`

The benefits of innovation and improvement within the Healthcare and Pharma sectors would, as you might imagine, have a major impact upon the wellbeing of many worldwide. We'll discuss the context for innovation in this sector, and cover the following areas where quantum computing may facilitate large improvements:

- Drug discovery
- Last mile drug distribution
- Cancer diagnosis

The term *last mile* is used to refer to the final destination of a distribution network. In this context, it would refer to the capability to get quality healthcare to the rural population in emerging markets.

These examples are not the exhaustive set of healthcare use cases that can benefit from quantum computing. However, they should bring to life the potential benefits of the technology.

The rally for innovation

It is critical to understand the pain points in the healthcare and pharma value chain to spot opportunities for emerging technologies such as **artificial intelligence** (**AI**), Blockchain, and quantum computing. Over the last few years, AI has been trialed and employed at an unprecedented scale to solve some of these issues. IBM have been quite vocal about their Watson-enabled healthcare capabilities.

Yet, there is a lot of work to be done to make healthcare seamless, cost effective and inclusive across the world. Even in developed economies such as the US and the UK, healthcare is one service where consumers (patients) would like to see major transformations.

There are several innovative trends like remote consultation using apps like Babylon, or clinical decision support using IBM Watson, or drug discovery using AI applications. IBM Watson have tried to create the **Robo Doctor**, but they have big challenges due to the lack of focus with their approach.

Thanks to the convergence of wearables, **Internet of Things** (**IoT**), and analytics on IoT data, it is now possible to make several health decisions instantly. These tools also help insurance firms price the premiums that customers pay.

On the other side of the spectrum the pharma supply chain is shouting out for more innovation. The supply chain is inefficient, opaque, and is ripe with counterfeits due to lack of governance and controls.

That is not to say that we haven't made big strides in healthcare. The life expectancy for AIDS victims is now nearing the normal life expectancy. Polio was eradicated successfully in India. Regenerative medicine is focused on methods to regrow, repair, or replace damaged cells. It can help people suffering from osteoarthritis, which is a growing problem with 30% of adults expected to suffer from it in 11 years. This list of advancements goes on, yet there is still much to achieve in the field of healthcare and medicine. Source: `https://www.weforum.org/agenda/2019/05/healthcare-technology-precision-medicine-breakthroughs/`

At my **Venture Capital** (**VC**) fund Green Shores Capital, we come across healthcare businesses that have the potential to create impact at a huge scale. Technology could bring healthcare to the *last mile* in emerging markets like Asia and Africa. It could help pharmaceutical firms model results of trials much more easily than before, and reduce time-to-market for drugs. Technology could help identify genetic diseases like cancer much faster, and with better accuracy than ever before.

Every time I see a funding request with a deck explaining a ground-breaking healthcare opportunity, I am filled with hope. That's why healthcare is so special. We continuously look to refine our investment thesis at my fund. One aspect we agree on unanimously is that health and wealth were two industries that we could not ignore. I believe that innovation and investments in healthcare perhaps have the most societal impact. In the following sections, we will see the opportunities that healthcare offers for technology.

The AI doctor

It all started in February 2011 when IBM's Watson competed in a television show called Jeopardy against the top performers of the show, Ben Jennings and Brad Rutter. Until that point, the most a computer could do was to answer questions that had very straight and factual answers. Computers have been historically very bad at coping with questions that have involved subtleties in the interpretation and answering process.

The Jeopardy show saw IBM Watson put together information from different sources and interpret an answer from that. Prior to this point, programs that were developed to perform human-like interactions were thought to be clever algorithms. However, with IBM Watson the process changed. Watson was fed with millions of books, encyclopedias, novels, and any other reference texts available.

Every time a question was posed, Watson would identify a list of possible answers, and a set of evidence for each of the answers. The quality of the evidence was assessed using natural language processing. Based on the quality and the relevance of the evidence, answers were given a ranking. There are several algorithms performing the same exercise simultaneously. As more algorithms rank an answer, the confidence level for that answer increases. As a result, Watson presents the answer to the question.

A few years ago, when I was working at PwC, we were evaluating IBM Watson to provide answers to regulatory and legal questions. The idea was that millions of legal and regulatory texts would be fed into IBM Watson. After a period of training Watson, that IBM termed "Watson going to school," it could be put in action for commercial use.

I had the opportunity and the responsibility of being part of the board that evaluated IBM Watson through the evaluation process at PwC. One of the biggest challenges we faced at that time was for IBM Watson to understand legal and regulatory language. The idea was that the understanding should allow for natural language conversations with the user.

Over a period of time, Watson would be trained by legal and regulatory experts through a process of asking questions. When Watson answered questions, the trainer would provide feedback on the answer. After several repetitions of this process, Watson was supposed to learn and provide more accurate answers over time.

This was exactly the vision that IBM had for healthcare. Data from medical records, research, information on clinical trials, books on medicine, and other reference materials were fed into IBM. At the time of a consultation, the doctor would interview the patient and the medical assessment would be assisted by IBM Watson.

As the patient provided information about their health, the consultant would use IBM Watson to refer to a vast base of information. IBM Watson would use the wide knowledgebase it possessed to find information pertinent to the patient's diagnosis. The consultant could then refer to that information to assess the patient and provide health advice.

The vision around IBM Watson was to use it as an AI doctor to provide treatment to oncology patients. However, over the years, the performance of the system hasn't met expectations. IBM have over 13,000 healthcare clients trying the solution. Despite that, Watson's accuracy has been short of expectations, leading to churn of hospital clients. This has also resulted in fall of revenues of 6% from cognitive technologies in 2018. Source: `https://seekingalpha.com/article/4212897-watson-failing-deliver-ibm`

The primary reason for the low accuracy rates of IBM Watson is the lack of high-quality specialized data. IBM went after a very broad use case in healthcare. Therefore, the data sourced for Watson's engine was broad and shallow. However, for AI's accuracy to improve, data needs to be narrow and deep. High quality data in the field of application is required to make it a viable model for AI.

The two healthcare areas chosen for the work were oncology and genomics. Both these fields were complex areas for AI, and the medical jargon presented a major hurdle to overcome. In 2018, the leadership at IBM Watson saw a change due to the negative PR that all these challenges resulted in. Watson's health chief Deborah DiSanzo stepped down and was replaced by John Kelly who was then the senior vice president for Cognitive Solutions and IBM Research.

Efforts to use AI in healthcare has its success stories too. As per comments from one of the clinics in Highland Oncology Group, Watson achieved 78% better performance in pre-screening process for clients. However, quantum machine learning can help the field of healthcare more due to its inherent ability to model nature.

In July 2019, Accenture was successfully granted its second US patent for quantum computing. The patent was for their "quantum computing machine learning module" that trains AI models to choose between classical and quantum computing modules depending on the suitability of the task. Source: `https://patents.justia.com/patent/10095981`

Accenture has had major breakthroughs in molecular comparison using quantum-enabled methods. They have partnered with firms called Biogen and 1-Qbit to create quantum computing models that add efficiencies to diagnosis and the drug discovery process.

Last mile healthcare

Recently, I interviewed the head of AI/quantum research of Amrita University, where I graduated from in 2003. She explained to me the use cases of machine learning in healthcare, and more importantly in an emerging markets context. We also discussed how quantum machine learning could help take the capabilities to a whole new level.

Amrita University is based out of a village called Ettimadai, 20 km from the city of Coimbatore in South India. Ettimadai is home to the Engineering college of the university. My professor Dr. B. Rajathilagam, who taught me **Database Management Systems (DBMS)** and **Object Oriented Programming** 20 years ago, is now leading AI and quantum machine learning research.

One of the key criteria for her is the outcome of the research work. Throughout our conversation, she was stressing the importance of making an impact in the society through her research work. So, we spent some time discussing the problems her PhD and masters students were trying to solve.

Amrita University's management have adopted 101 villages that are mostly inhabited by tribal people. Most of these villages do not have a hospital and the nearest hospital is at least 20 km away. Providing that last mile healthcare has been quite a challenge in these parts of India.

Providing last mile healthcare involves the following steps:

- Continuous monitoring of health conditions
- Cloud hosting the data
- Identifying the individuals and their data
- Performing diagnostics on the data
- Providing immediate remedy

And the process can be repeated. How can technology help with each of these steps?

Monitoring health conditions can be automatic or manual. There can be a doctor visiting these villages at regular intervals and conducting basic tests and electronically capturing the results. The process can also be automated through diagnostic devices using IoT.

The automated capture of health conditions can also be performed using drone cameras. Deep learning image recognition algorithms can be employed to identify symptoms of issues such as anemia, depression, and dehydration. This capability can be enhanced by quantum machine learning that can provide diagnosis results with varying degrees of confidence across different health conditions.

The **quantum image processing (QIP)** enriches the capabilities of existing image processing techniques. Using classical information processing techniques requires a lot of computing resources. When this is done using QIP, the storage of N bits of information happens in $log(2N)$ qubits. The two image processing methods that sound promising are **quantum Fourier transform (QFT)** and **quantum wavelet transform (QVT)**. The added advantage of using qubits to store imaging information is that they can leverage properties like superposition.

A central office in every village could host some of these basic diagnostics devices. Villagers can come into the offices, identify themselves using the national ID card (Aadhaar) and use the device. The device would send the details to a cloud-hosted server with an identifier to the villager.

Once data is uploaded, machine learning algorithms will assist human doctors who will make the diagnosis and prescribe medications remotely. Medicines will be distributed to these villages as prescribed. This process of distribution can be made efficient using quantum annealing processes.

Let us assume that amongst the 101 villages, about 50 of them had about 5 sicknesses each. That is 2,500 different health conditions needing treatment. Say, each of these conditions on average need 2 medicines for treatment. That would require 5,000 medicines (2500*2) to be distributed under these assumptions.

The logistics of sourcing and distributing these many medicines everyday is no mean feat. Not all these medicines can be sourced from the same supplier. Road conditions, weather conditions, and the severity of illnesses will all need to be taken into consideration while calculating the optimal way of delivering medicines to these villages.

Remember the travelling salesman problem we discussed in *Chapter 2, Quantum Computing - Key Discussion Points*. It is an excellent model use case for quantum computing and a way to address problems in logistics that involve several correlated variables. In this scenario, the friction created by a lack of infrastructure is an important variable to model in.

An adiabatic quantum annealer can be used to solve this problem. Road conditions, weather conditions, and severity of illnesses can be modeled into the annealer. The optimal solution to distributing the medicines would be derived from the lowest energy-level solution of the annealer.

The energy space of the annealer would be created by adding all the real world problems into it. Correlations between one village having an increased sickness and its neighboring village being affected by it is yet another important factor to model in. When all these variables are coded in, we would see an energy space with peaks and troughs.

We then use quantum tunneling to traverse through this energy landscape. In the process, troughs are identified without having to climb the peaks. In the end, the optimal solution is given by the lowest energy level of the system.

It is also true that all this distribution can be achieved manually by hiring a team of low skilled labor. This is especially true in India, where labor is cheap. However, for a scalable model that can be replicated elsewhere in India and across the world, it is essential to bring together the power of several emerging technologies.

In Ghana, medical supplies were recently distributed through drones with 100% accuracy. The cost of scaling this in a big commercial setup makes it unsustainable at this stage. However, as drone technology goes mainstream, last mile delivery of healthcare will be one of the major use cases and the intelligence driving these drones could be powered by quantum computers.

We will need to bring together a whole suite of technologies to make this possible.

- IoT for data capture
- Blockchain for data integrity and patient identity management
- Machine learning (classical and quantum-based) for diagnosis
- Quantum annealers to model distribution of medicines
- Drones to perform distribution of medicines

Many of these areas are under research at Amrita. They are working with healthcare device providers to build the infrastructure on the ground. Their researchers are looking into the software algorithms that will help with several of these use cases from diagnosis to drone intelligence.

I can't thank my professor enough for giving me a glimpse of what is possible with the convergence of these technologies. In the West we often live in a bubble and fail to think of such basic problems that could be solved at scale. However, when we manage to do it, we see leapfrog moments happen across the world. When healthcare in these villages is made possible through technology, it could be a case study for other parts of the world to follow.

Cancer diagnosis and treatment

We briefly touched upon the applications of quantum machine learning in diagnosis of diseases and their treatment in the previous section. Let us spend a bit more time trying to understand some areas where quantum computing can have a profound impact.

Humanity has ever fought to cure illnesses, and advances in healthcare and medicine have overcome many of them over the centuries. One illness we still haven't got a handle on is cancer. Billions of dollars are being invested into the field of oncology; identifying and treating cancer. There are also initiatives around developing vaccines for some types of cancer.

However, the process of identifying and treating cancer is no easy task. There are about 200 types of cancers in the world.

Cancer cells are present in most of our bodies, yet they only become a problem when these cells grow rapidly and dominate the healthy cells in the body. This can reach a level where the normal cells cannot perform their functions in the human body. Causal triggers that lead cells to become "cancerous" are still not completely understood.

There are several potential causes of cancer. If a healthy human being is continuously exposed to carcinogenic materials, that could trigger the cancer cells. Other reasons include exposure to radiation, smoking, and lack of physical activity. As one of these external factors triggers cancerous behavior of cells, the subject starts to see the symptoms.

The varied nature of triggers, the different types of cancers, and the way they manifest as symptoms make timely diagnosis harder. Cancer cells come together in the form of a tumor. The size of the tumor, the status of the tumor (malignant or not), and the metastasis state determine the kind of treatment to be provided.

Metastasis indicates the spread of cancer from one part of the body to another. The part of the body where the cancer has occurred and the speed at which the cancer cells spread are factors to be considered in the treatment.

A research paper launched out of the Technocrats Institute of Technology in Bhopal, India identifies a method to use Shor's algorithm to identify cancer treatment. The method proposes using Shor's algorithm on the dataset recursively to identify cancer type. The dataset includes tumor size, metastasis state, and node status (malignant or not).

Shor's algorithm is used to parse through the data and identify the stages of the cancer. This is followed by agglomerative clustering to logically group the results. This process using quantum algorithms has been proven to be much faster than the classical methods to identify and categorize cancers. Classical methods take hours to get to the results, whereas this method has been shown to get results in seconds. Source: `https://www.omicsonline.org/open-access/quantum-computing-based-technique-for-cancer-disease-detection-system-jcsb.1000095.pdf`

The preceding method uses Shor's algorithm to arrive at a categorization and identification of cancer types. However, patient requirements for treatment are varied and complex and could range from surgery to chemotherapy. That is more of an optimization problem and will depend on whether the patient would benefit from a specific type of treatment.

Optimization problems can be solved by quantum annealing. Factors involved in the diagnosis, the attributes of the patient, and the part of the body affected by the cancer cells will need to be modeled in the energy space. Current processes involve going through several hundred variables to identify an optimal plan that will kill cancer cells without affecting healthy cells.

The lowest energy state of the system will identify a treatment plan for the cancer cells. Using quantum computing can also provide a holistic view of all options and their suitability, with their associated degrees of confidence.

Drug discovery

Drug discovery is the process by which new medicines are discovered, tested, and brought to the market. The cost of bringing a new drug to the market for pharmaceutical firms is approximately $2.6 billion. The process takes several years with several stages of clinical trials to get through before going for a regulatory approval.

As a result of this process, over 90% of candidate drugs fail on the way to the market. Different factors such as disease type, biomarkers, and industry affect the success of the drug discovery process. Some fields have lower success rates. Based on several studies, oncology has a success rate of about 5%. Source: https://www.ncbi.nlm.nih.gov/pubmed/29394327

There are several attempts to use machine learning to predict the results of clinical trials, so that the time taken to get the drugs to market is lessened. One of these attempts focuses on modeling the behavior of healthy cells and cancerous cells to varying levels of sugar and oxygen levels.

Differences between the behavior of healthy and cancerous cells is demonstrated by data from their lipid, enzyme, and protein profiles. This data is useful in turning the drug discovery process upside down. The field has been taking a trial and error approach for far too long and needs a more scientific approach.

Several start-ups are looking to make this process better for the pharmaceutical industry. They use a mix of both classical and quantum computing-based machine learning. Benevolent AI is a London-based start-up that sources data from several clinical trials and patients' records and models the relationships between them.

Natural language processing techniques are used to provide insights to scientists going through the drug discovery process. The algorithm uses several dimensions of data across diseases being researched, the symptoms of the disease, the proteins involved, and the drug that is being proposed.

Using this intelligence, firms can shorten their drug discovery cycle and get their drugs to the market much faster than in a conventional approach, thereby saving billions of dollars for the pharmaceutical industry.

Another key area where quantum machine learning can be used is in the field of protein modeling. The human body is made up of billions of cells and proteins are essential components of these cells. The structure of proteins and their folding mechanism is critical to understand the behavior of cells.

Protein folding was first brought to light more than 50 years ago by a Nobel prize-winning scientist Anfinsen CB. We have made excellent strides in understanding the importance of proteins in our functioning. We have identified that protein folding is related to Alzheimer's, diabetes, and Parkinson's disease.

Proteins are made up of amino acids, and when these building blocks come together, they can take different shapes. Aberrant protein folding can cause several diseases. Also, as we age, the body struggles to stop misfolded proteins from getting created. That explains why we become less immune to diseases as we grow old.

There are several attempts to model protein behavior. However, this is a challenging process as it depends on the polarity of amino acids and how they interact with the aqueous environment in the cell. Modeling protein behavior is crucial to our understanding of diseases.

Classical computers haven't been able to do that very successfully. There are firms like XLabs in San Francisco that are working on solving this fundamental problem using quantum computing.

Biogen has worked with 1-Qbit and Accenture to identify potential solutions to treat neurodegenerative conditions like multiple sclerosis, Alzheimer's, and Parkinson's. Patients with these conditions will benefit the most once there are industrial solutions identified.

Two quantum computing patents were awarded to Accenture, who are already creating pilots to address the drug discovery problem at scale once it is industrialized. One of the patents (patent number 10095981) focuses on solutions using a multi-state quantum optimization engine. The engine calls different quantum devices based on the tasks to be solved. The devices called by the engine could be an annealer, a simulator, or a gate-based quantum computer.

The other quantum computing patent (patent number 10275721) awarded to Accenture was for a machine learning module that had the ability to route tasks to a classical or a quantum device based on the nature of the task.

The multi-state quantum optimization engine is used to develop a breakthrough quantum-based solution for molecular comparison. This solution is expected to speed up drug discovery exponentially. See the following sources to find out more:

- https://www.ncbi.nlm.nih.gov/pmc/articles/PMC6205278/
- https://www.quora.com/Why-is-protein-folding-an-important-problem-What-are-its-applications
- https://patents.justia.com/patent/10095981
- https://patents.justia.com/patent/10275721

We have discussed the applications and benefits of machine learning and the scale at which it can be achieved using quantum computing within healthcare. In the next section we will look at some of the issues that Blockchain can solve. Yet again, we will see that there are hardly any collision points when it comes to commercial applications of the two technologies.

Blockchain in healthcare

One simple Google search on Blockchain's applications in healthcare will return you a world of information. However, many of those applications of Blockchain do not really seem to need Blockchain at all. Most of these applications can be performed with traditional DBMS. Blockchain would create additional overheads and scalability challenges in an already difficult value chain with several pain points.

Having said that, there are areas within healthcare where Blockchain technology can help in its current form. If some of its technology limitations are resolved, it can be more useful. One of the key areas where Blockchain has potential is health insurance. I didn't discuss insurance in any detail in the financial services chapter, but I am one of those who believe that Blockchain will help transform insurance more than banking.

Insurance

Many of us have gone through a tough time making a claim on an insurance policy. It is harsh on customers if insurance firms identify loopholes in their terms and conditions to not pay customers' claims. For a good part of my life, I avoided insurance wherever possible, as I genuinely believed that it was more of a hassle. However, when I had a family, I had to make sure I had them all covered with health insurance.

That didn't make my experience with insurance better. A few years ago, my wife fell sick, and I called up my health insurer. We had submitted her health details when signed up and the sickness had nothing to do with any of her past conditions. We even had our consultant's opinion that they weren't related conditions. However, the insurer refused to pay the claim, because they decided that the condition was not new.

As our focus at that time was to get her treated, we just went through the process without the insurance cover. Had that process costed us a lot more, or if this had happened to people with less financial ability, there would have been lives at stake. It was a painful experience for the entire family.

Since then, I have been on the wrong end of bad behavior from insurance firms or middlemen selling insurance packaged up with other services of theirs. Thanks to all those eye-opening experiences, I believe this is a field where smart contracts will have to be used. I can see a convergence of applications of several technologies to make health insurance work.

I changed my medical insurance provider in hopes of finding a better service.
I now use Vitality, who are more technology-focused. They have managed to create
an ecosystem that feeds information to them about their customer. For instance,
my Fitbit and my wife's Apple Watch are both connected to the Vitality App. My
monthly premium is decided by the data that these smart devices send to Vitality. If I
spent a month with a lot of activity, my insurance premium is lower, and vice versa.

This is a pretty good start, where insurance firms provide a transparent framework
to collect premiums. They can go further in protecting customers when they really
need it by building a seamless process and experience into their claims process.
The process could look something like this:

1. At the time of signing up for my insurance, I provide my insurer my health
    details.

2. They verify this information with my doctors.

3. A smart contract is created for two aspects of the insurance:

    ◦   The framework to compute the premium.

    ◦   A clear set of rules to release the claim.

4. The insurer uses smart devices that gathers data about the customer and
    periodically sends it back to them.

5. The insurer can use that data to price the premium.

6. If the smart device at any point identifies a scenario where the insurance
    claim must be released, it should happen seamlessly.

7. For instance, if the data from my wearable device identifies that I am sick,
    and if that hasn't been registered as a pre-existing condition, there needs
    to be a process to release the claim automatically.

8. The claim process could be triggered by the insurer (instead of the customer
    going after them).

9. The trigger may have to be followed by the customer having to approve the
    release of the claim and acknowledging that the wearable device was right
    in raising the red flag at the right time.

There shouldn't be any manual intervention from the insurer needed in the claims
process. They can artificially create subjectivity in the favor of the insurer. With real
time data capture by the integration of IoT, they can be more proactive with their
customers. Hence, they can respond to claim scenarios in real time, even without
the customer having to chase them for it.

It is not just the customers who will benefit through the proper digitization of health insurance. Insurance firms can create several insights using health data they capture from these IoT devices. This data could be put through machine learning models to then predict any future health issues the customer could be vulnerable to. This can help them warn their customers of a potential future condition.

What would be more useful for an insurer is their ability to use this health data, and price future insurance premiums of a customer. If the wearables from a customer indicates an increase in inactivity, decrease in sleep, late hours spent at work, reduction in water consumption, and irregular heartbeat patterns, it could indicate that the customer has a higher risk of falling sick.

Let's say that the data captured through a wearable device indicates that the risk of a customer getting a heart attack has increased. The insurer could reach out to them about it and proactively ensure the customer understands the status of their health. If this warning is ignored by the customer, then the insurer could indicate that it would increase their premiums.

On a similar note, let's say that a customer made a claim to cure an illness. If their health data post-treatment was captured by the insurer, it might show that the customer was getting their health back on track. In this instance, the data could be used to reduce the premium of the customer, thereby rewarding good habits and behavior.

In all these scenarios, intelligence can be used to optimize the premium amount the customer would pay. The benefit of Blockchain in these scenarios is to contractually structure the premium amounts and the release of the claim money if the intelligence adds up.

Another emerging use case is the use of facial recognition technologies. SenseTime is the world's largest AI start-up that grew from a piece of research to a $4.5 billion company in four years. They have an interesting use of facial recognition technology in insurance. If a customer made a claim, they would be put through an interview process.

The AI engine scans the customer's face during the interview and based on the facial expressions can provide an integrity score. This integrity score is used to decide if the claim is truthful or not. An improvisation from there would be to create a smart contract which would trigger the claims payment if the integrity score is over a threshold.

One of the key applications of Blockchain is immutable traceability. Across the world, counterfeit drugs has become a thriving industry due to lack of traceability and handshake mechanisms through the supply chain. Let us now look at how this can be fixed using Blockchain.

Pharmaceutical supply chains

We discussed how quantum machine learning could help with the drug discovery process and reduce the cost and the time to market for the pharma industry. However, the supply chain that the industry relies on today needs a major face lift. This is especially true in several emerging economies, where counterfeit drugs are costing the pharma industry several billions every year.

A PwC report on counterfeit drugs call it out as the most lucrative illegal market making over £150 billion a year. The more worrying number is the "millions" being killed consuming these fake drugs. In developed markets about 1% of the drugs available are fake, but this number goes up to 70% in markets like Africa.

Thanks to the digital economy, counterfeiting is carried out globally in recent times. According to the **World Health Organization (WHO)** about 50% of drugs sold online are fake. The fight against fake drugs has been widespread, yet has only yielded sporadic results.

Despite the efforts of organizations such as Pharmaceutical Security Institute, the US Food and Drug Administration and the WHO, much is still to be done. Pharmaceutical firms struggle to invest into fighting fake drugs because they are already burdened by high drug discovery and regulatory costs. Therefore, keeping the drug market clean is not in their list of priorities.

As a result, we still have a thriving drug counterfeiting market. In over 50,000 online sites selling drugs, 95% of them have no regulatory approvals and industry standards. As a result, the counterfeit drug market has been categorized by big corporations and organizations as an unaffordable vulnerability. However, over 450,000 people die of ineffective and counterfeit drugs for malaria every year. Any factor that kills so many people every year needs to be dealt with in an organized fashion. The following chart from the PwC report highlights the money made by counterfeit drugs:

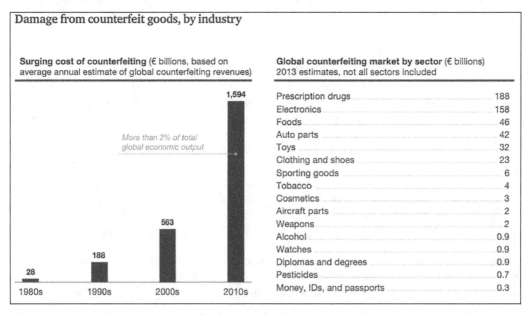

Damage from counterfeit goods, by industry

Surging cost of counterfeiting (€ billions, based on average annual estimate of global counterfeiting revenues)

More than 2% of total global economic output

1980s	28
1990s	188
2000s	563
2010s	1,594

Global counterfeiting market by sector (€ billions) 2013 estimates, not all sectors included

Sector	€ billions
Prescription drugs	188
Electronics	158
Foods	46
Auto parts	42
Toys	32
Clothing and shoes	23
Sporting goods	6
Tobacco	4
Cosmetics	3
Aircraft parts	2
Weapons	2
Alcohol	0.9
Watches	0.9
Diplomas and degrees	0.9
Pesticides	0.7
Money, IDs, and passports	0.3

Figure 1: Statistics relating to the counterfeit drugs market. Source: https://www.strategyand.pwc.com/report/counterfeit-pharmaceuticals

The solution to this problem that several institutions and the pharma industry came up with was mass serialization and tracing the medicines across its supply chain. Mass serialization involves the use of a bar code on the packaging of the drugs. The drugs and their corresponding codes are centrally registered at the point of manufacturing. The bar code is then scanned across several steps in the supply chain to ensure they are looking at the same drug.

However, the challenge is that many of these systems have been cracked by the counterfeiters. As a result, only a fraction of the counterfeiting attempts has been fixed by bar codes and mass serialization efforts. A better solution that is harder to crack and more secure is required to address this industry and fight an organized battle against fake drugs.

As mentioned earlier in the chapter, I grew up in a village in south India. I have seen the negative impact of broken healthcare for a good part of my life. India is arguably the global hub for counterfeit drugs. Following are some statistics that are worth knowing about India and its role in the counterfeit drugs market:

- The Indian pharma industry is the third largest in the world in terms of consumption
- However, 35% of fake drugs across the world come from India
- India exports drugs to over 200 countries in the world

Needless to say that for the benefit of the world and India, the drug supply chain in India needs a serious revamp.

In *Chapter 14, Interview with Dinesh Nagarajan, Partner, IBM,* when we discussed the applications of Blockchain, we saw that supply chains were one of its key industry use cases. Blockchain can be an excellent tracking mechanism for industries like food, pharma, and goods. I see several start-ups across the world leveraging the tracking feature of the Blockchain framework.

A start-up called Chronicled, based out of the US, set up a Blockchain consortium for healthcare called MediLedger. The Blockchain would be used to register and track every hop the drug takes through its supply chain. One of the key principles of the ledger is that only manufacturers can create and attach identifiers to the drugs. If the drug's identifier gets tweaked anywhere else in its supply chain, it would be marked as fake by the Blockchain.

At least in the US, the **Drug Supply Chain Security Act (DSCSA)** is enforcing pharma companies to have systems that are interoperable and can help track drugs through the supply chain. Using Blockchain can ensure this interoperability comes out of the box, and doesn't have to be developed through an expensive system and process integration work.

The advantages in using Blockchain in this space are as follows:

- The rules that the consortium must work with can be pre-agreed and coded into the Blockchain.
- There is no single entity that can go and change the supply chain details.
- The Blockchain allows for entries and no deletions are allowed. Therefore, every entry into the ledger is audited and tracked.
- The decentralized nature of control, along with the preceeding features, make it hard to tamper with.

The MediLedger consortium used **zero-knowledge proofs (ZKPs)** to enforce governance and controls without individual nodes (firms) having to share detailed data with each other. ZKP is a simple framework that allows for someone on the Blockchain to provide the right level of information to demonstrate they satisfy a condition.

For example, if I am placing a request for a loan to a bank, the bank will need access to my credit score. With ZKP, the bank would perhaps just need a range that my credit score falls within, to decide on my loan request. In the ZKP model there is a prover (me) and a verifier (the bank). I should be able to convince the bank that the information I provide to them is complete and genuine. However, there should be no further information shared with the bank.

We live in a world where every little bit of data we generate is being used by tech giants like Google, Facebook, or Amazon to provide better services to us. They also resell the data to third parties and make money. In such a scenario, ZKP acts as an excellent way of ensuring users are in control of their data that is being used by these service providers.

Coming back to our healthcare example, a system like MediLedger could offer the right level of information transparency to thwart faking attempts. At the same time, where there are sensitive drugs being transported, the information wouldn't be too readily available to all parties. It is early days for Blockchain in drug supply chains, but the technology has looked promising in most of the supply chain use cases.

Let us now move on to the next use case of Blockchain, which is record keeping. It is essential that patient records are stored in a safe and secure way. It is perhaps as important to ensure the patient owns their data. Let us look at this in detail in the next section.

Healthcare data exchanges

One of the biggest challenges in the field of healthcare is the availability (or rather the lack of it) of quality data. At many points in the healthcare value chain, access to patient's health information can help with better decision making. Real world health data helps the quality of research, health consulting, and drug discovery.

There are ways to create mocked-up data for all research. However, it often fails as a good proxy for real patients' health data. In the past, I have always been willing to give away my health data for research. Every time there was a health review process, and I was asked to choose if my data could be used, I would respond "Yes".

More recently however, I have started to get a bit cautious about data privacy and security implications. There is another key reason to have caution when it comes to sharing my data with healthcare organizations. I am a firm believer in self-sovereign identity. Therefore, I believe that when my data is being used somewhere it needs to be attributed to me in some shape or form.

There are no systems that bring all these three together, namely, privacy, security and self-sovereign identity. If there was a mechanism where I could share my health care data anonymously, where it is used for research or health consulting purposes, I may be more willing to do it.

Apart from being safe and secure, I expect to have traceability of where my data is being used and how much money a third party has made using my data. There needs to be a pre-agreed mechanism, so that I can benefit monetarily from sharing my data.

A survey by Ponemon Institute across 503 respondents identified that about 86% of them have seen medical issues that occurred due to misidentification of patients. 80% of respondents believed that positively identifying the patient through biometrics could improve cashflow to the hospital. Source: `http://promos.hcpro.com/pdf/2016-national-report-misidentification-report.pdf`

There are a few firms trying to address data sharing, copyright, and the intellectual property market using Blockchain. It gets more interesting and challenging with healthcare data sharing. Firms like HealthVerity and Doc.ai act as marketplaces for healthcare data using Blockchain.

Through this marketplace, individuals can allow for their data to be used in specific research. As this research yields returns through medical breakthroughs; the spoils of the initiative are split across the data providers. Data used by the research is held in a temporary space until the research is completed, and then deleted.

Although the Blockchain is currently initiated by these startups, the plan is to evolve the ecosystem like an Ethereum ecosystem. This would help genuinely decentralize ownership and management of individuals' data. In this model, anyone who wants to sell their data can put it up on a marketplace. Third parties wanting the data can bid for it and utilize it. The Blockchain network can verify the transaction and commit it to the chain. The nodes involved in the verification can be rewarded for it.

As this process of decentralized governance of data sharing scales, healthcare marketplaces can go mainstream. Let us now look at how smart contracts can make medical research more efficient.

Research governance

In *Chapter 8, The Impact on Governance*, we saw how Blockchain is being used across the world for effective operations of governments. In principle, the Blockchain framework can be utilized for any context where contractual terms are agreed before initiating a process. As the process progresses, every time a contractual term is satisfied, a set of actions would be triggered.

In tracking these contractual obligations on a Blockchain, every step of progress can be digitally timestamped. Service level agreements can be initiated and enforced based on these contractual obligations. However, the most important aspect of using smart governance using Blockchain is that human biases in contractual decisions can be eliminated.

Healthcare research has been an operationally inefficient machine for a long time. Some of the inefficiencies within healthcare research are:

- Objective of the research and success criteria is often not agreed beforehand
- Lack of a design with milestones throughout the research process
- Researchers are affected by human biases and can change criteria mid-way through the trial
- Negative results are not generally published
- Interoperability across healthcare systems is hard to achieve, therefore, data sourcing and integration can be a challenge
- Audit trail of the research steps are often missing, so it is harder to identify lessons learned from historical information
- A real time view of where the research is unavailable to most key stakeholders involved

With all these pain points, healthcare research is really shouting out for a solution to achieve operational efficiency. Blockchain can help with this as we consider the following steps:

- All the key stakeholders in a piece of research are registered as a node on a Blockchain
- The terms of the research, the outcomes, and the success criteria of the outcomes are agreed upfront
- All intermediate milestones are understood with an indicative timeline agreed
- Publishing policies for both success and failure of research activities are agreed

- Any data sourcing/sharing requirements from multiple systems are identified and can perhaps be sourced as an Oracle into the Blockchain

The benefits of getting all these agreed and onboarded into a Blockchain are immense. Every single friction point highlighted earlier can be resolved, and the process can be seamlessly managed and monitored on a near real time basis. However, loading healthcare data onto a Blockchain is not without its challenges.

Healthcare data is more sensitive than most other information, and there are serious regulatory implications for any breach identified. Therefore, data might have to be shared in a consolidated and relevant fashion. But third parties using the data shouldn't be able to identify the patient who owns the data. The other challenge is more political in nature.

Pharma players have historically been resistance to change. Moving from paper-based records to electronic records in the US took a major regulation (the HITECH Act) to be enacted. So, how they embrace Blockchain as a technology paradigm at scale is yet to be seen. Unlike other technologies, for Blockchain to be meaningful, most key stakeholders in an ecosystem must be on the chain.

Therefore, if a good percentage of the pharma industry do not want to adopt Blockchain, it becomes increasingly hard for other players to make any impact using the technology.

Conclusion

I have perhaps narrated more stories in the healthcare chapter because I can relate to many healthcare scenarios personally. The field has several pain points across different parts of the world. The developed world is focused on adding efficiencies to existing processes like patient identification, record keeping, data sharing and privacy. The emerging economies on the other hand have more fundamental issues to resolve.

Emerging economies have a last mile problem in delivering basic healthcare to its population. Being able to provide timely, effective healthcare at scale is perhaps the biggest issue facing mankind today. In regions like Africa, Asia, and Latin America, there are millions of people who do not have access to basic healthcare.

As we focus on bringing innovative ideas to transform healthcare, it is critical to address both the developed markets and the emerging world. The scale of the challenges is big enough that it is not enough to just use individual technologies and provide piecemeal solutions.

Being able to treat diseases like cancer with more accurate diagnosis and treatment plans is a major leap in healthcare capabilities. The modeling of protein behavior can help us create drugs that would solve degenerative neural conditions such as Alzheimer's. The efficiencies that quantum computing can bring to the drug discovery process can shrink the trial period from over a decade to a few years, effectively saving billions of dollars.

Technologies that tackle all touchpoints in the data value chain need to be used. IoT and data-capturing healthcare devices are needed to receive health data from patients. This information must be safely and securely stored in a system. It is then important to use this data to create intelligent insights. Diagnosis and decisions on treatments will need to be made based on this intelligence using machine learning. This entire process could be tracked on a Blockchain to provide the right levels of transparency and privacy at the same time. There are still protocol level improvements, on chain and off chain designs needed to overcome regulatory challenges using Blockchain. However, as the technology matures, and several architectural solutions evolve, data regulations should no longer be a stumbling block for healthcare.

Over the course of writing this book, I have had conversations with healthcare experts across the globe. One discussion that has had the most impact was my interview with Dr. B. Rajathilagam, my professor. Maybe, I related more to it because I spent four years of my life in and around those villages. Maybe it is more inspiring because it is a healthcare application. But most of all, maybe, that is where we could help save lives and see tangible results on a daily basis.

Healthcare innovation will continue to inspire me, and I hope we see more and more exciting technologies that can transform people's lives.

7

Interview with Dr. B. Rajathilagam, Head of AI Research, Amrita Vishwa Vidyapeetham

I did my Bachelor's in Engineering at **Amrita Vishwa Vidyapeetham (AVVP)**. I graduated in 2003 and moved to Mumbai for my first job as a software consultant. If someone asked me if there was a period of my life that I would want to relive, it is without a doubt the time I spent at this amazing institution. Over the years after I graduated, AVVP has only got better, and I feel jealous of the current students!

The reason why AVVP has become one of the top 10 institutions in India is largely due to the quality of the teaching faculty members. When I meet my start-ups at Green Shores Capital (my fund), I often tell them that founders need to be storytellers. The best storytellers often grow faster than the rest, as they can paint their vision so well that people feel inspired and want to be part of the start-up's journey. That is true with teachers too. The difference is that teachers are a lot more selfless than start-up founders, who often have dreams of making billions.

The best storyteller I have had in my life is my mom. She was an amazing teacher, and, thanks to her, I am who I am today. The second best is without a doubt Dr. B. Rajathilagam (BRT), who blessed us with her lectures for 3 years of our university life. When I meet her, I jokingly tell her that I don't remember the **Object-Oriented Programming Systems (OOPS)** concepts she taught us anymore; but I can never forget the lift/elevator example she gave us to bring those concepts to life.

Over the past few years, I have been continuously in touch with BRT over various initiatives. She has been leading AI and machine learning research within the university for some time. The best aspect of the research done at the university is that it is focused on solving social problems identified locally in India.

We have been discussing how research students at the university could receive support from across the globe. We have also evaluated start-ups that shared synergies with research work within the university. So, I had a good understanding of the real-world problems that the research team in the university was trying to solve.

As a result, I knew I would get some invaluable insights for the book if I could interview BRT. She agreed to help straight away. In this chapter, BRT brings to life the kind of social challenges that emerging technologies such as AI, quantum computing, and Blockchain can solve. The interview script follows:

Arun: Ma'am (that's how I address her throughout our conversation), thanks for your time. It's great to have the opportunity to interview you for the book. Can you please tell me a little bit about your career, your current role in the university, and how you are involved in the quantum computing space?

BRT: My exposure to quantum computing started with my research in feature engineering. I found that we had reached a saturation point in feature engineering where we were not able to capture minor details in signals, images, videos, and so on. I think there are so many areas that conventional algorithms were not able to capture. We had reached a bottleneck where the performance did not meet our expectations. Therefore, I was looking at algorithms to overcome these limitations during my research. I found that quantum computing principles inherently have the nature and the ability to solve these limitations.

One of the fundamental concepts for quantum mechanics is group theory. Group theory defines the characteristics of atomic particles in quantum mechanics. It offers mathematical representations and abstractions that can help you with a real-world problem that you are trying to solve. Some of the multi-dimensional problems that we are working on can be represented by group theory.

I started looking at algorithms using the principles of quantum mechanics. Using group theory techniques, we developed feature filters (**G-lets**) for signals, and those filters could also work for multi-dimensional signals. There is a natural flow in that mathematical abstraction that captures quantum mechanics. Therefore, it works more seamlessly on a quantum computer than on a classical computer. We then made a quantum algorithm for signal processing in order to capture the features. Following that, we also made a classical version of that, although it cannot be compared to the quantum version.

The exciting part for me was that, even with a simple version of that algorithm adapted for a classical computer, it outperformed many of the existing conventional feature algorithms. For example, let's say you are listening to a human continuously speaking and then you occasionally hear a bird signal – the signal frequency keeps changing. Let's say you must capture the point at which the signal transition happens from the human voice to the bird signal. That can be very difficult at times using existing classical algorithms.

In a quantum computer, you should be able to do these operations in parallel. That was an important capability of quantum computers that made them very exciting for me. That capability then moves us into machine learning. Machine learning requires a lot of features and a lot of data for us to understand the underlying patterns. Therefore, if you can handle so much data and look at the patterns, quantum computers turn out to be a better option. So that is how I started looking into quantum machine learning, though I still work on classical machine learning as well.

I am looking into companies coming up with simulators for quantum computers. We have D-Wave's quantum computing set up in NASA's Quantum Artificial Intelligence Laboratory (QuAIL). I follow these companies closely and I have noticed that in the last 5 years there has been a surge in the interest in quantum computers.

Of course, there are roadblocks. One of the key obstacles to overcome is the hardware. How do you maintain this kind of atomic particle setup at room temperature? It is a real challenge, especially when we want quantum computers to scale commercially. However, annealing techniques are arriving sooner than we initially anticipated. Optimization using annealing has become more successful now, and that will be a big boost to the field. That is because annealing methods have been thought through from the ground up using quantum principles.

Although big firms like IBM and others focus on universal gates, I don't think it will be commercially viable for another 20 years or so.

Arun: So, you think simulators would be the first to take off?

BRT: Absolutely. Writing quantum algorithms is not going to be easy for first timers. They will start with simulators as they will be able to understand the environment.

Arun: This is precisely the input I received from Fujitsu's chief scientist. He mentioned that optimization solutions would be the low-hanging fruit in this space as annealing takes the lead. Gate-based solutions will perhaps take longer.

BRT: Yes, that is going to take time because the semiconductor industry is still working hard on how to get it all working in manageable ambient temperatures. We also need to address error rates. These are two major obstacles that the industry is working on. Researchers are working really hard on error correction goals.

Arun: I have spoken to someone who is doing his research on Noisy Intermediate Scale Quantum (NISQ) techniques for quantum error correction. He stressed that this was a critical space where infrastructure must improve to keep the error rates lower. So, tell us about the interesting work you're doing in your research at the moment.

BRT: As part of the research work, we are doing simulations and real data analysis. In a simulator, we're able to model the scenarios and parameters we choose. Therefore, the complexity of the algorithm is something designed and decided by me. As the complexity of the problem is designed by me, I can expand it as I choose to. Where I see a challenge (with traditional methods), I can choose to do it in a quantum simulator. One of the use cases we are working on is traffic incident detection.

Right now, we do not have any infrastructure in India that monitors traffic, except in some complex signals, on the highways, and at major junctions where you have some cameras. In other parts of the world, along with the road infrastructure, they have built a digital infrastructure. That digital infrastructure simply does not exist in India. What's stopping us is the cost of creating this infrastructure. For example, the cameras we currently have will not be useful at night or in bad weather. If you have to set up a radar to overcome the technical limitations, the costs of implementing it for 1 kilometer is 30 lakhs Indian Rupees (~ £32,000). Lower cost radars have challenges with noisy signals.

Arun: So, it's not sustainable.

BRT: It is not a sustainable solution at all. They are trying out a 3D radar at a difficult junction in Delhi, but the distance at which it can work hurts the feasibility of the solution. Now let's look at the other existing technologies – sensors, cyber physical systems, IoT devices – where will you put them on the road? Again, the range at which they work is a challenge. Actually, there is an opportunity here for someone who is able to build systems capable of overcoming these current limitations.

Arun: So, thinking about a solution to this problem, can we not have IoT devices installed on cars, buses, and motorbikes? There could be IoT devices attached to these vehicles with real-time tracking. It would be an easier way of knowing the state of the entire traffic system at any point of time. If there was a central traffic management system that these IoT devices connected to, we could first capture traffic data in real time to manage traffic. But also, we can do predictive analytics to say that (for instance) 2,000 vehicles go through a junction every day at a specific time. We can plan traffic regulations and management resources accordingly. Is that in line with what you find?

BRT: That will address one part of this big puzzle. However, the range of these IoT devices, the speed at which vehicles move, and the lack of good connectivity will limit the efficacy of the solution. With 5G technology, you are going to have better solutions. But, as we see it today, connecting quickly, transmitting data in real time, and acting on it has practical difficulties. It's not because a software solution is not there.

Arun: If hardware solutions have limitations, can drones help?

BRT: Yeah. Drones are another aspect of a potential solution. You can add other solutions on to that to make it holistic. You can have an aerial view of the world with drones. Maybe during peak hours, you can fly drones in specific parts of the traffic system. All of them will connect to a hierarchical network and you can build a solution. You see, it is totally a multi-dimensional problem to solve. Coordinating this across a busy city in India is still a long way off at this stage.

Arun: Yeah, there is a correlation/interdependency problem here as well. Let's say, 10 people are driving into a junction and they can all be correlated to each other. So, if you want to model the behavior of this traffic, we need to model how the 10 people influence each other.

BRT: Look at the spatial-temporal impact on the entire city and on the specific road. Let's say that one road is blocked, and people are driving through an alternate route, so that they don't get into this jam. This may cause the alternate route to get blocked too.

All the surrounding areas start getting clogged and you have a bottleneck there. In order to disperse traffic, it is not about working out a single point in the system; you need to have a coordinated effort to do this, so that you prevent traffic jams in the first place, and should they happen, you need to disperse them as quickly as possible.

Arun: So where are we with this research and the solution?

BRT: We are looking at a radar that can work at a better range. There are some retired Indian Space Research Organization (ISRO) scientists who were working in radar technology. We also have a retired wing commander from the Indian Air Force, who has worked with radar technologies. We are working with them to come up with a radar solution. We see that secondary radars are a better solution to this problem. Radars will be here on the roadside as you can have them in the vehicle. You can call it an IoT device or you can purely call it a radar. Coupling technologies (radar and IoT) can help us improve on the network formation itself. Technology within the vehicles solves only part of the traffic management solution.

The government of India is largely focused on building the physical road infrastructure first. Cyber-physical infrastructure and digitizing the network of roads only comes after that. Therefore, it is up to institutions such as ourselves to come up with innovative solutions for these problems.

Some of the solutions we come up with can be suboptimal initially. But we can start a conversation with the government about where the gaps are. If we can build a quantum solution, we can demonstrate to the government the efficacy of said solution at a small scale and show them where they need to be investing to scale the cyber infrastructure of roads across the country.

Arun: But do we need a quantum solution? Can we not achieve this using classical computers?

BRT: I think a quantum solution can definitely help due to the complexities involved. The first reason is the amount of data and the interrelationships that you have to look at. Correlation and covariance within the data will have better visibility in a quantum solution. You're going to be able to visualize it better. Otherwise, you will have to analyze one dimension of factors and may not be able visualize and analyze multi-dimensional data.

That is where quantum machine learning can do a better job than is possible with classical computers.

Arun: So, are there any other smart cities use cases you are looking at for your research?

BRT: We have learned about non-polynomial (NP) problems. Quantum computers are expected to solve NP time problems. I saw an interesting link where a company has put up their GitHub code for the traveling salesman problem, which is a NP problem. If we can start solving NP problems, then we open up a huge set of problems that we could not consider before, and we will get fresh solutions for these problems through the power of quantum computing.

Now that you have an option with quantum computing, there's a whole new way to solve NP problems. Machine learning in today's world is largely thought of only with the capacity of a classical computer. When we have quantum machine learning going mainstream, we would be operating at a totally different level, solving non-polynomial type problems.

Arun: Interesting. This again takes me back to the conversations I am having around logistics. You spoke about the traveling salesman example. On a similar note, getting optimal flight routes across the world is a problem we struggle with using existing technologies. At the moment, it is not done with any kind of seamless method. Logistics, therefore, is going to be one big area for annealing-based optimization.

BRT: Yes, logistics is a big industry that could greatly benefit from quantum techniques. As some of the key logistics problems are optimization-based, we can use quantum annealing to identify solutions for this industry.

Going back to the smart city use cases, I would like to make one last point about geospatial data. Satellite data can help with infrastructure projects in a city. For example, when you want to build an apartment, you may want to understand the shadow impact, the visibility impact it has on the rest of the place, and so on.

We can model flooding in a city; we can model fire escape routes and the positions of CCTV cameras to ensure maximum coverage. There are so many such aspects that we can find answers to when we use geospatial data for smart cities.

Many of these problems are also optimization based, and can be solved using quantum annealers.

Arun: We (at Green Shores Capital) have invested in a firm called GYANA and they are already working on some of the use cases of geospatial data you mentioned. It is indeed a powerful tool in a smart cities scenario. Would you like to make any other points on smart city solutions using quantum and classical machine learning techniques?

BRT: Well, we could move on to healthcare now. You were mentioning about optimization problems. Why do we go for optimization in numerical computations? Precision in numerical computations make a big difference to the results we get. In machine learning and deep learning techniques, we rely on optimization techniques to improve our calculations. That precision of calculations can be handled better in a quantum computer. For instance, Python is a programming language that doesn't in itself restrict me in terms of the size of a number and the number of decimals that I want to calculate, but the classical computer I am running it on does restrict me, purely due to the hardware's inherent limitations.

The kind of precision computation we can achieve using quantum computers depends on the number of qubits. Now, let's take a healthcare and pharma example. Sickle cell anemia disease is prevalent in tribal populations in India. People with this condition have distorted red blood cells. This can be a hereditary condition as well as, in some cases, one caused by the environment. If you look at the patients, they are in pain most of the time. As part of their treatment, these patients get a painkiller.

These patients are treated with a drug dosage in milligrams. To provide this treatment at scale, we will need to have a treatment plan for each patient and know how much dosage needs to be prescribed at a given point in time. This process combined with the logistics of distributing the medicines can get very complicated very quickly.

In India, tribal health is managed by primary healthcare centers or *super specialty* hospitals. How many primary health care centers are there in India? 69% of our population live in villages. Many villages do not have primary healthcare centers and, in many of these primary health care centers, doctors are often not available (sometimes, they simply might not show up!).

Forget about ICUs, casualties, emergencies, and other extreme circumstances. Even daily health, a painkiller, a paracetamol, is often not something that a villager in India has access to. That is the current situation.

Machine learning supports very minute diagnosis and suggestions on drug dosage. With the help of historical data, medical experts can make a more accurate diagnosis. A digital remote healthcare solution powered by machine learning can make a big revolution in the healthcare sector, not just in diagnosis, but also in the efficient distribution of drugs to the rural population.

We are working with some tribal people who live within a 15 km radius from our university campus. The nearest government hospital that they have is at a 35 km distance. Even transportation is a major challenge: they have just one bus that shows up once a day. Just once a day!

There are 450 people in one village and 150 people in another village. There is a bus that would come at 7:00 AM in the morning. That is the only transportation available for them. If there are any emergencies, they must call emergency services. This is something very common in India. Well, in this situation machine learning-powered digital solutions can make a big difference due to the precision in the treatment and distribution of drugs. In the existing *super specialty* hospitals, we can integrate digital solutions for remote consultation.

Even the logistics around the treatment can be managed. *Super specialty* hospital infrastructure in every village is not going to happen. Doctors will not come to the villages in person. We will need a global solution that is digital.

Arun: How do you gather intelligence around who needs the medicine on a regular basis? If there are 600 people in a village and if 10 of them are suffering from the condition, there needs to be a solution to first identify the demand for a medicine. There needs to be a logistical solution to suggest an optimal route that a distributor can take regularly. How do you gather the intelligence on the ground for all that? Are there any IoT devices?

BRT: Yes, IoT devices can be used to collect information. Wearable devices can be used as community kits. There are companies who come down to villages and collect data using such kits. But there is no single solution to data collection. There is lot of opportunity for researchers and industries to build solutions for diagnosis data collection from communities. We will need IoT devices that have non-invasive sensors, and ones that are accurate as well.

We are looking at ultrasound sensors that use the blood flow and provide data points for diagnosis. The traditional *Nadi* (pulse diagnosis) treatment we have in India has been using this technique for centuries.

 Nadi Pariksha is the ancient Ayurvedic technique of pulse diagnosis that can accurately diagnose physical, mental, and emotional imbalances in the body. It is a non-invasive science that helps reach the root cause of a disease and not just the symptoms.

There is also research where they take a picture of the eye and the blood vessels in the eye. Using that, they identify the part of your body where there is a problem. Researchers have published on this topic too. My point is, we may have to look beyond sensors to scale this into a viable model. You need to have better medical devices that can capture enough data.

We have a small clinic within our campus. There is a small laboratory testing set up within the campus. We are collecting data to see what we can do at this stage for some of the tribal population who come to work at the campus. One of our PhD students is working on this.

Thankfully, there is no problem with funding here because, for tribal welfare, the government is ready to spend good amounts. It's not a purely commercial solution, so there are not many takers from the private sector though. Otherwise, we would have had a solution long before now.

Arun: In this context, how can a quantum device help? Is there a use case at all?

BRT: It is early days, but when quantum computers become mainstream, we should be able to scale some of these innovative solutions. On the ground, we can think of small quantum devices that can help with better data processing. With the help of **5G**, we can make IoT devices powered by qubit circuits.

On the healthcare front, we also have Amrita's *super specialty* hospital, which is the fifth largest in India. We get the most advanced technologies in that hospital, which is perhaps one of the best in India. Any treatment you can get outside India is available in that hospital. Recently, they performed kidney surgery on an **unborn** baby successfully.

However, we know there is a lot more we can do using innovative solutions. For instance, let's take a patient in the ICU with a heart condition. Their condition generally doesn't just deteriorate all of a sudden. There are often small signals that a diligent human eye can perhaps notice.

But such signals are not easily captured by machine learning today. These signals are very mild, and often go unnoticed by humans due to the amount of patient data they have to review. This is where quantum technologies can help.

Healthcare solutions need to be capable of mirroring nature. In that sense, quantum computers should be more effective in healthcare than classical computers have been. With artificial intelligence and machine learning, we can put all the data we have captured and make progress. So, that's healthcare.

Arun: Sounds good; shall we talk about cybersecurity? I think that is an important area that both quantum computing and Blockchain technologies overlap with.

BRT: Yes, I would like to talk about Blockchain in this context. Blockchain and quantum computing have cryptography as a common element. But I fear it might be the end of the road for Blockchain (once quantum computing becomes mainstream). Blockchain, in its current shape, may no longer be relevant in the quantum world. The Blockchain community needs to adapt quickly to stay relevant.

I hear quantum-resistant ledgers can potentially change that status quo, but I am not a Blockchain expert. So, I don't know.

In terms of cybersecurity, quantum cryptography is unbreakable as of now. The reason is if somebody listens to the information, they will disturb the setup. China is a leader in this space, as they have recently demonstrated satellite communication using entanglement. They have successfully managed to transfer information over several thousands of miles using this quantum principle.

Coming back to entanglement, I think there are still several use cases and opportunities for this quantum property that we haven't really explored. Secure transmission of information using quantum cryptography does not need as much of an infrastructure as gate-based quantum computers need. As a result, they (quantum cryptography and information security) are going to be mainstream sooner than gate-based solutions.

Imagine the last two use cases we have discussed – medical data and cryptography. One of the challenges we have had with cloud adoption in finance and healthcare has been data security. If we can bring together quantum cryptography and medical data, and offer that as a service, it could be quite revolutionary to the industry.

China has managed to get well ahead of other countries in this space (quantum cryptography), and India is not doing enough.

Arun: That nicely leads us into another question I had for you. In the UK, we have a nice government-supported program called Innovate UK. I understand they have invested over £400 million in quantum computing R&D work. Also, Canada has invested similar amounts, but China is perhaps spending the most in this space. They have a few billion dollars' worth of R&D money allocated to quantum computing research.

At this rate, with very little R&D allocation for quantum computing, won't India fall behind? We are already lagging with Blockchain and innovation in that field due to the ban on cryptocurrency. How do we play catch-up with such a lack of support from the government?

BRT: Most of the commitments toward funding from the Indian government have been toward research led by the Indian Institutes of Technology (IITs). Prime Minister Narendra Modi has been quite good in general. He has introduced something called Institutes of Eminence and that will include other top educational institutions, like Birla Institute of Technology and Science (BITS Pilani) and Manipal University.

It will also help us collaborate better with global universities and recruiting foreign faculties. From a funding perspective, however, most of the funding is allocated to IITs, and the rest of the institutions only get a fraction of the allocated budget. With a lack of an ecosystem for quantum computing, I don't think we will be able to compete with China. Even countries like the UK may struggle to compete with them, as China has allocated 10 times more capital for the R&D than the UK, for example.

Countries need to remember that R&D and successes we see with technologies like quantum computing are like successes countries saw in defense and military technologies during the Cold War period. If China gets to quantum supremacy first, I would be surprised if they shared the technology with India or the US. They will use it to their advantage to stay ahead in information warfare.

Arun: That was a good comparison exercise between India and China. As always, China are a few years ahead. Let's talk about the semiconductor industry and how that will be affected by quantum computers.

BRT: Semiconductor devices are an interesting space. If you look at qubit circuitry, we have silicon chips and hydrogen atoms being used to make them. MIT recently published an article in *Nature* that hydrogen atoms can be used to make qubits at room temperature. I follow this research closely. I have some material science colleagues. One of them is working on hydrogen fuel batteries.

The spins we use for superpositions in quantum computations – that characteristic is common across quantum computing and material science.

Material scientists already have such devices that trap ions. That is one place where I think the semiconductor industry could look up to the material data science industry to build better devices. If you think about it, quantum computers have particle physics as a fundamental element, and we have so many different types of particles. We haven't really tried all of them to form qubit circuits. They all come with different characteristics, so depending on the suitability, we may potentially have quite a lot of options for qubit construction.

A deeper understanding of particle behavior could disrupt the qubit development industry. We may not see a monopoly in quantum computers (hardware) as we have seen in classical computers from a few semiconductor firms.

Another point I would like to make is that quantum computing research can only be successful when we have multi-disciplinary experts coming together. Computer scientists, physicists, and material scientists are all needed to create meaningful innovation in this space. That is only happening within communities like MIT, and we will need that awareness and capability across the industry globally. At this point, I see only a very few institutions in India working in this space. ISRO is looking into it, but even there only from a satellite communication perspective.

That is why having a more holistic ecosystem is so critical for quantum computing and innovation around that.

Arun: There are quite a few important points there. The thought about semiconductor industry becoming a lot less monopolized is interesting. I think that might be a refreshing development when it happens. I don't have any other questions, ma'am. Thank you so much for your time and your insights.

BRT: Thanks for reaching out to me, and I am glad that we could make this happen.

Conclusion

Even after almost 20 years of listening to BRT at university, she inspired and enlightened me with several industry insights during the interview. The enthusiasm she has for technology was very evident, especially if you had the privilege of listening to the recording of this interview. In the absence of that, I will quickly list the key takeaways from this interview chapter.

We touched upon how quantum machine learning could change lives in rural areas. BRT brought to life the opportunities that she has identified while working with villages in India. However, if that is executed at a small scale, there is no reason why such technologies can't be scaled in other rural parts of the world.

I was particularly moved by her healthcare examples. If a solution like the one she mentioned was implemented using a central digital infrastructure, powered by quantum machine learning, the industry could be more efficient and effective. She also touched upon several other healthcare use cases like diagnoses using machine learning, and how quantum computers can add value there.

I have used this interview as an inspiration for the smart cities chapter. Some of the points discussed in this interview have been explored in much more detail in that chapter. One of the key points that BRT touched upon is the importance of an ecosystem, and how a technological advantage could help nations get their noses ahead in an information race.

Finally, her insights about the semiconductor industry and how that could transform with quantum computers was interesting. The world could do with more competition in this space as different solutions for qubit circuitry emerge.

We have two more interview chapters that will touch upon topics such as error correction and cybersecurity-related quantum computing applications.

8

The Impact on Governance

Governance refers to how government and civil society arrive at a decision in meeting the needs of the populace. It is the mechanism of running a government using a set of principles defined in a constitution. Politics involves the art of governance, but is often considered to go beyond governance; it is also the means by which an individual or an organization establishes and enforces governance.

This chapter touches upon how both governance and politics have sought to utilize emerging technologies in recent times to deliver public sector services.

Governments across the world work on several mandates depending on local priorities. Governments of developing countries focus on judicial effectiveness, poverty eradication, healthcare, and basic necessities for its people. In the more developed parts of the world, government integrity, financial freedom, and business freedom are all important aspects. In states that have public healthcare and welfare, unemployment and healthcare benefits are important aspects that citizens expect.

Despite differences in priorities for governments across the world, one aspect is largely common across governments; they have been slow in going digital and embracing innovation when compared to their private sector counterparts. There are very few incentives to do so. With businesses in Financial Services or healthcare, there are competitive reasons to adopt innovation. Without a technology edge, they would often quickly become irrelevant. However, due to the lack of competition, governments have no such pressure.

This is not to say that governments have no drive toward digitizing their functions. In the developed world, with high internet and mobile penetration, several public offices have gone digital. The tax office, driving license authorities, and more importantly, visa and immigration services have all been digitized. However, more could be done here.

There seem to be more emerging technologies being used in campaigning for an individual or a party to get elected to office. This drive for technology is perhaps missing after they win the elections. Individuals and parties contesting to form governments have employed behavioral and predictive analytics using social media data. Trends and patterns in social media are understood and used to exploit the emotional leanings of voters, to win over the electorate.

As a result, social media has been the tool for top political parties and leaders to push their agendas. Be it the American election in 2016, or the Brexit referendum or the Indian elections of 2014, social media has played a large role. Efforts to use social media for election propaganda have now taken a new dimension with the application of **Artificial intelligence (AI)**. This technology has been used for sentiment analysis and in understanding sensitive words that would trigger a particular voter reaction.

The use of AI to understand voters can be scaled to a whole new level using quantum computing. AI can currently perform sentiment analysis, but it falls short when it is used to model voters' behavior in an election. In order to model election results, it is essential to model the correlations between different regions of a country. That would provide information regarding how certain shifts in voter perspective in one part of a country would affect voters in other regions of the country.

In this chapter, I discuss the applications of quantum machine learning in election modeling. QxBranch, a firm based out of Washington DC, led by CEO Michael Brett and Chief Data Scientist Max Henderson, have modeled the American election of 2016 using quantum machine learning.

Apart from the applications of AI and quantum machine learning, Blockchain also has several use cases within the public sector. We have also seen instances of governments piloting emerging technologies such as Blockchain. Switzerland, Estonia, and Dubai have been trialing Blockchain across several aspects of governance. Central Bank Digital currency, a key financial service use case of Blockchain, could help bring transparency to taxpayers and curb corruption. This chapter will touch upon the uses of Blockchain technology in these contexts. Let us first look at the use of social media by political and social organizations across the world over the last few years.

Social media in politics

As social media became mainstream, organizations have started to depend on it to understand the sentiment of their customers. AI algorithms that looked at Twitter data to understand any negative trends or reputational issues have been useful with the management of perception. Organizations using these tools have managed to be more proactive with their engagement models with their customers.

> *"A good reputation takes years to build and a second to destroy."*
>
> *– Warren Buffett*

Organizations that intend to engage proactively with their customers will need to stay on top of social media sentiment toward their brand. It is critical to have engaging conversations to stay relevant in a fast-changing world of Millennials and Generation Z customers.

The 2016 American elections saw data analytics employed in an election campaign. The extent to which it was used is debatable and has created controversies at the highest levels. However, the use of artificial intelligence and behavioral science to engage with voters has since proven to be effective. Channels such as Twitter and Facebook allow politicians to interact directly with their voters.

> *"I like it because I can get also my point of view out there, and my point of view is very important to a lot of people that are looking at me."*
>
> *– Donald Trump*

In India, Prime Minister Narendra Modi has been quite successful with his social media campaigns during the elections in 2014 and since then. By Q2 2019, he had over 45 million Twitter followers across the world. After Donald Trump, who has 65 Million followers, Modi has been the most successful in rallying his followers on social media.

It is also remarkable to note that during his time in office between 2014 and 2019, Modi never faced the press even once. In spite of that, he has been quite successful in creating a channel of conversation with his followers. He has set up a marketing capability as part of his campaigns that has helped his party win by clear majority. This was the first time that any Indian party had won an election with a majority since 1984.

As politicians look to use technology in a top-down fashion, citizens who want their say in policy making have made clever use of social media too. Citizens use social media to garner support for key campaigns. In April 2019, several thousand activists took to the streets of London urging UK politicians for more measures to curb climate change in London.

In 2017, about 2 million people in Chennai gathered at the Marina beach to protest the ban on their tradition of bull fighting. The government initially banned bull fighting as it was under pressure from animal welfare organizations. However, locals argued that their form of bull fighting was not harming animals, unlike in other parts of the world. Bull fighting was used as a means to find the strongest bull in a community and was essential for that breed of cattle to thrive.

These protests were orchestrated through social media. They were peaceful and mostly led by Millennials and Generation Z citizens. It went on for a week and resulted in the ban being reversed by the government of India. Protesters also agreed for regulatory oversight as the bull fighting was taking place to ensure that animals weren't harmed.

Social media has become the primary tool for citizens, activists, and lobbyists to drive political decisions through campaigns. It has also helped politicians and stakeholders in governments to create a perception that they were accessible and just a message away from voters.

Conversations that resulted from this convergence of behaviors provide rich data that can be used to understand priorities of citizens in different parts of the country. They can be used by politicians to further customize their message to their audience. Messages can be targeted at audiences of a certain age, gender, community, region, or a combination of these. This has hopefully set the context for the next section, which is about how artificial intelligence helps with election modeling.

Election modeling

Thanks to the big data boom, modeling solutions to a problem using AI algorithms is now possible. One of the key areas where predictive analytics firms have been working is in the field of modeling election results.

Historically, election results were modeled using two key methods. Voters were asked before elections about whom they would vote for, and this method was termed an opinion poll. The other means was when voters were asked who they voted for when they exited the polling booths. This method was called exit polling. Exit polls were typically more accurate in predicting the election results than opinion polls.

The accuracy of exit polls has been challenged in recent times. In the past three Indian elections and the most recent Australian elections of 2018, exit polls have been inaccurate.

As predictive analytics and statistical modeling have become more mainstream, several economic indicators and their correlation to election results have been modeled. The results were surprising, as key economic indicators seem to have minimal impact on elections. For example, the **Gross Domestic Product (GDP)** in the US could explain only 33% of elections that took place post World War II. In the period before the World War this number fell to 23%. Source: `https://fivethirtyeight.blogs.nytimes.com/2011/11/18/which-economic-indicators-best-predict-presidential-elections/`

Unemployment rates did a poor job of predicting election results. I would expect citizens of a country to vote for a government that brought down unemployment and vice versa. For instance, in the UK, unemployment rates were at their lowest for 44 years in 2019. However, voter sentiment in 2019 for the incumbents, the Conservatives, was generally negative – likely due to their handling of Brexit.

In many of the developed countries, the correlation between unemployment and election results is rarely noticeable. In the emerging markets, unemployment has been a major problem for households. For instance, the correlation between election results and unemployment in Latin America can't be ignored.

Coming back to the US elections, none of the them had any supporting information that unemployment was a good indicator of election results. We may also need to consider the fact that this analysis was done with data from only 16 American elections. This might be too small a sample space to provide meaningful correlations with election results.

Social wellbeing is another dimension that we might look to in order to help explain election results. Indeed, research to identify correlations between election results and social wellbeing and happiness factors have yielded beneficial results.

Researchers consolidate all these factors into something called "National Happiness" as a key performance indicator of an incumbent government to get re-elected. In May 2019, the New Zealand Government revealed that in times of populist policies, they were moving to a "wellbeing" budget for their citizens. The Prime Minister, Jacinda Ardern, is expected to announce a budget that addresses issues such as mental health, child poverty, and social inequalities.

This regime in New Zealand had already brought in policies to ban plastics and fight climate change. However, in doing so, Jacinda Ardern has also been criticized for not focusing on policies that addressed the bottom line, especially at times when the country was facing an economic slow down.

Economic and social indicators have both been combined to predict elections in the past. Another important pattern that is evident in some parts of the world around the time of elections is called "Political Business Cycles." This is a trend where a ruling party starts making voter-friendly economic policies a few months ahead of the elections.

Political business cycles have been observed as a common occurrence in emerging economies, where the voting population are less aware of these blatant tricks by political parties. In more developed parts of the world, political business cycles are far subtler.

Despite these political, economic, and social tools that could influence election results, the deep-tech newcomer and arguably the most powerful of all techniques in the politician's arsenal is social media. The idea is to use social media to model voters' behavior, create conversations to address the sensitivities of voters, and instigate certain favorable behaviors through these subtle techniques.

Another observation from the 2016 American election was that most forecasting models failed to predict the final outcome. The failure of these predictions is attributed to their inability to model correlations between states. That is precisely the limitation that quantum annealing can address. In the next section, we will go into the details of how quantum machine learning and quantum annealing techniques were brought together to model the American election.

Quantum machine learning

QxBranch, a quantum computing firm based out of Washington DC, has come up with a quantum machine learning approach to model the American elections. They used the 2016 American elections to create their machine learning model. A fully connected graphical model was identified as the best fit for correlations between the American states. The following diagram shows an example of what a graphical model could look like.

One of the key challenges associated with connected graphical models in modeling correlations across variables is in implementing them using classical computation. The models were powerful; however, they could not be generated using existing computing infrastructure. Recent developments in quantum computing have addressed the computational power needs to train these models. Graphical networks are now a realistic option when dealing with correlated variables.

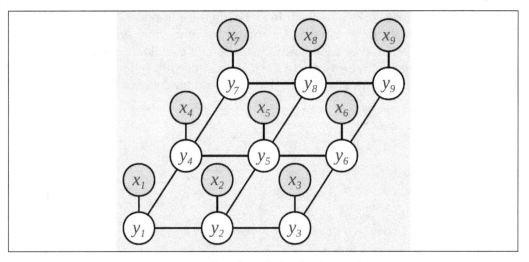

Figure 1: Illustration of a graphical network
Source: https://medium.com/@neerajsharma_28983/intuitive-guide-to-probability-graphical-models-
be81150da7a

Let us now look at BMs, a deep learning technique that has been used in the modeling of elections.

Boltzmann machine

An interesting area of research within the quantum machine learning space is deep quantum learning. This involves studying the impact of quantum devices and algorithms on classical deep learning models such as graphical models and **deep neural networks (DNNs)**.

In 1985, Geoffrey Hinton and Terry Sejnowski invented an unsupervised deep learning model called the **Boltzmann machine (BM)**. In doing so, they sparked the development of several neural networks called deep models. The BM is based on Boltzmann distribution, which is part of Statistical Mechanics.

One of the applications of a BM is in modelling the impact of parameters such as entropy and temperature on quantum states. Hinton famously referred to the illustration of a nuclear power plant as an application for understanding BMs. A BM is a powerful graphical model that can be categorized as a DNN.

Traditional neural networks models didn't have their input nodes connected. The BM is fundamentally different in that, the inputs are connected. As these nodes are connected to each other, they exchange information (of correlations in our elections example) and self-generate subsequent data. Hence, they are called a generative deep model. *Figure 2* represents the BM that has its nodes connected.

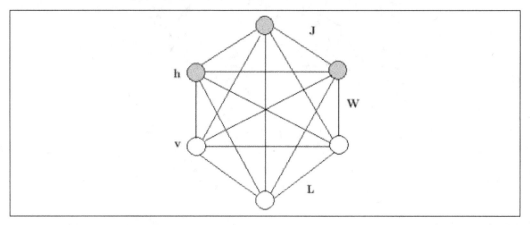

Figure 2: Hidden and visible nodes in a Boltzmann machine

Gray nodes in *Figure 2* represent hidden nodes, and white ones are visible nodes. Visible nodes are the variables we measure, and hidden nodes are those we don't measure. The machine first needs data to be input. Once data is input, the nodes learn their parameters, patterns in the data, and correlations between these variables and form an efficient system. As a result, a BM is categorized as an unsupervised deep learning model.

Despite offering a powerful model, BMs can be hard to train. Their training costs using classical computing infrastructure can be prohibitive, thereby limiting their mainstream industrial applications. However, with quantum computing infrastructure, training such networks seems more feasible.

QxBranch have used quantum annealing devices produced by D-Wave systems to implement BMs for elections modeling. These devices can deal with the computational requirements of the algorithm much better than classical computers. Certain types of energy landscapes in an annealing process can be explored more effectively using quantum computing due to the superposition and tunneling properties. As a result, we can train BMs to address the complexities of election modeling.

In an annealing process, the system is set in a ground state and then the adiabatic evolution process begins. If the process is slow enough, the system should provide optimal results in the end state, which will also be a ground state. However, there is a probability that the system may not end up in a ground state. Thus, by using BMs to model the correlation and quantum annealing to identify the low-energy state, the solution to an optimization problem such as election modeling can be achieved.

The following sections describe the experiment performed by QxBranch on the American elections of 2016 using a D-Wave quantum annealing machine.

QxBranch election model

In the modeling of the US Presidential election in the BM, a US state was represented by binary units. The presidential candidate who won the most electoral votes in the simulation was classified as the winner of the elections.

The state of voting results was mapped to a candidate. For instance, Democrats would be 1 and Republicans would be 0. Each state in the model had different weights assigned to it. The weights of the states were determined based on their influence on the national vote.

Modeling the first-order moment terms involved identifying the probability of a state voting for a candidate. The data to model this was sourced from FiveThirtyEight. The data involved the time-averaged polling results of the states. Therefore, if the chance of a Democratic candidate winning New York was considered 70%, then the first-order moment of the variable assigned to represent New York would be 0.7.

The projected vote share for both candidates per state was acquired for a period of 6 months leading up to the elections. These projected vote shares were used to calculate the first-order moment terms for each state. That was the easy part of the model. Calculating the second-order terms was harder. The second-order terms involved modeling the correlations between states. This could be explained as the likelihood that two states will end up with the same voting results in an election.

In identifying correlations, it was established that states that voted for the same party were highly correlated and vice versa. In the model, high correlation was represented by high second-order moments, and low correlation was represented by low second-order moments. Correlations were influenced by demographic, geographic, and in some cases economic factors.

Data from the last 11 US presidential elections were used to identify correlations between states. Where two states had consistently voted for the same party, the correlations were higher, and where states voted for different parties throughout history, correlations were lower.

Amongst the correlations derived from the data from previous presidential elections, higher weights were assigned to more recent election data. For instance, a correlation between two states in the past five elections would have higher weights assigned than a correlation identified in elections prior to that.

Due to the hardware limitations of the quantum computing infrastructure, the model had to be simplified using a few basic assumptions. The D-Wave 2X system couldn't embed the 50 American state model and the Washington DC province. So, Washington DC and Maryland were omitted as the likelihood of them turning to Democrat victory zones was nearing 100%. Once the model was largely in place, it had to be trained using data at regular intervals.

The next section goes into the detail of what the model achieved, and how the results compared to existing methods used to predict and model election results.

Primary experiment

This section describes the experiment conducted by QxBranch using DWave quantum annealers. The process of training the algorithms and the results achieved have also been evaluated.

Training of the BM with election data commenced once the variables and the data needs were identified. The DWave quantum annealing device was used to train multiple, fully connected BM with data from June to November 2016. However, training had to be performed every 2 weeks, rather than every day due to limitations. Training the network involved 150 iterations with randomized coefficients.

After the first set of training, a fortnightly process focused on the first-order moments. They were conducted to achieve convergence of the results to a stable summed error. This phase of training involved 25 iterations, with minimal changes to the first-order moments.

Each qubit result was mapped to a state. This was to find which candidate "won" a sample. The number of electoral votes a candidate won was added to the model. In this way, each sample resulted in a candidate winning or losing.

The number of samples that were won by Clinton was identified. This was then divided by the total number of samples to arrive at the probability of a Clinton Win.

A function of the time-weighted arithmetic mean was needed to get the mean forecast of the election results.

Through the experiment, a few well-known voters' behavioral patterns were observed. States that had heavy Democratic or Republican leaning had very low correlation coefficients. States like Illinois and Nebraska were identified as firm holds for Democratic and Republican candidates, respectively. States with the highest correlation coefficients were the heavily contested states.

Let's now look at how QxBranch's work compared to an existing election polling method. FiveThirtyEight is a website that provides election polling results. They have been doing this since 2008 and, in 2010, became a licensed feature on New York Times magazine. It would be worth comparing the QxBranch's approach with FiveThirtyEight to understand the effectiveness of QxBranch's algorithm.

Like QxBranch's model, where they identified states that swung the election results, FiveThirtyEight's forecasts had a metric called "tipping-point Chance." They define this metric as "the probability that a state will provide the decisive vote in the Electoral College". On election day, 7 out of the 10 states they ranked as the highest tipping-point chance states were similarly in the list of the 10 most correlated states in the QxBranch model.

In summary, the methodology that QxBranch used consisted of modelling the first-order terms and the second-order terms. The first-order terms involved identifying the winners of a state, and the second-order terms identified the correlation between states. And despite the complexity in the algorithms, with very little simplification, the quantum infrastructure was able to produce good results.

The real test for the algorithm is when America goes to the polls in 2020. Will this model help identify the winners beforehand? It would be good to see how this model needs to be tweaked when used in other democracies in the world. In any case, without a doubt, technology would affect democratic processes in the coming years across the world.

Let us now look at where Blockchain is being used in public sector activities across the world.

Blockchain, governance, and elections

Governance is one of the key design principles of Blockchain. This makes the technology a good fit for government and some of the public sector use cases. Identity management, e-governance, elections, and land registry management have all been trialed using Blockchain.

It would be beneficial to understand different strategies used for governance within Blockchain. Once we understand the framework from a governance perspective, we can discuss how it is used in several countries across the world.

Governance models

The focus of this discussion is the application of Blockchain in the governance of organizations and nation states. However, it is essential to understand the governance models used by Blockchain. This would help us relate how it could be used as a model for governing a nation.

Several Blockchain governance strategies have been used by key Blockchain networks as building blocks for their platform/protocols. The commonly known governance strategies are as follows:

1. On-chain governance
2. Benevolent dictator for life
3. Core development team
4. Open governance

On-chain governance

In this model, the governance rules are stored on the chain in smart contracts. The smart contracts offer the governance required in the Blockchain and procedures to change them are predefined. When there is a need to modify the rules of the Blockchain, users can rely on built-in methods.

Benevolent dictator for life

This approach is perhaps the simplest method to govern a Blockchain. In this model, the creator of the Blockchain is the final authority on all decisions regarding the Blockchain. Despite its simplicity, this model results in highly centralized decision making. In times of crisis, this can help in quick action; however, centralized decisions have their own risks too as it can lead to misuse of power.

Ethereum uses the "benevolent dictator for life" mode of Blockchain governance. Even though users and developers offer their inputs to the roadmap of the Ethereum Blockchain, Vitalik Buterin is the final authority on key decisions regarding the Ethereum roadmap.

Core development team

Firms running Blockchain protocol businesses have the unenviable challenge of first building a developer community before going to market to win customers to use their Blockchain. After the **B2C** (**Business to Customers**) and **B2B** (**Business to Business**) models, Blockchain has introduced the **D2D** (**Developer to Developer**) model. This has highlighted the importance of developers in business models. Developing a community of contributors has become as critical to a Blockchain business as acquiring clients.

Due to this fast-changing landscape, it is only fair to make developers part of the governance model in a Blockchain. A subset of the most active developers decides the functionalities that should be included in a Blockchain. The control of the Blockchain development and release roadmap is with the core development team.

This strategy is already used in open source programming projects, where developers have the final say on what is part of a rollout of the project.

Open governance

The "benevolent dictator for life" model is perhaps the most centralized form of governance. As governance models evolved, Blockchains used the open governance model. Here, the team making the decisions for the Blockchain is chosen by the users of the Blockchain themselves.

The open governance model is used by Hyperledger to make decisions on their technology roadmap. Their **Technical Steering Committee** (**TSC**) consists of users and developers and is the final authority when it comes to technology decisions.

Every year, the TSC is chosen from a group of dedicated users and developers within the Hyperledger community. This also allows active developers and users to have a say in key decisions. Community development within Blockchain ecosystems is so critical that involvement in governance has become a key motivation for engagement.

This also helps in making sure that any critical decision in the network is made with most users and developers in mind. As governance of the Blockchain largely rests within a small team that is chosen by the network, this perhaps reflects the structure of democracy across the world. This can also be the right balance between a highly centralized and decentralized governance philosophy.

Now that we have reviewed the governance models within Blockchain, let us look at Blockchain's applications in governance. Several countries across the world began Blockchain experiments within their public sector functions. One of the leading "Blockchain for Government" initiatives was Smart Dubai.

Smart Dubai

In January 2017, Dubai launched an initiative for all its government transactions to go digital. It would be powered by Blockchain technology with a plan to launch by 2020 and with a vision to cut 100 million paper transactions per annum. Thanks to Smart Dubai, over 130 projects in partnership with government and private sector entities have been launched.

Some key initiatives of Smart Dubai include the Dubai Data Initiative, the Dubai Blockchain Strategy, the Happiness Agenda, the Dubai AI Roadmap, and the Dubai Paperless Strategy.

In February 2017, a public and private sector initiative was kicked off. A pilot using IBM Cloud and Hyperledger for trade finance and logistics was launched in partnerships with key financial services players like Emirates NBD bank, Santander, and Aramex.

In Q2 2017, work on digital passports was initiated by Dubai's Immigration and Visa Department. The system brought together biometric verification and identity trust frameworks. It was powered by Blockchain technology in partnership with a UK-based firm, Object Tech.

Another initiative with government and private sector organizations followed. ConsenSys was named as the city advisor for Dubai Blockchain initiatives. IBM and ConsenSys led the build out of Blockchain applications across public sector offices covering policing, electricity, human development, and water.

The Dubai Land Department launched a Blockchain initiative for land registry. They also extended Blockchain for tenants to make their payments digitally without having to provide any documentation.

Towards the end of 2017, Dubai announced a Sovereign cryptocurrency called EmCash. This would be used across the country in retail outlets. A Blockchain firm, Pundi X, has created a **Point of Sale** (**POS**) device that would accept EmCash. The plan is to create over 100,000 outlets accepting EmCash over the course of the next few years.

The Smart Dubai initiative works on four key objectives:

- Integrated daily life services
- Optimized use of city resources
- Anticipate risks and protect people
- Enriched life and business experiences

They plan to achieve this by 2021 and are well on their way to doing so at the pace they have set for themselves. the Smart Dubai initiative has managed to create regular headlines about using or trialing an emerging technology to add efficiencies to public sector processes. It has always been quite difficult to execute initiatives where a public-private sector partnership was required. However, that has not dampened the spirits of the Smart Dubai initiative.

Digitizing public sector and government processes is a space to watch for all key nation states who want to digitize their capabilities. It is certainly more of a marathon than a sprint, and is prone to take longer than a private sector project. However, as Smart Dubai initiatives mature and take shape, they can be a case study for the world to learn from. While we cast admiring glances in the direction of Dubai's work in this area, there is yet another country that has taken Blockchain use cases to its citizens across the world. Let us now look at Estonia and how it has leveraged Blockchain to bring e-governance.

e-Estonia

It is hard to ignore Estonia when the topic of discussion is e-Governance and digitizing public sector processes. It is an example of how a nation could embrace emerging technologies to make public sector services instantaneous, seamless, and cost effective.

Estonia gained independence from the Soviet Union in September 1991 after 57 years. One of the key milestones was achieved in 2000, at the turn of the millennium, when a digital signature was given the same legal value as a wet handwritten signature. As a result, digital ID supported by a short code became a possibility.

This breakthrough allowed for an avalanche of public sector digital initiatives. The Tax and Customs Board became the nation's first public sector office to offer e-services. They allowed individuals and businesses to submit tax returns online. This also became the building block of the digital society portal called e-Estonia, a digital platform that puts more developed parts of the world to shame.

e-Estonia was supported by the launch of X-Road, a digital exchange system where organizations could exchange information securely. Banks, telecoms companies, the land registry, and tax services became part of this platform to function in harmony. The statistics regarding the growth of X-Road is inspiring. Key metrics captured as part of X-Road and, more broadly, the digitizing Estonia initiative are as follows:

- More than 1,000 organizations signed up to this platform, including 99% of state services.

- 52,000 organizations across the world are involved in this initiative indirectly.

- Each year, 500 million queries are handled by the system, saving 1,400 years of working time.

- Over 98% of Estonians have an ID card, which includes a chip and enables individuals to access services online.

- 50 million digital signatures annually, saving them five work days every year.

- The economic impact of going digital is worth 2% of the country's GDP in efficiencies.

- About 98% of all tax declarations in Estonia are now filed electronically, with the process typically taking about 3-5 minutes.

- The one-click tax return system was hailed as one of the key benefits of e-Estonia.

In 2005, Estonia became the first nation on the planet to hold national elections with an online voting option, and was the first to do so in parliamentary elections in 2007. With all these digitizing initiatives, it is no surprise that they were one of the first nations to embrace Blockchain technology.

Despite the digitizing efforts, there were challenges posed to the e-Estonia initiative; one being that a large amount of public sector data was vulnerable to cyber-attacks. The efficiencies achieved through all the digitizing efforts would be of no use if the system's security was compromised.

As a mitigation to the risk identified, Blockchain technology was trialed and helped the initiative's rhetoric, which was, "no one – not hackers, not system administrators, and not even the government itself – can manipulate the data and get away with it." Estonian cryptographers who developed the Blockchain made this statement to describe their intention that all ecosystem stakeholders would be kept honest.

In March 2019, as the nation went to elect their next government, 44% of voters used the digital voting platform called i-voting. The previous elections had 31% of voters using the system.

The number of people who used their mobiles to vote increased from 12% to 30% from the previous elections. This has aided a steady increase in election turnout as it went from 47% in 2005 to 64% in 2019.

Source: `https://e-estonia.com/solutions/e-governance/i-voting/`

The i-voting system used Blockchain to add transparency to the process. Election results were announced immediately after the voting closed. One can argue that in a small nation with very little population, it is perhaps not as operationally challenging to achieve real-time election results. However, this is the way forward for the rest of the world.

Estonia's land registry and healthcare systems are also using Blockchain to create transparency. Patients' medical histories are stored in the Blockchain and can be used by doctors to make assessments during emergencies. Patients can also access their digital medical history online. It also allowed for complete transparency if patients wanted to know which doctors accessed their file.

The system facilitated 500,000 doctor queries and 300,000 queries by patients every year. The data generated by the system was critical to inform policy decisions from the Ministry of Social Affairs, so that resources can be spent and allocated accordingly.

The success of e-Estonia and its platforms, such as i-Voting and X-Road, has been acknowledged globally. The X-Road system is being rolled out in countries like Iceland, Finland, Kyrgyzstan, Azerbaijan, Palestine, Vietnam, El Salvador, and Argentina. Let us now look at how Estonia have enabled non-Estonians to access its public sector services through e-Residency.

Estonia and e-Residency

In December 2014, Estonia launched a e-Residency scheme that allows non-Estonians to access its digital services, including company formation, banking, payments, and taxation. The scheme has been a big success and has attracted top talent from across the world.

- Over 40,000 people across 150 countries have been granted e-residency so far.
- Over 6,000 businesses have been established, contributing about 10 million euros (£8.6 million) through taxes.
- The country aims to have 10 million e-Estonians by 2025 and create a "single market" of e-services between countries.

> *"Even though there are only a little over a million of us, thanks to Estonia's capabilities, we can make ten million payments, perform ten million requests, and sign ten million contracts in just ten minutes. Even ten times larger states cannot beat us. But the good news is that it is possible to join our exclusive club of digitally empowered citizens."*

> – *Kersti Kaljulaid, President of Estonia*

Estonia is where the digital transformation of government services using technologies such as Blockchain and AI has been realized. As a result, other nations are drawing inspiration from their platforms. The e-Residency goes one step further and attracts people across the world to start businesses in Estonia.

The start-up community in Estonia has been thriving, thanks to its digitizing efforts. The ease of starting a business and running a business are critical to an early stage venture. If the operational pain points of running a business is taken care of, firms can focus on their core value proposition. Be it telecoms, fintech, or cleantech, Estonia has Europe's highest concentration of start-up firms. Some interesting statistics about Estonia's start-up ecosystem are as follows:

- Over 550 start-ups are based out of the country, which has just over 1 million people.
- Over 3,763 people were employed by start-ups in 2018.
- These start-ups raised 320 million euros (£275 million).

Estonia may not be able to claim a leapfrog impact, as witnessed in perhaps Africa's m-Pesa success or China's Alibaba and Tencent wave. However, with the use of Blockchain and cutting-edge data intelligence, they have shown the world the possibilities of digital governance.

The use of Blockchain in European public sector organizations doesn't end with Estonia. Austria have made headlines through their initiatives, too More on that in the next section.

The Vienna token

One of the interesting aspects of Blockchain technology is that some of the leading ecosystems of the technology exist outside of Silicon Valley. Traditionally, most emerging technologies have their inception and big players based out of the bay area; this was possible due to the flow of capital and the risk appetite of investors in the valley. Be it classical computing firms, social media, artificial intelligence firms, or even a good number of quantum computing firms, they all have a strong link to the valley.

However, that is not quite the case with Blockchain. The initial boom of the technology had its epicenter in Asia. Europe came a close second in embracing and adopting the technology. Several European hubs, including the Crypto Valley, emerged and allowed the region to take a lead. Family offices and institutional investors have supported the rise (and the hype) of the technology in a way that only Silicon Valley had boasted in the past.

Vienna has been at the heart of some of the recent Blockchain industry developments. One of the key initiatives is the notarization of **Open Government Data (OGD)**. This is about facilitating the use of food stamps by local government employees. Vienna is also setting up a Blockchain-based token to incentivize citizens for good behavior.

One of the first thoughts that hit me about this system was its similarities to China's Social Credit System. China has been trialing an AI-driven Social Credit System to reinforce good citizen behavior. However, it has been a controversial scheme (according to the West) that shunned consumer data privacy. Private sector firms such as Alibaba were also engaged in providing the data required to make this scheme happen. An example of this system would be where citizens could access day-to-day facilities like transport depending on how well they have paid their credit dues.

However, Vienna's "Culture Token" is planned as a reward for any good behavior of a citizen. Citizens can use the token to get access to arts and culture in the city of Vienna. The scope of the rewards is planned for expansion across several other citizen services.

The scheme is helping Vienna authorities in Vienna to reduce their carbon emissions by rewarding citizens for walking instead of using their cars in the city centers. In the long run, the Culture token could be used across several other key initiatives and transition into a Vienna token.

Let us now look at how the United Nations has used Blockchain technologies across its initiatives globally.

United Nations and refugees

The United Nations has been at the forefront of public sector innovation using Blockchain. Several UN initiatives have been launched over the last few years that have resulted in tangible benefits in keeping track of aid, curbing corruption, and most importantly, ensuring accountability in the value chain.

Organizations such as the UN face several operational challenges in dealing with financial and government organizations. Many of these organizations are based out of parts of the world where the regimes are hostile and corruption levels are high. Ensuring the effective distribution of humanitarian aid through a transparent platform is a challenging process.

As a result, beneficiary data is at risk and can be a source of financial mismanagement and corruption if financial aid is not traced to the last mile. In order to address these challenges, the UN's **World Food Programme (WFP)** has launched a programme called Building Blocks. The research that backed up the core thesis of Building Blocks showed that the direct transfer of aid funds to beneficiaries was the most efficient and benefited the local economy.

However, achieving disintermediation and bringing complete transparency to the flow of money in the charity/aid industry is no simple feat. The UN's WFP distributed record cash transfers of $1.6 billion in 2018. They needed a technology platform to do this more effectively and efficiently.

The Building Blocks programme was launched in 2017 to do just that. In 2017, the WFP began a proof of concept in the Sindh province in Pakistan to use the capabilities of Blockchain for authenticating and registering beneficiary transactions. The technology removed the intermediaries and allowed for a secure and fast transaction between the WFP and the beneficiary. By 2018, the platform had over 100,000 refugees on board. They could get their irises scanned to prove their identities and pay for their groceries.

The Building Blocks platform used a permissioned version of Ethereum Blockchain. In a year's time, the platform was rolled out to two refugee camps in Jordan. The food voucher system that was in place until then, was quickly replaced with an iris scanning checkout for groceries and food. As the refugee information was integrated with UNHCR (the UN's Refugee Agency), biometric authentication was used to record every transaction and the beneficiary behind it.

This has saved 98% of the transaction fees in the camps. Building Blocks is now due for an upgrade. They are now exploring using mobile money in the refugee camps in Jordan. That would also scale quite quickly in providing an economic identity for refugees who often live and work across different countries. As refugees' identities are managed on a Blockchain and their transactions are registered, it would be easily accessible for authorities who want to understand their financial background.

In an interview with Coindesk, Robert Opp, the WFP's director of innovation and change commented on the key achievements of the programme.

"All 106,000 Syrian refugees in the camps of Azraq and Zaatari redeem their cash transfers on the blockchain-based system. So far, more than US$ 23.5 million worth of entitlements have been transferred to refugees through 1.1 million transactions. By March 2019, Opp expects that an additional 400,000 refugees will receive their assistance through a blockchain."

Families in need in these countries do not have to wait for weeks to receive their cash. In the past, they have had to depend on corrupt officials in intermediary organizations to receive the funds. Often, a good portion of the money was paid to the intermediaries who distributed the cash, both for operational and corruption-based reasons. However, all these parties can be disintermediated with this technology.

Over the last two years, I have had the pleasure of discussing this use case with three different Blockchain start-ups. Disberse, AidTech, and Agriledger are all focused on bringing accountability to charity and UN-led initiatives. Disberse and AidTech use Blockchain to bring the key stakeholders in a charity/aid transaction on to their network. Transactions get tracked in real time, and offer instant reporting and transparency.

On the other hand, Agriledger is working with the United Nations to provide end-to-end traceability for food produced by farmers. They are working on a prototype in Haiti with the UN and have started on projects in China and Africa. Another start-up, Banqu, led by a refugee from Africa, also focused on providing economic identities to women in Africa.

Agriledger have their work cut out as they attempt to add efficiencies to the food supply chain with the help of the UN. Farmers could own their food produce and logistics and other middlemen in between can offer their services and take a cut of the revenues. This brings transparency to the food supply chain and allows farmers to price their products with more information at their disposal. Customers buying food can also clearly trace the item back to its source.

Conclusion

At the Singapore Fintech Festival in November 2018, Narendra Modi, the Prime Minister of India, delivered a keynote speech. He mentioned that start-ups used jargon such as Blockchain to increase their valuation with investors. Never in the past thirty years have I seen an Indian political leader pay attention to innovative trends. It may be an indication of the maturity of the Indian start-up ecosystem, but it is also due to the focus that the government devotes to technology

Governments and governance have been a brick and mortar story for centuries. Digitizing government offices and processes hasn't been high on the agenda for most nation states. However, that has changed in the past 10 years. With countries like Estonia, Dubai, Georgia, India, and Singapore exploring several digital initiatives, we are certain to see several leapfrog moments and case studies that can be replicated elsewhere.

Voter behavior has never been as well understood or exposed as it is today. Social media and the data that voters generate during the times of elections is a vital tool that can, at times, work against them. Thanks to deep learning algorithms and quantum computing, politicians can model voter behavior in a country and plan their campaigns accordingly. This intelligence can also help them decide policy decisions and hopefully enforce better governance.

All this points to a welcome trend that governments are increasingly cognizant of the competitive edge over information that these technologies can give them. It is a day and age where nation states don't go to war using nuclear arms, but through data and information. One way to equip themselves is by redirecting defense budgets to developing cutting-edge technology.

With better governance over citizens' behavior, traceability of the cash in their economies, and an improved understanding of the sentiments of voters, governments will have the required tools to make well-informed policy decisions. In the past, most policies were made through models and frameworks that didn't have the data management capabilities that are on offer today.

Another key takeaway is that some of these technologies are quite affordable and democratic and that it is not just the big economies who can afford to use them in a meaningful way. On the contrary, smaller economies like Estonia have become fast adopters of Blockchain and data analytics.

It is also essential that organizations like the United Nations embrace technologies such as Blockchain and AI to create impact at scale. The charity/aid value chain, which is inefficient and corruption-prone due to local authorities and intermediaries, can be fixed. As these technologies are used to bring economic identity to refugees, national borders become irrelevant. Governance can be truly global.

9
Interview with Max Henderson, Senior Data Scientist, Rigetti and QxBranch

Just before I started to write this book, I felt I had a good grasp of the industries and use cases that I would be focusing on. I had a vision for the flow of the book, and the real-world problems I would be covering. However, through the research I have done over the course of writing the book, I realized there were areas that I should be touching upon that I hadn't planned to. The interview with Max Henderson was certainly serendipitous for me as an author, and something I hadn't planned for. I hope it will bring to light an interesting application of quantum computing for you, the reader.

Max Henderson and I have been social media acquaintances for some time. We have interacted with each other's posts, however, we never took the next logical step of sending a personal message to each other and saying hello. It was early in 2019 that I reached out to him to have a conversation on what he was doing at QxBranch. At that time Max was only at QxBranch and his additional role at Rigetti only materialized later in the year.

I knew that Max was working on a really interesting problem – modeling the American elections. He had done some work with the 2016 elections, which I discussed in *Chapter 8, The Impact on Governance*.

I was keen to understand the backstory of how he identified this as a problem that he could model using a quantum computer. I reached out to him.

Max was very happy to talk, and we had an initial discussion about what he was working on. He confirmed that he was working on quantum machine learning to identify a solution for election modeling. He also clarified that he was a data scientist who was into business development. That meant he was in the business of simplifying the narrative around quantum computing.

That was exactly the kind of person I was looking for. I told him I would like to write about his work in my book. Max was open to the idea, and we closed the call with a view that we will sleep on the idea.

A few days later, I wrote to Max with my thinking on what would be a good way to capture what he was working on within quantum machine learning. Max liked it, and we agreed to do a recorded interview.

The interview is captured below. One of the key takeaways for me from all this is the effective use of social media. In my opinion, social media can't be a medium that can connect people the way a face-to-face conversation does, however, it can help to build relationships that can lead to mutually beneficial results. Let's now get into the interview:

Arun: Hi Max, thanks for joining me today. Let's kick off with a bit of an introduction about yourself. Let's talk about yourself, your background and about your firm and how it all happened.

Max: Yeah, basically my background was in Physics. I got my Ph.D. in Physics from Drexel University in Philadelphia. I was doing biophysical models of neural networks to try to explain how our brains might change as we get older using simulations. That naturally got me really interested in machine learning algorithms because those are nicely abstracted versions of biophysical neural networks. They allow us to capture some of the really powerful things our brains do, using simpler models.

At the same time, I was working at Lockheed Martin as an intern. Back in 2011, they bought the first commercially available quantum device. I experimented with quantum hardware ever since 2011. So originally, we were looking almost exclusively at optimization types of problems and over time, quantum machine learning became much more promising.

I continued those avenues of research and now I am at QxBranch, which is also working in a similar space. A big part of my job is helping the firm identify pain points across the different lines of businesses we operate in. There are hard computational problems that we look into, and my role is to identify quantum computing solutions for these problems. It is quite interesting to come up with new ways of solving these problems with a more holistic and scalable perspective.

Arun: You mentioned your expertise in quantum machine learning. Let's spend some time on machine learning and talk about some of the driving factors as to why it is more relevant today than ever before. We have seen a massive explosion of data in the last decade or so. Social media has led to this volume of data that we can mine. These are good times for **artificial intelligence (AI)** to exploit and go mainstream, which is what we see happening across industries. However, AI and machine learning have been around conceptually for quite some time. So, what has happened in the last five to six years that has made AI a real thing? What is your take on how we could make *AI on steroids* using quantum computing principles?

Max: Broadly speaking, you know machine learning is a field that has grown over the last few decades. Ever since the 1980s, there have been some very powerful tools. In those times there were some very powerful models that simply weren't practical because we didn't have enough data. Also, we didn't have big enough computers to make them work. The big data era and the era of cheap computers have really allowed machine learning to go from a research topic to an incredibly powerful tool.

Every Fortune 500 company on the planet is looking into machine learning now. There's a similar extension that we could think about with quantum machine learning. Even though we have massive amounts of data points and more powerful computers than we used to, there are still some computationally difficult problems where classical computers just get stuck. Especially if they want to be exact about the solution.

Quantum machine learning really started out by looking at a particular type of machine learning problem. Things like searching unstructured lists, and a couple of great theoretical models (PCA, clustering, and so on), are areas where quantum seems to give you a speedup compared with any known classical algorithm. But there's a whole bunch of practical hurdles encountered when dealing with these algorithms that make some of those approaches really difficult.

 Some of these speedups delivered on these models through quantum algorithms have been *de-quantized* recently. There are new classical quantum-inspired algorithms that have matched the performance of these quantum algorithms.

Over the last five years pretty much every quantum machine model was sort of stuck in terms of being able to run on physical devices until we solved some foundational scientific problems that allowed for much larger, error-corrected devices. What's happened in the last five years is that people have really looked at using quantum computers in slightly different ways than originally intended, and they're a bit more experimental.

One that has received considerable research interest is using adiabatic quantum devices like those that D-Wave produces to model Boltzmann distributions, which are at the core of a lot of powerful graphical models. Some of these problems just cannot be effectively estimated using classical computers at scale. That is because it boils down to trying to sample from an exponentially large number of states, which you just can't do with classical computers as the problem gets bigger and bigger.

Adiabatic quantum computing (AQC) is a model of computation that uses quantum mechanical processes operating under adiabatic conditions. As a form of universal quantum computation, AQC employs the principles of superposition, tunneling, and entanglement that manifest in quantum physical systems.

Source: `https://oxfordre.com/physics/physics/view/10.1093/acrefore/9780190871994.001.0001/acrefore-9780190871994-e-32`

Simulated quantum annealers seem to be performing just as well as the real quantum annealers for certain modeling tasks.

We believe that by mapping certain graphical models to this spin-glass Hamiltonian, you might be able to get a better representation with a finite number of measurements to train these really powerful models. We have used D-Wave devices to map these graphical models. There is another whole topic area that really didn't exist until 2016 and it's really seen an explosion in recent times: it is an area of research that I would call *quantum feature extraction algorithms*.

Some examples of this are quantum reservoir computing and quantum circuits learning. We just published a paper at QxBranch on quanvolutional neural networks. Basically, the idea is that using the universal gate-based quantum circuits, you can pass classical data through those and extract data by measuring the final state. You could sort of think of this as doing some kind of nonlinear function interpretation of the original data.

That is basically what the most sophisticated machine learning models are doing anyway. They're trying to extract nonlinear data using classical transformations. The idea is to see if we could use quantum circuits of various types, flavors, initializations, and ways of encoding. To then decode the information, we use quantum nonlinearities to extract useful features from classical data that could be used in a broader machine learning context. So that's an exciting and very new line of research in the quantum machine learning world that's getting some real attention now.

 For instance, consider an exercise to build an algorithm to identify a cat in a three-dimensional space. We will first need to identify the features from the data available (colors, shape) that can be used by the algorithm to identify a cat. This exercise of separating useful information from all the other data points could be done by a quantum computer. Once the key data points are identified, then a classical computer can be used to identify that it is a cat. A quantum computer can spot features even in a noisy environment.

Arun: One of the topics that keeps coming up and that you kind of alluded to is that there might be some kind of hybrid model between classical and quantum computing that might accelerate the mainstream adoption of quantum computing. I have recently spoken to Fujitsu, which has a digital annealer based on quantum principles, but it is not really a quantum infrastructure. However, it seems to solve problems better than classical computers. Is that [hybrid model] something you think is going to be a trend?

Max: That's a really good question. There is an entire field of research that would broadly be called quantum-inspired applications. Just like you were saying, they are taking some kind of a lesson from quantum mechanics, but they are still realized completely using classical computers. There is some reason to think that there is a really promising path there because we can deploy real-world applications using that infrastructure.

We have somewhat perfected classical computing in a sense. We have built very large, very fast, very parallel classical computing capabilities at this point. We believe that there are shortcuts, in a manner of speaking, where people can kind of model an approximation of a real quantum computer at a much larger scale in connectivity using these kinds of approaches. There might be some reasons to look at that kind of an implementation to solve certain types of problems. So yeah, annealers are a great example. Rigetti and Fujitsu have got simulated digital annealers, and that goes to show that people within the industry are clearly understanding the way in which this space is evolving.

We just finished building our own large quantum simulator through a project with Innovate UK. This is an active research area, which is probably a very good stepping stone between the purely classical computing world and the "real deal" of quantum computers. There's quite a lot of interesting quantum-inspired solutions and it doesn't just mean trying to simulate quantum systems using classical computers.

There are also examples of people trying to do innovative algorithms. Ewin Tang is a pretty famous person in the quantum computing community because she actually discovered an algorithm that gave an exponential improvement for recommendation systems using a quantum-inspired approach. She actually de-quantized a quantum computing algorithm in what could be considered a field of quantum-inspired research in the classical computing world. People dig in deep to see if quantum algorithm speedups hold when you *level the playing field* and allow classical computers to have the same access and query properties as the quantum algorithm.

An example of de-quantization is the recommendation algorithm, where a classical algorithm was developed after its quantum counterpart and had similar performance. A recommendation algorithm, for instance, helps Amazon to predict what a consumer would prefer to purchase based on their purchase history.

Ewin Tang solved the recommendation problem using a classical algorithm that runs in poly-algorithmic time. Therefore, the classical algorithm had the superior performance of the quantum algorithm developed by Kerenidis and Prakash.

There are certain problems right now that benefit from a quantum speedup, and there may be a classical [algorithm with similar speedup] if you make some assumptions about what you can sample from and query efficiently [from the input dataset]. There may be certain classical approaches that can give you an improvement over what was previously thought to be possible using classical algorithms.

Ewin Tang's famous paper really showed that, in thinking about a quantum solution, you can actually come up with novel classical approaches. That paper in particular is the kind of shining light that you look for in a field that is looking to break into creating real-world impact.

We need to really be precise about understanding what assumptions go into some of the papers claiming an exponential speedup. Tang basically put some of those assumptions under a microscope, and when she did that it opened the doors to a new classical idea. If you're taking this approach, this whole *"quantum-inspired"* field is a really interesting area, especially in the near to medium term.

Arun: Absolutely, I think this is perhaps the way forward too, Max. I think there will be a period where this hybrid approach could be the bridge between the classical and the quantum eras. It is also going to help us because the stability of these *"quantum-inspired technologies"* is going to be much better than current quantum infrastructure.

Now let's come to you. What are your focus areas at the moment? What are the interesting problems that you're working on?

Max: As I mentioned before, one of the interesting things that we published, and that I was the first author on, was what we call a quanvolutional neural network, which is my own coinage. It's basically combining quantum with convolutional and is essentially like a quantum version or an extension of a classical convolution or neural network. You touched on this idea that hybrid quantum-classical systems are probably where we're going to see the most traction in the near term. I think that's absolutely correct. So, this is really another step into better understanding how quantum can very explicitly fit in as just a component of an already existing paradigm.

We're still in the early days of pursuing and characterizing convolutional neural networks, and I am very excited about that. We are still very active in investigating and characterizing Boltzmann machines in various forms for autoencoders and quantum approaches on adiabatic devices like the D-Wave or simulated ones. So that's another research area that we're working on with a lot of researchers.

Arun: Great, thanks for that. Now, let's come to the specific paper that we've been discussing for some time. Tell us about how you arrived at that. What made you think, *"okay, I'm going to solve that problem?"* Also, tell us about the process. You would have gone through a process of data collection, putting the data through this engine you have built, and you would model something out of it, then source additional data and test the model with that data, and so on. Please can you walk us through the process? That would be really interesting for people to read about.

Max: Yeah, absolutely. I first had this idea pop into my mind during the 2016 presidential race. Before the race was actually over, I was working at QxBranch and thinking about the possible negative side effects of the fact that all of the US states more or less are *"winner-takes-all"* in awarding their electoral votes – unlike a lot of other countries where they would break those down and be a little bit more proportional.

For instance, if you have the majority in Pennsylvania you get all of those electoral votes. That made me really think, *"oh this is so interesting, you can almost model this like a binary system of quantum bits."*

At the end of the day, when you make a measurement, each of these states is making a binary choice, which is just like what happens when we measure a quantum system.

People basically didn't think too much about the correlations between states. So, if you are looking at New Jersey, your results should be very correlated with the results of New York because the populations are very similar; both similar demographics and in a similar part of the country. You would assume that New York and New Jersey should be much more correlated when you make a single measurement than, for instance, New York being correlated with Arizona; those are very different places with very different people.

The idea eventually emerged out of the fact that the election maps well into a binary system. Also, the fact that there are correlations between states gave birth to the idea of trying to put this on a quantum computer. With quantum computers, the strength really is that they are intrinsically correlated systems. You can't affect one piece of the system without affecting the rest of it. There was a machine learning algorithm called the Boltzmann machine that I had already done a decent amount of research with on early-stage quantum devices. It had all the ideal properties for expressing the exact type of problem that is the US presidential election.

Really, you need a model that would assign a probability to every possible outcome. So, if you have 50 states, there are 2^{50} possible outcomes. If you are doing a true forecast, every potential outcome is non-zero, even though some of those outcomes have very low probabilities. So at the end of the day, the best forecast would have the ability to create accurate probabilities for all measurable outcomes and then sum up all those things together to give a true probabilistic forecast.

The reason why that is very difficult in practice is because there's a whole bunch of possible outcomes, and no one wants to crunch all those numbers. People typically make approximations, or they will ignore the correlations between states, because then it's very easy to model individual states and just add up all the individual results. We got the idea that maybe we can map this onto a quantum system. While the system is in superposition, it is theoretically in all possible states at once. By making a finite number of samples, we might get a very good approximation of that full distribution of probabilities by taking advantage of the fundamental physics driving that system.

In a nutshell, that's why we felt this is a powerful modeling approach. This is a very difficult distribution of probabilities to do classically, but we think there is a bit of a natural fit for quantum computers. Putting it on a quantum computer such as those made by D-Wave was an easy choice for this kind of modeling work. As we went through the process, we were able to successfully generate results that passed all the litmus tests you would want.

We got data from FiveThirtyEight, who is the leading institute for doing this kind of mathematical modeling for elections. By the end of the process, we were forecasting results that matched the general trend lines that FiveThirtyEight were producing themselves. At the same time, our models were a little bit more bullish on Trump than the FiveThirtyEight models were – and that was an interesting result.

We're not saying that the quantum approach is superior. However, we do really believe that getting a good approximation of an exponentially large number of possible states is a difficult problem that these quantum systems may just do more naturally and more natively than classical computers. We are looking at redoing this study for 2020 and trying to do it live this time. We think that these are early days for quantum computers, but this is a really good fit for the type of problem that might be good on near-term devices. It's also a small enough problem that you can actually now fit the whole US election on a D-Wave.

It will be a fun thing to see what comes up in the next election cycle.

Arun: We'll know that in a year's time, I guess. You touched upon an interesting point, Max, which is that people quickly tend to pick variables, or rather ignore the correlations between the variables. That makes things easier, but potentially less accurate. For example, in the financial services sector when people are doing portfolio rebalancing, changing the weights on a particular asset class is going to have an effect on another allocation within the same portfolio.

Correlations make this whole modeling and the task of optimizing a lot more complex. We come across **principle component analysis (PCA)** in financial services. That simplifies the optimization process. Is that something that's being considered with your quantum solutions?

Max: Yes. Portfolio rebalancing is actually one of the exact use cases we have investigated for using quantum computing for financial applications. I think there will always be folks that are trying to implement simplification methods that attempt to get rid of the computational burden of dealing with correlations. Depending on the actual system you're dealing with, there may be simplifications that can allow you to do more or less. You can get rid of those complexities and still represent the problem well.

However, in certain other problems that tend to be within highly correlated systems, those approximations may not work as well. It varies on a problem-by-problem basis. It also depends on exactly how good your results need to be. In the extreme case, where you want to accurately model interactions of a system with correlations, you can't make approximations and expect that the results are going to be as good. There are definitely techniques that can help get around the problems, but it depends on the situation and what fidelity you need.

Arun: Thanks for that. I have a couple of questions for you bundled into one. If you had a crystal ball and I asked you where you would be with QxBranch in a couple of years' time, what would you say? The second half of the question is, what is the one biggest hurdle on your roadmap? The one thing that, if solved, would make your life so much easier?

Max: Yeah, that's great. I'll reference the quantum computing stack just so we have a common reference point. The quantum computing stack describes the different levels that different companies are being built of, in order to do different things in the emerging quantum computing ecosystem. At the very bottom of the stack are companies or research groups building quantum hardware devices. These are people actually in a lab trying to build new types of quantum computers, and QxBranch is sort of at the opposite end, at the top of the stack. We are trying to build the software layer on top of all the bottom and the middle pieces. It would be used by a quant someone who works in quantitative analysis, a data scientist, or a software developer, to take advantage of quantum algorithms without needing to know quantum physics. These users will be very much like your average data scientist in today's world; they may not know how a transistor works, but they do not need to – even though their computer is using quite a few of them. That's sort of the direction that QxBranch is going in: building software that takes advantage of quantum, for users who do not know quantum physics.

We are looking to continue doing work with individual companies to figure out where their hardest problems are. Then we are looking to make quantum algorithms and applications that are easily accessible by the types of folks that don't need to know how the algorithm works but need to know how such algorithms would fit into their use cases. That's sort of where QxBranch has put its stake in the ground. We are a quantum software company at the top part of that quantum computing stack. We are going to be releasing version one of our software platform for doing exactly that in a few weeks.

Arun: Great to hear that, Max, and good luck with the launch of your software. So, what are your challenges? What is hampering your growth or progress at this point?

Max: Referring back to the quantum computing stack, depending on where you are in the stack, your challenges will be different. For people at the bottom of the stack, the challenges are truly research and scientific challenges. To build better quantum hardware, you have to figure out techniques that can increase the coherence time of the qubits, so that you're getting lower error rates. You have to figure out layouts that allow your qubit systems to scale. There's a bunch of engineering and physics problems for the hardware providers to solve.

For the software providers, there are different sets of challenges, and some of those things are figuring out how to bridge the divide between technologists and the subject-matter experts. In an organization like a bank, people who will be working on quantum computing are not so abstracted from the complexities of quantum computing yet. They can't be completely oblivious to how quantum computing works. It is a little bit of a middle-ground phase where the people that are going to get the early benefits of quantum computing are also going to need to understand a little bit more about how quantum computing works. There have been challenges in just working with customers to help make sure they understand the fundamental technology well enough, so that they can understand how it might impact their business.

Additionally, quantum software is always going to be limited by how the hardware progresses. We can build some good software tools, but if there eventually aren't the hardware tools to plug into that software framework, quantum application firms solving specific industry problems are going to be hard-pressed in that regard. You know, we aren't the ones trying to push forward that part of the stack. So, we are dependent on the hardware providers ultimately making good quantum hardware that we can show has relevance to business applications. So, I think that's sort of the challenge for the people at the top of the stack.

Arun: So, let's hope for better innovation across the stack, so that one party is not bottlenecked by another. On that note, Max, I think we have come to the end of the interview. I would like to thank you again for your time and amazing insights.

Max: You are welcome, Arun. Keep me posted on how the book is shaping up.

Arun: Absolutely.

Conclusion

The discussion with Max helped expand my horizons around the applications of quantum computing. Until I stumbled upon Max's work, I had understood the applications of quantum computing in financial services, logistics, healthcare, and other traditionally data-rich industries. However, politics is a new industry in this context, and it is very data-hungry.

The other interesting point that Max shared with us was on the pain points across the quantum computing stack. It is critical to note here that there is innovation across the quantum computing tech stack, and each layer of the stack (be it hardware or the application) has its own challenges. A slowdown in innovation in one part of the stack has a profound impact on innovation throughout the rest of the stack.

Very much like the discussion with Dave Snelling, Max also felt that there might be a hybrid step in the evolution of quantum computing. The hybrid step could involve a neo-classical computing method. In *Chapter 5, Interview with Dr. Dave Snelling, Fujitsu Fellow*, we saw how the digital annealer could be a bridge between classical and quantum computing.

However, the most important takeaway from this chapter for me would be how people who lead the formation of democratic administrations rely on cutting-edge technology. Social media data is a critical component in making this work for all parties interested in understanding the voters. I hope that we will see more groundbreaking results when Max uses his application in the 2020 American elections.

10

The Impact on Smart Cities and Environment

Technology has made our lives better. However, much technology that has been to our betterment has unfortunately been to the environment's detriment. Can we maintain our modern lifestyles whilst moving towards living more sustainably? This chapter focuses on applications of quantum computing and Blockchain for smart city and environment use cases, and how those applications might lead us to some answers.

We are the smartest species that ever walked the earth. Nature has endowed incredible physical and mental powers on human beings. With great power comes responsibilities too. As we start deploying technology and human resources to make our lives better, it must be done in a sustainable fashion. We need to be mindful of the fact that we share the world with our friends from the animal and plant kingdoms. More importantly, we must consider the kind of world that we want our future generations to inherit.

Innovation across all levels of society will need to be aligned towards the long-term wellness of the world we live in. Apart from being tech-rich, smart cities could also mean greener cities. In this chapter, I cover how technology can be used for applications such as traffic management, waste management, and climate modelling.

So why do I care?

Just over 26 years ago, I was travelling with a group of friends and my teacher to sit an exam. The means of transport we took to get to the exam center was a bullock cart. It used to be a common sight in my village in Tamil Nadu in India. The village is called Melagaram, about 5 miles from the border of Tamil Nadu and Kerala, at the foothills of the Western Ghats mountain range.

There used to be a time when we could go to the terrace of our house and see the waterfalls called Main Falls. It is one of the top tourism spots of southern India, regularly visited during the months of June to August by people across the globe. It is a beautiful village, and I still have dreams of working from "Home," as in from my village.

The school where I spent most of my years was called Hilton Matriculation School. It was led by a charismatic Mr. Bell; someone we all respect and love. We all have many memories of the school. It was based just a mile away from the foothills of the mountain range that formed the border of the two southernmost states of India. The monsoons would bring rains, and we would be able to see the waterfalls we call Old Falls from the windows of our classrooms.

The school had a beautiful garden, and even the school canteen ("mess" as we called it), was in the middle of the garden. Our commute to the school every morning in the school bus would go through lakes, green fields, waterfalls, vast stretches of dense vegetation, and little streams. Come to think of it, it was more of an excursion every day than a commute that my kids take to their schools in the UK today.

Our home, which was a few miles from the school, had a green neighborhood too. We had an anthill opposite our house, just about a cricket pitch's distance away from our main gate. Surrounding our home were green fields where rice was cultivated. Many of our neighbors had cows, hens, and haystacks, and we would play in those fields all day long.

During the monsoons in June and July and again in November, we would collect little red-colored velvety bugs in our pencil boxes. I lived in that village until I was 15, before moving into the hot, humid, crowded, and polluted city of Chennai for my higher secondary schooling.

I almost took the green hills, beautiful landscapes, and the mild drizzles in my hometown for granted. Chennai was a shock to my system. I would cycle to school, and when I got home, I would have to wash the black soot off my forehead. In the summer months, the tar on the road would melt. I knew I had left paradise in search of a better life. It shouldn't have to be like that.

There is a reason why this chapter brings together smart cities and the environment. Smart cities are not just about filling our cities with devices that track citizens' behavior. They are not just about getting data from these devices and making real-time decisions to optimize the functioning of the city. They are also about ensuring that a city doesn't have to lose its greenery to be smart and sophisticated.

Every time I look to share interesting content on social media, my first picks would be about environmental awareness, climate change, and plastic pollution. These are stories where someone leads the cleaning-up efforts of a plastic-polluted beach or creates hundreds of acres of forest land after quitting a highly paid job. These stories inspire me.

So, how are emerging technologies useful in creating smart cities? Recently, I was driving my Tesla from London Heathrow to my home in Kent. In the passenger seat was a friend who has been an engineer at Intel for the last couple of decades. We were discussing how the artificial intelligence powering Tesla's self-driving engine would work if deployed on Indian roads.

Traffic management is a good use case for quantum computers. The machines will need to be supported by data from IoT devices and geospatial data from telecoms providers. Emerging economies, where traffic management is a major challenge, have piloted artificial intelligence to get better at it. However, the problem is far from resolved.

As the world focuses on making our cities better, it is critical to ensure we don't harm the environment in the process. Efforts towards smart cities should also be about protecting the environment. Climate change has been a topic of discussion at the highest levels across the world. Nature documentaries talk about the melting of polar ice and its impact on wildlife and weather patterns.

There is still a debate on whether climate change is just a cycle that we might have to go through, or whether it is something manmade. Some argue that it is only a theory without enough data points, and some argue that over the last 10-15 years humans have caused a large part of climate change.

Is this something that technology can help assess? Start-ups like PolArctic are modeling the melting of arctic ice and the variables causing it. It is a difficult task to get a comprehensive model of climate change and variables around it. Quantum computing is perhaps the best platform to model how nature works. Technologies in the past have not been so successful at this task. Modeling nature or physics into a classical computer is much harder than it is with quantum computers.

When we model climate change, we get into the realms of interdependent variables. In this chapter, I discuss efforts to make our lives better through smart city innovation, and our world better through innovation to understand nature better.

Smart cities

Smart city initiatives across the world involve using data-capturing devices across a city to offer contextual and optimal services to the people in the city. The smart city market is expected to be anywhere from $700 billion to $2.4 trillion by 2025. It is hard to get to the right figure, but it is a huge global market across the developed world and emerging economies.

There are several smart city use cases that involve Blockchain and quantum machine learning. Some of the areas we'll touch upon in this chapter are:

- Parking
- Traffic management
- City planning
- Trash collection

Smart parking

Typically, in smart city projects, we see governments working closely with the private sector to deliver results. For example, an initiative within the UK aims at making parking cars more efficient. The process involves getting vehicle data and parking slot availability in real time. While there are several apps to hold parking data, the data standards to bring them all into a central repository to offer intelligence is missing.

Therefore, the UK government made an announcement in May 2019 about standardizing data across the parking applications that are available. This data would include the availability of parking data, permitted times, and prices. This would be accessible to all car drivers through a consolidated platform. Source: `https://www.gov.uk/government/news/uk-on-verge-of-revolution-to-make-parking-easier-and-help-british-high-streets`

The challenge with such initiatives is that the people of a country are sharing a huge amount of personal data with their government. Centralized holding of such data makes owners of data concerned. It offers opportunities for hackers, but also allows policy makers access to certain types of data that citizens may consider an intrusion of privacy.

Blockchain could help decentralize the ownership of such data. Even a permissioned blockchain, where a pre-agreed consortium of entities could act as the gatekeepers of public information, could be better than a completely centralized setup. A purist may not want to call a permissioned ledger a blockchain, but in my opinion it would take the centralized world a few iterative upgrades before it could get to appreciate purely decentralized ecosystems.

There are protocols like the **delegated proof of stake (DPoS)** that can have a small group of nodes validating transactions. While they do not have privileges to change transaction details, they can sign and broadcast transactions across the network. In DPoS protocol the delegates are chosen by the network through votes. Therefore, if there is a node that is a dishonest delegate, it can be voted down by the network.

These protocols can act as a bridge to moving to a decentralized data world. However, I still believe there will be a certain level of centralization even in the target state. Coming back to our smart city example, the use of Blockchain, combined with good metadata management, could be the future for data privacy. There are firms like people.io and Nuggets.life in the UK that are focusing on solving these issues with data privacy.

While smart parking could be of significant value in countries like the UK, traffic management is well done in that part of the world. In many parts of emerging markets, traffic management is a major issue. Let's now see how technology can help with that.

Traffic management

The moment I think of traffic management, the picture that I get in my head is the chaotic roads of India. Managing and regulating the roads of countries like India is one of the biggest challenges for today's technologies. When I moved to the UK 15 years ago, I went through the process of unlearning and relearning my driving skills.

I am now more comfortable driving on UK roads than on Indian roads. More versatile drivers can comfortably drive in both countries, but the intelligence engine that sits in my brain struggles to do so. It takes a great deal of effort for the human brain to adjust to the complexities of transitioning between two very different environments. It will likely be some time before AI has reached the level of sophistication needed to cope in such scenarios.

However, that is not to say that efficiencies cannot be achieved by deploying cutting-edge technologies in these contexts. In my conversations with the Head of Research at Amrita University in India, she revealed research efforts were in progress for traffic management using machine learning.

During my discussions with Fujitsu, they revealed that their quantum-inspired Digital Annealers also solved the traffic management problem. They have deployed their solution in a warehouse distribution scenario and achieved 45% efficiency in identifying optimal routes.

The application of geospatial data combined with data from sensors and radars can help manage traffic effectively. Thanks to the penetration of mobile phones across the world, geospatial data from mobile towers is available in most parts of the world. Proactive identification of crowding can be achieved using this data. Patterns from historic data can also predict the probabilities of traffic jams.

While it is easier to identify crowding in one part of the city using this data, it is harder to predict it ahead of the crowding. Radars are deployed in emerging markets to identify crowding at a traffic junction, however, they are not scalable due to the hardware costs, and the challenges in capturing and transmitting large amounts of data in real time. In India the cost of a radar sensor can be up to £40,000, which makes it an unviable option for widespread deployment.

Traffic cameras combined with image recognition algorithms could identify crowded junctions. This, when clubbed with drones, can be useful in the real-time management of traffic jams. However, smart cities must move towards predictive modeling of traffic jams and identifying solutions for them.

In a recent experiment in Chennai, India, there were 64 cameras set up in a busy part of the city. In a day about 90,000 traffic rule violators were identified and fined. Breaches identified included wrong-side driving, no entry violations, jumping signals, and triple riding. That shows the efficiencies to be had even when such controls are implemented at a small and limited scale.

Geospatial data can identify the flow of traffic. This data can help model how many people from one part of the town drive to the other and at what times of the day. Patterns in this data can be captured. However, the harder behavior point to model is how an increase in traffic, an incident, or a roadblock in one part of the city can affect traffic in the rest of the city. This is where quantum annealers can be used.

During quantum annealing the information required for optimization is fed into a physical system. Modeling a traffic management problem on a quantum annealer is very similar to the travelling salesman problem, as discussed in *Chapter 2, Quantum Computing – Key Discussion Points*. The quantum system is prepared in a superposition of many possible solutions of the problem. The probability of different possible solutions evolves through the annealing process.

As the annealing process takes place, the lower-energy options emerge as the likely solutions to the problem. The probability is the highest for the solution identified by the ground state of the system. The Hamiltonian function used by this process manages information on the energy levels of the system.

There are two aspects to consider with traffic management in a busy city. One is the ongoing occurrence of traffic jams and how they are resolved, and the second is predicting the occurrence of traffic jams. Real-time data capture can allow resources to be allocated to areas where there are traffic jams.

The ability to predict traffic jams can allow the planning of roadworks, accident management, and management of traffic through the city more efficiently. As autonomous vehicles start becoming mainstream, an integrated infrastructure to manage traffic becomes increasingly important.

City planning

In many parts of the world, city planning and governance is performed by the councils and public sector bodies managing the city. The process that we will touch upon involves understanding the impact of new buildings, flyovers, parks, and roads on the lives of the citizens.

New buildings, parks, and road infrastructures are important additions to a fast-evolving city. However, they affect the carbon footprint of the city, the drainage infrastructure, rainwater management, and traffic control as well. Geospatial data combined with 3D-modeling techniques is required to optimize the use of city space for the wellbeing of its citizens.

Waste collection

As automation takes over the world, there is research being done by several firms to identify its impact on jobs. As per a recent report from the company PwC, the UK's waste management industry is expected to be affected by automation the most. As listed in the following figure, over 62% of jobs in the industry are at a risk of being replaced by machines.

Employment shares, estimated proportion and total number of employees at potential high risk of automation for all UK industry sectors			
Industry	Employment share (%)	Job automation (% at potential high risk)	Jobs at high risk of automation (millions)
Wholesale and retail trade	14.8%	44.0%	2.25
Manufacturing	7.6%	46.4%	1.22
Administrative and support services	8.4%	37.4%	1.09
Transportation and storage	4.9%	56.4%	0.95
Professional, scientific and technical	8.8%	25.6%	0.78
Human health and social work	12.4%	17.0%	0.73
Accommodation and food service	6.7%	25.5%	0.59
Construction	6.4%	23.7%	0.52
Public administration and defence	4.3%	32.1%	0.47
Information and communication	4.1%	27.3%	0.39
Financial and insurance	3.2%	32.2%	0.35
Education	8.7%	8.5%	0.26
Arts and entertainment	2.9%	22.3%	0.22
Other services	2.7%	18.6%	0.17
Real estate	1.7%	28.2%	0.16
Water, sewage and waste management	0.6%	62.6%	0.13
Agriculture, forestry and fishing	1.1%	18.7%	0.07
Electricity and gas supply	0.4%	31.8%	0.05
Mining and quarrying	0.2%	23.1%	0.01
Domestic personnel and self-subsistence	0.3%	8.1%	0.01
Total for all sectors	**100%**	**30%**	**10.4**

Sources: ONS for employment shares (2016); PwC estimates for last two columns using PIAAC data

Figure 1: Figures predicting jobs put at risk due to automation

Source: https://www.pwc.co.uk/economic-services/ukeo/pwcukeo-section-4-automation-march-2017-v2.pdf

I would interpret the preceding statistics about the waste management industry differently. The high percentage shows us that there are many efficiencies to be had with the waste management industry with a little bit of intelligent automation. The specific area of focus for this discussion is the waste collection process.

The current process of waste collection involves trucks going through every street in a town and collecting the trash from the bins. In the UK, there has been pilot testing of bins with sensors. These sensors could provide information on how full the bins are so that collection is needed only for the fuller ones. Sensors on the bins could also send alerts as they fill up.

A pilot with Rugby Borough Council in the UK, using solar-powered smart bins, helped reduce waste collections from 51,000 per year to 1,509. As this process goes mainstream, there could be further efficiencies to be had. For example, quantum annealers could inform waste collection trucks of the quickest way to collect the trash.

From a sustainability perspective, sensors inform councils about the homes that have the lowest level of trash. Councils could have smart tax system that provide a rebate for homes that trash the lowest amounts. We could take it one step further to identify homes that trash the most plastics and charge them more tax for that. As the internet of things goes mainstream, the application of quantum computing can help achieve impact at scale.

Climate modeling

Apart from a few climate change sceptics, most people appreciate that climate change is an important phenomenon that we cannot ignore anymore. According to the **World Wildlife Federation (WWF)**, the earth is losing 18.7 million acres of forests per year, or the equivalent of 27 soccer fields every minute. This is a serious problem, as forests are carbon sinks because trees absorb and store carbon dioxide.

There is a hypothesis that climate change or global warming is a cyclical event. Since the last cycle that saw the ice age, global temperatures raised between 3°C to 8°C over the space of 10,000 years. It is the current scientific consensus that carbon emissions due to human actions have been a large factor in accelerating this cycle of climate change. Research by the **Intergovernmental Panel on Climate Change (IPCC)** has identified that there is a 90% chance that recent climatic change is associated with human actions. Source: https://www.ipcc.ch/

Carbon emissions and increases in temperature have also been documented over the past 200 years and are found to closely correlate. There is a significant likelihood that such emissions are playing a causal role in temperature increases, due to the fact that greenhouse gases such as Carbon dioxide (CO_2) are known to trap heat in the atmosphere, leading to increases in global temperatures. Reference: https://www.nature.com/articles/srep21691

However, it is not all doom and gloom. Nature has weird ways of resurrecting life out of disasters. There was a recent article about Chernobyl in Ukraine that fills me with hope. The Chernobyl incident that happened three decades ago was so bad that the word "Chernobyl" is now synonymous with disaster. In 1986, the nuclear reactor at Chernobyl suddenly released a large amount of energy. This was followed by radioactive contamination that was airborne for several days. The death toll from the accident is estimated at thousands of people.

Since the disaster struck in what was then a region of the Soviet Union, an area of 2,600 square kilometers has been abandoned. However, three decades later both plant and animal life has returned to Chernobyl. A recent article about the resurging ecosystem in the area describes how plants have adapted to even radioactive environments. The Business Insider article states that Chernobyl has better plant and animal life today than it did before the disaster in 1986. Source: `https://www.businessinsider.com/chernobyl-exclusion-zone-animal-refuge-2019-5?r=US&IR=T`

This goes to show that if systematic efforts were put into bringing back forests we have lost, the impacts of climate change could be reversed. Bringing back forests takes a few decades. Therefore, it is imperative that we get a handle on climate change with the help of technology in the meanwhile. Whilst long-term reforestation efforts present a promising mitigation solution, we will also need to be able to manage the climate extremes we are currently experiencing across the world. A two-pronged approach would be needed to effectively manage climate change.

There are two key areas of climate change modelling that technology can help to facilitate:

1. Quantum annealing and machine learning can help us to predictively model spatial and temporal climatic conditions across the world, enabling us to anticipate and manage extreme weather events across the world.

2. Quantum computing can help us to identify and quantify the most influential drivers of climate change, which in turn will inform global mitigation solutions.

The first is a tactical exercise that can help us predict, monitor, and manage extreme weather patterns across the world. The second one is a more strategic and experimental approach, where we identify key lifestyle changes humans have to embrace to combat climate change in the long run.

Understanding climate changes would need data on several variables – those variables known affect a region's climatic conditions. They are:

- Biogeography
- Atmospheric circulation
- Oceanic circulation
- Earth's tilt

Biogeography

Biogeography refers to the spread of plants and animals across the earth. As we discussed earlier, it is critical to have the optimal mix of land, ice, plants, and animals. Plants and animals compete for land when there is too much ice cover, as they did during the ice age. Climate change through the ice age period pushed species like the mammoth and the saber-toothed cat into extinction. However, the climate change we are more likely to encounter is the melting of ice. This might lead to the extinction of animals that live in the polar regions.

The extinction of animal species influences the vegetation patterns of the earth, which in turn affects climate patterns. There have been instances where the introduction of certain animals like beavers in to an ecosystem changes the natural landscape and the climate patterns of a region. This phenomenon is termed a "feedback loop." Beavers affect the flow of streams and rivers, which in turn affects vegetation. As vegetation patterns change it results in new species of animals arriving to further influence the landscape and the balance of life. Source: `https://www.nature.com/articles/nature10574`

Hence, an understanding of how the biogeography of a region, continent, or even a planet affects the climate patterns over thousands of years is essential. There is inherent interdependence between the evolution of animals, plants, landscapes, and climate patterns. Such environments are termed "open systems"; these systems are incredibly complex due to our inability to control the variables within the system, and the tendency for the variables to interact with one another. These attributes make it extremely difficult for classical computers (and indeed climate scientists) to model these behaviors.

Atmospheric circulation

The movement of air in the earth's atmosphere starts at the equator. The high temperatures at the equator causes air to rise. As air rises it gets colder and causes condensation, leading to rain. This is an important phenomenon that affects the weather and vegetation patterns across the world. As air moves from areas of high pressure to areas of low pressure it creates dry and wet areas of the world.

Air movement from the equator to 30° north and south of the equator is what creates deserts. As this air has very little moisture, this part of the world receives less rainfall. This region is referred to as the Hadley cell. As shown in the following figure, each of the regions have a specific air movement pattern and are named differently. The movement of air creates a cycle of evaporation, condensation, and precipitation influencing weather patterns across the world.

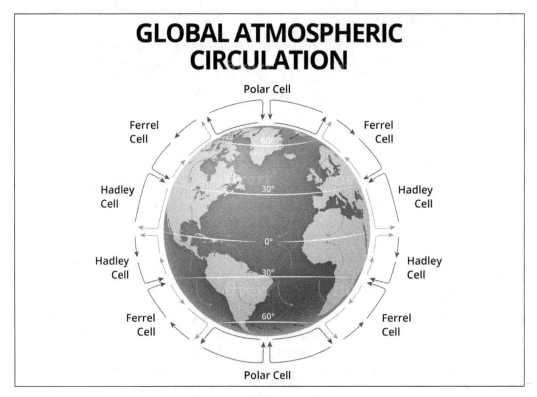

Figure 2: Illustration of global atmospheric circulation

Ocean currents

Ocean currents have an impact on weather patterns across the world. Temperatures in the oceans flow in a three-dimensional pattern, namely east to west, north to south, and the surface to the depths. Winds in tropical oceans blow from east to west. As a result, coastal areas of land masses have a temperature gradient from east to west. For example, the western part of the pacific is 8°C warmer than the eastern part.

However, as trade winds weaken, the warm water moves towards the east due to gravity. When this warm pattern of weather moves eastwards to the coastal areas of South America, we see the El Niño effect.

El Niño causes the North Western part of South America to heat up. As the warmest part of the oceans' surface generates the most evaporation, we see tropical storms move eastwards too. This affects weather patterns across the earth. The El Niño effect happens once every few years, and scientists haven't been able to predict it accurately.

Earth's tilt

The earth's tilt has an impact on the atmospheric circulation of winds. Thanks to the tilt, the air on the surface is deflected. The deflected air flows to the right of its initial trajectory in the northern hemisphere, and vice versa in the southern hemisphere. The earth's revolution in its orbit around the sun creates climate cycles.

These cycles are 100,000 years long. During these cycles the earth's tilt changes from 21.5° to 24.5°. As the tilt affects the solar input, ocean currents and atmospheric circulation, it has a marked effect on climate cycles.

Quantum computing solutions

As there are several interdependent variables, as described previously, affecting the climate of the earth, it is hard to model climate patterns meaningfully using classical computing methods. Quantum computers should have the ability to deal with the data requirements to model climate change. The first step needs to be about determining conclusively that climate change is being caused by human actions.

In January 2019, Exxon Mobil partnered with IBM's quantum computing capabilities for environmental modeling. Modeling nature can be better done by quantum computers because nature is effectively quantum mechanical. To do this in a classical computer requires the translation of physics into computer science before loading it up into the computer. In a quantum computer, physics is encoded in its native state. There is no translation and so no loss of information in the process. Therefore, simulating its behavior should be more accurate with a quantum computer.

In my recent conversations with a physicist, he mentioned that quantum computers should be great tools to model physics. Aside from the improvement in the crunching abilities of the quantum computer, the fact that it mimics nature allows for better modeling of nature's behavior, if properly utilized.

The University of Southern California is also working on solving the climate change puzzle using quantum computers. As quantum machine learning and annealing processes go mainstream, there will be several solutions that we will use daily to understand the impact we have upon the environment. We will be able to predict weather conditions better and more effectively manage extreme conditions.

Conclusion

The application of quantum machine learning and annealing techniques within smart cities and climate modeling is still at a very early stage. In comparison to financial services and healthcare applications, these applications are still well behind. While smart city applications of emerging technologies can perhaps wait, it is critical that we get a firm understanding of climate change.

The emerging impacts of climate change are perhaps some of the most important phenomena affecting our lives, and the lives of future generations. It is imperative that policy makers leverage technologies such as quantum computers to drive decision-making at the highest levels. A top-down approach to climate change will help us as citizens to combat the long-term effects of human action on our planet.

We have so far covered the applications of quantum computing in the field of healthcare, financial services, and smart cities. In the coming chapters, we will look at its applications in logistics, which struggles with some of the hardest problems to solve using classical computers. We will also look at quantum-resistant ledgers, which can be used by the Blockchain community to be quantum-ready.

11

Interview with Sam McArdle, Quantum Computing Researcher at the University of Oxford

In several previous chapters of this book, I have touched upon the barriers for quantum computing to go mainstream. One of the major barriers with quantum computing is the challenges with error correction. In a classical computer, bits have two states, "0" and "1." Therefore, error correction is a lot easier. In a quantum computer, qubits can exist in superpositions at any point in time during the calculation. As a result, it is harder to observe and correct their values without disrupting the calculation.

Error correction within quantum computing is a fascinating space and there are several techniques being explored. Hence, I wanted to dedicate one interview, and thus a chapter, to this topic. I met Sam McArdle at a quantum computing event at the University of Bristol. He made a presentation at the event on his research at the University of Oxford. The research focused on quantum error correction.

Sam's presentation at the event was fascinating, mainly because he simplified the narrative. He still got technical where he had to during the presentation, but it was clear that the audience were engaged in his speech and followed up with several interesting questions. That was in line with my way of looking at this technology. Despite the complexities within the Math and Physics of quantum computing, there is always room to keep it all simple from a use case perspective.

As a result, I reached out to Sam about the book and asked if he would be willing to be interviewed for it. I wanted to keep the focus of our interview on error correction and his research at the University of Oxford. Sam kindly agreed, and after a couple of email interactions, we managed to do a recorded interview session. The interview is as follows:

Arun: We're recording now. Thanks for making time, Sam.

I recently had a chat with the CEO of a company who is creating quantum computing solutions for healthcare. He told me something that we all know about but don't quite put it the way he did.

It was that classical computers take a concept in Physics, use Math to translate it to computer-understandable code, and then replicate Physics based on the code. It takes three hops before it gets Physics to look like Physics on a classical computer. Quantum computers just naturally model Physics without as much translation. Therefore, there is less loss of information while simulating nature using quantum computers. It's interesting because we are here to discuss loss of information within quantum computers. Let's touch upon error correction in quantum computers and why that is different from error correction in a classical computing context.

Sam: Let's first touch upon errors in the context of classical and quantum computers. In a classical machine, you have to consider "bit-flip" errors; the probabilistic flipping of a bit from zero to one. These are also present in a quantum computer. However, quantum computers also suffer from another type of error, called phase-flip errors, which also need to be corrected.

These errors can be addressed using error correction techniques. In classical error correction code, we can take many copies of our bits and perform majority voting schemes. Therefore, you don't need much in the way of error correcting properties in classical computers, with the exception of hard drives and other things that are going to store memory for a long time.

These have some redundancy built in, which stops the degradation of information over time as well, but their fault level is low. It's approximately one part in 10^{15}. In today's classical computers, we focus more on handling errors that occur programmatically. Therefore, in a classical computer, we don't really worry about error correction as a limitation.

In contrast, a quantum computer is much more sensitive to the environment. Therefore, error correction is a lot more delicate. If it was approximately one part of 10^{15} in a classical hard drive, it is closer to one part in 10^2 or 10^3 in the quantum computers we have now.

If you're going to run a calculation for a long time, you need to correct against imperfections arising from interaction with the environment. There are ways of doing this using quantum error code. It is another level of difficulty in the sense that, when we use classical error correcting code, you can just directly interrogate the information in your device. The most common one that people talk about is repetition code.

If you want to store a single bit that is "0" or "1", you can just copy it three times. If there is an error, it is very unlikely that there are going to be two bits affected by it. One error is the most likely thing that's going to occur, in which case when you look at your three copy bits, two of them are still the same and one of them might have changed. You can majority vote. You can see what errors have occurred and fix them. It's different in a quantum computer.

Quantum computing takes advantage of two main quantum effects: superposition and entanglement. Superposition is the famous Schrodinger's cat type effect – the ability of particles to be in two places at once, or quantum bits (qubits) to be in a joint state of zero or one at the same time – with the outcome only being revealed upon measurement. Entanglement can be loosely defined as a stronger-than-classical correlation between two particles, whereby it doesn't really make sense to think of the two systems that are entangled as individual entities anymore. These two effects can be combined to give quantum computers their touted advantage over their classical counterparts.

However, quantum information is delicate, and these same effects can become rather damaging. In a quantum computer, error correction gets more difficult because you can't copy information across and you can't directly interrogate the quantum bits, because that would reveal in what state they are and interrupt your whole calculation. You have to be smarter about how to interrogate the system to try and learn what errors have occurred and find ways to correct those.

Our quantum computer has to sit in some kind of environment. The qubits in the computer interact with the environment. This manifests as a degradation of our quantum state, essentially forcing it to decay back to a classical state. Even though experimentalists try to shield their quantum computers from the environment (by keeping them at low temperatures, encased in vacuums, and/or shielded from magnetic fields), error rates are still much larger than one would find in a classical computer. Consequently, without any protection from errors, the quantum nature of the system will quickly decay away.

We can provide a level of protection for our quantum systems using error correcting code. Loosely speaking, this represents the logical zero and one states of a qubit by encoding them in a highly entangled state that is spread over many qubits. We can make cleverly designed checks on our qubits that won't tell us exactly what the state is, but can at least tell us if certain errors have occurred, where they are, and how to correct them.

Arun: Interesting. Thanks for that. Can we discuss a few approaches that we have today for quantum error connection? What are the most common and the most popular ones?

Sam: The primary approach used for error correction is based on code. Most code that people are trying to experimentally realize across the world, can be described by the *Stabilizer formalism*. It is essentially a mathematical formalism that nicely encapsulates how your code behaves. It gives you good ways to describe code behavior and makes it easier to work with.

The *Stabilizer formalism* has led to a bunch of good code, some of which is more experimentally accessible than other code. A widely studied code is known as *surface code*, which is a little different to some other ones as it has topological properties.

It depends on the topology of surfaces. The appealing thing about *surface code* is that you can realize it just with an array of qubits laid out in a grid with nearest neighbor interactions. If you're trying to build your quantum computer with solid state qubits, superconducting ones or silicon, that is a very attractive architecture because that's kind of the natural interactions for your system.

The other useful thing about the surface code is that it has got a very high *threshold of the code*. At this point you say: *This is the physical error rate in my system.* And the threshold says: *If I can get that error rate below a certain value, then I can make my code bigger. I can keep making the overall error rate in the computer lower.* Then error correction becomes effective. If you're above that threshold, it doesn't make sense to do a correction that's going to make everything worse.

Notably, at the error rates that people are achieving in their hardware systems, it gives hope that if those systems can be scaled up while the quality stays high, that kind of code might be experimentally realized. Error rates that some research groups are achieving in their hardware systems are now comparable to our estimates of the surface code threshold.

If these systems can be scaled up while maintaining these error rates, then this may be a promising route towards large scale quantum computers.

Arun: Thank you, that an interesting overview on the about surface code. We've also come across NISQ computing. Why is that important from a quantum error correction perspective? What are the future possibilities using NISQ?

Sam: NISQ stands for Noisy Intermediate Scale Quantum computing. In the era we're in now, we have small quantum computers. If you want to do error correction, you need much larger ones. In a fault-tolerant quantum computer, you will generally have thousands of physical qubits for error correction. If you want to implement the surface code, you might need a thousand physical qubits to encode one error-corrected logical qubit.

A logical question to ask would be, *why don't we do calculations on the noisy qubits we have*? If you're going to do that, the algorithms that you run can't be too long. If you run them for a long time, there's more chance that errors build up and ruin your calculation.

With NISQ, you don't do any error correction; you just run your algorithm. This may work well in use cases like chemistry simulation.

However, in such scenarios, the algorithm runs with much shorter circuits. When qubits are noisy, the coherence time is low. Shorter circuits typically have lower computation time that can arrive at the results quicker with fewer errors.

NISQ takes a very different approach to that of quantum error correction. NISQ normally involves trading one long circuit for lots of repetitions of much smaller ones. After each repetition, you re-initialize the system.

If the quantum circuit that you apply is short, then one might hope that the circuit could be implemented before errors are able to accumulate. As such, to do a calculation involving 100 qubits, you just do the calculation with the 100 noisy qubits that are available, rather than trying to encode 100 error-corrected qubits into 100,000 noisy qubits.

Clearly, a 100-qubit machine will be easier to build than a 100,000 qubit one, but in order to make the NISQ proposal realizable, algorithms must work with short circuits.

NISQ algorithms have been developed for problems in chemistry, machine learning, optimization, and a range of other problems. However, one issue is that it is difficult to show that a NISQ algorithm will possess any advantage over the classical algorithms we currently use.

There is ongoing research to demonstrate that circuits can be made small enough to lessen the effects of noise. While error mitigation techniques have been proposed that can aid in achieving this goal, there is still a lot of work before we can get to noise-tolerant short circuits. As such, the next few years will be very interesting in this space, as groups around the world develop larger NISQ machines (50 to 100 physical qubits) that can test these algorithms.

There is a hybrid approach towards NISQ where the quantum computer does something that's hard classically and the classical computer does something that it finds easy – like an optimization subroutine. You iterate through this process and that helps you to solve the problem you're trying to deal with, whether that's machine learning, or optimization, or chemistry.

There are error mitigation techniques that work by just taking more data than you would need naturally to solve the problem and then combining it in clever ways, effectively taking an average that allows you to cancel out some of the noise. These techniques can be very useful. They may play a key role in deriving us anything useful out of these NISQ quantum computers. But they are also not a substitute for error correction in the long term. They can only tolerate small amounts of noise.

Arun: Conceptually, this is similar to the evolution of cloud computing – particularly Amazon Web Services (AWS). In the initial days of AWS, the allocation of resources on their infrastructure was done based on low time utilization and then almost became a new business model altogether. Let us move on to the next point of discussion.

There is a strong argument that quantum computers may not go mainstream for at least another 10 years. If quantum computing gets through some of its major hurdles in the next 5 to 10 years, even then I think some of the hybrid solutions like digital annealers could still be relevant. The cost involved in going mainstream with quantum computers would still be high. But then, in hopefully 15 to 20 years, an acceleration could happen to make the cost benefits of quantum infrastructure more attractive.

Are there any particular subjects of research that you are closely following? Any areas you think will help accelerate the field of quantum computing?

Sam: On the one hand, experimental groups are trying to implement these error correction procedures. That involves computer modeling of routines they're going to implement, to model what the types of errors are, and the best ways to overcome those.

When you introduce this code, you are introducing additional overheads for the computation. There are scientists who work on trying to find more resource-efficient ways to implement a given algorithm in certain code. There has been a lot of work done on that recently, which has reduced the overhead (of error correction). Some of these calculations are within the field of chemistry.

On the other hand, there are a lot of researchers who will research more exotic varieties of code. Rather than the ones that are already in existence, they'll look at new varieties that people haven't studied as much before. They hope that they may have some advantages in terms of how the algorithms can be expressed in that code or if it's better at correcting errors, or if it's more suited to a certain type of hardware than other types of code.

Arun: That's definitely an interesting insight. I do hope that all the hard work converges to something meaningful. What would some success in this space do to quantum computing applications in industrial scenarios?

Sam: While there is currently hope that NISQ algorithms may lead to useful applications of quantum computers within the next few years, this is currently unproven, and will require testing on real hardware systems as they become available. In order to run the provably fast algorithms developed for chemistry, machine learning, optimization, or cryptography, it is expected that quantum error correction will be necessary, as the circuits required are long.

As such, new developments in quantum error correction will hopefully reduce the resources required to implement useful algorithms. This includes both the spatial resources (the number of qubits required, which determines how hard it is to build the quantum computer) and the time resources (how long the algorithm takes to run).

Improvements in the former of these metrics will mean that useful quantum computers will become available for industrial applications sooner. Improvements in the latter mean that quantum algorithms could become competitive with their classical counterparts for smaller problem sizes, again meaning that they may find use in the nearer term.

As such, improvements in quantum error correction techniques should be considered just as important as both algorithmic advances, and hardware developments, as a step toward the goal of realizing industrially useful quantum computers.

Arun: Great. We will close off with one last question. There are several industrial scenarios that quantum computers can be useful in. There is huge potential within logistics, and portfolio rebalancing within financial services is interesting too. There are a lot of possibilities. What are the use cases that you can think of and is there anything in particular that excites you?

Sam: The ones you've mentioned are good applications, in the sense that people have done a lot of research into solving machine learning problems, optimization problems, and problems in finance in general. The simulation of physical systems using quantum computers interests me.

Quantum computers may be interesting in the pharmaceutical industry in trying to work out how a drug is going to work. If you offered them the opportunity to take a molecule, look at it in a computer, and work out how it is going to interact with other molecules. That could be important to them.

Similarly, if you're a big materials company, you do things with catalysts. A study of how a catalyst reacts with chemicals and speeds up the reaction is a good area. Industries that are focused on coming up with new materials that can withstand certain challenges can look at quantum computing solutions, too. For instance, batteries for electric cars are an example of where the best material to be used for energy efficiency and fast recharge may be researched using quantum algorithms.

An area of focus is the simulation of a molecule that is present in bacteria that are able to use nitrogen in the atmosphere to produce fertilizers. This process happens in nature in ambient pressure and temperature. The industrial process we have today for fertilizer production is energy-intensive. There has been research to determine whether error-corrected quantum computers can aid in the simulation of this molecule, which may provide novel insights into this process.

If you could learn how that nitrogen-converting bacteria works and replicate its behavior, that could be a huge energy saving that is really useful for the world. Similarly, there are range of chemical materials that we would love to understand better, but we can't just yet. With quantum computers, we may be able to simulate those systems and that's going to give us a whole new understanding of materials system, and ultimately may even allow us to design our own molecules with the properties that we want them to have.

Arun: Thank you very much for that, Sam. On that high note, let's close the interview.

Conclusion

We have so far been focusing on industrial applications of quantum computing in all our interviews. We have touched upon applications in financial services, healthcare, smart cities, and even politics. The interview with Sam had a different focus, and that was deliberate. I wanted to focus on one of the key barriers for quantum computing going mainstream – high error rates.

We discussed why error correction in a quantum computer is harder than in a classical computer. The superposition property of qubits makes it harder for us to capture their states. When we observe qubits, their states collapse. These properties of quantum computers make them useful in solving complex algorithms and make information on quantum computers more secure. However, they also make error correction harder as we cannot observe or copy over the information easily.

We touched upon techniques like using shorter circuits and using certain code for certain algorithms and NISQ in detail in this chapter. Sam brought these complex concepts to life with a simplified articulation. He described error correcting of the methods and touched upon the impact some of the breakthroughs could have on quantum computing. We also discussed applications that are possible when error correction within quantum computers is no longer such a big barrier. For instance, modeling Nitrogen fixation in computers can help the world in many ways.

Once we are able to simulate the Nitrogen fixation process that happens in nature using quantum computers, we will be able to understand better the feasibility of replicating it in an industrial scenario. That could save energy and cut carbon emissions. There are many such applications that could have big impact on our lives and our planet.

In summary, the field of error correction within quantum computers is vast enough for a whole book in itself. However, I wanted to provide an overview with inputs from a specialist in the field and bring to life the opportunities in the field of error correction.

12

The Impact on Chemistry

The term "quantum supremacy" was coined in 2012 by Caltech's John Preskill. Scientists foresaw a state where a quantum computer would be able to do a task that a classical computer could not. That is a very loose definition of quantum supremacy though. That is perhaps what allowed Google to claim that they have achieved quantum supremacy with their Sycamore chip.

The Sycamore is a 54-qubit processor that is able to generate random numbers. The algorithm used to do that would take over 10,000 years to do the same task using a classical computer, whereas it took 200 seconds on the Sycamore. IBM had its objections to this claim. They calculated that the entire quantum state vector of Google's Sycamore chip could be stored within Summit – the world's largest supercomputer, with 250 petabytes of storage.

Scientists who reviewed the work done by Google have revealed that the processor had high-fidelity and superfast gates. But is that what quantum supremacy is?

In all my conversations with quantum researchers, notably Dave Snelling at Fujitsu, they highlighted that we need to be careful about hype around quantum supremacy. They confirmed my view that the industry is clearly in its infancy, and any premature celebration could be counterproductive.

To come back to the question of quantum supremacy, in my opinion, it is less about the speed of calculations. Despite the generic definition of quantum supremacy, it is more about the ability to model particle physics within a computer in a way that has never been done before. It is more about solving problems that we couldn't even model accurately within classical computers. On top of that, with quantum annealers, combinatorial optimization problems with interrelated variables will get easier to solve.

This is perhaps most applicable to quantum computing use cases in chemistry and healthcare. We discussed the use of the technology in healthcare at length. In chemistry, one of the goals for researchers is to be able to solve the **Schrödinger equation** (**SE**) for atoms and molecules.

The SE for atoms and molecules describes the wave function that can be used to model the physio-chemical properties of these particles. Without getting into too much detail at this stage, the gist is that calculating molecular systems accurately has been a hard task for classical computers.

In this chapter we will primarily cover quantum computing applications within chemistry. We will touch upon organizations looking into this field, techniques that are employed, and algorithms that are being explored by researchers.

The applications of Blockchain in the field of chemistry are also interesting, but relatively limited to other industries. Apart from the applications of the technology in chemical supply chains, we are also starting to see potential applications in managing risks. Blockchain can be used for disaster recovery and business continuity management during emergency situations in the chemical industry. We will discuss that in this chapter too.

Let's begin by looking at how quantum computing can help us to compute chemical processes that are currently intractable with classical computing methods. Being able to model these processes will allow us to work towards solutions for longstanding industrial problems, as we'll see. Let's first look at the process of Nitrogen fixation.

Nitrogen fixation

Chemicals are everywhere. From the water we drink to the cells that make up our body, the fertilizers that are used for agriculture, the drivers of photosynthesis in plants – all these are based on chemicals. Understanding the behaviour of chemicals during a reaction is essential to predict the results of the reaction.

Let's take the example of fertilizers. Fertilizers are used in agriculture to increase crop yields. In the initial days, farmers were using natural manure such as animal faeces to improve crop production. It was in 1914 that the first synthetic fertilizers were used, and since then the industry has grown so much that, today, it accounts for 1.2% of global energy consumption.

Fertilizers are largely categorized across three nutrients: Nitrogen, Phosphorus, and Potassium. Nitrogen is the most important of all the nutrients. However, Nitrogen is fed to crops in the form of Ammonia (NH_3). The process of converting atmospheric Nitrogen (N_2) to Ammonia (NH_3) is called **Nitrogen fixation**.

This step is important for plants, as they can metabolize Ammonia, whereas Nitrogen is mostly non-reactive. The process of Nitrogen fixation happens naturally due to catalysis by bacteria using enzymes such as nitrogenase. The bacteria use these enzymes and convert Nitrogen (N_2) into Ammonia (NH_3). Nature makes it look very simple; in an industrial context however, it is not so straightforward.

The mechanism of producing Ammonia from Nitrogen in an industrial environment is called the Haber-Bosch process. This process is very energy intensive and accounts for 2-3% of the world's CO_2 emissions. This is not just because of the industrial process but also due to the demand for Nitrogen from the agriculture sector.

Nitrogen doesn't stay in the soil for a long time after application. Therefore, it must be reapplied to the soil. As a result, the consumption and demand for Nitrogen fertilizers is higher than phosphorus and potassium fertilizers. About 93% of the total energy consumed by the fertilizer industry is taken up by Nitrogen fertilizers.

This is a problem that is shouting out for a solution. How do plants, and the bacteria they utilize, manage to convert Nitrogen (N_2) into Ammonia (NH_3) without much fuss? Why have we taken such an energy-intensive approach to producing fertilizers? Could we replicate the reaction between Nitrogen and enzymes like nitrogenase in an industrial setup?

That seems like a solution that is worth exploring, and it is indeed a field of study for several quantum computing researchers across the world. It would help us reduce 2-3% of our CO_2 emissions, and eat our food guilt-free. Therefore, we will need to develop an understanding of nature's Nitrogen fixation process. But the reaction between Nitrogen and the bacteria is hard to understand, as classical computers do not have the ability to model it.

It is especially important to get into the details of the process where the cofactor of nitrogenase, known as FeMoco, goes through Nitrogen fixation. Experiments to get details of that reaction haven't been successful.

Chemical reactions must take into account electron correlation. This is where electrons in the atoms and molecules of chemicals interact with each other during a reaction. Due to the fact that electron correlation influences the movement of electrons within a quantum system, a whole new dimension of complexity is introduced. This impacts the outcome of chemical reactions and leads to simplified particle interaction modeling being inadequate. As a result, accurately predicting the results of chemical interactions is extremely hard. Highly accurate electronic structure models are required to model the behaviour of these particles.

Although there are techniques in classical computers such as **density functional theory (DFT)**, they still lack the quantitative accuracy needed to model chemical reactions. As a result, even a chemical reaction with just a hundred electrons involved in it becomes very hard for the computer to deal with. As a result, scientists are looking to quantum computing methods to solve this problem.

DFT is currently quite popular in obtaining approximate solutions to the Schrodinger equation of a many-body (multiple electrons) system. Source: `http://newton.ex.ac.uk/research/qsystems/people/coomer/dft_intro.html`

Quantum computers can model chemical reactions that happen in nature to create Ammonia, so that we can understand it better and possibly replicate it in an industrial scenario. In this case, scientists are exploring ways to perform simulations of interactions between nitrogenase and FeMoco in quantum computers. Algorithms like Trotter-Suzuki decompositions and truncated Taylor series are used to simulate chemical reactions, with varying degrees of precision. Source: `https://www.pnas.org/content/114/29/7555`

There are hybrid models being explored that use classical and quantum computers for different steps in the chemical reaction. Molecular structure optimizations within the chemical reaction can be performed using the proven DFT method in classical computers. DFT can also be used to validate the output of the quantum computer and feed back into the process of structuring the molecules. It is really for the computation of correlated energies between electrons that calls for quantum computers to be used.

Looking into the quantum computing part of the process, a gate-based approach can be used to implement a quantum algorithm and compute the behavior of correlated electrons. An experiment conducted by scientists titled, *Elucidating reaction mechanisms on quantum computers*, identifies three different gate-based approaches and the resources required in each of the approaches:

- The first method of implementing the quantum algorithm involved serializing the rotations.

- In the second method, Hamiltonians influencing the spin were executed in parallel.

- The third approach had rotations modeled separately and teleported into the quantum circuit when needed.

Using a combination of logical T gates and Clifford circuits, and surface code for fault tolerance, they have shown that the behavior of the electrons in a chemical reaction can be analyzed.

The combination of these options could take a year when serialized. However, when the first and third approaches are combined, the simulations could be done in days. The cost of doing that is high though, and would require 20 times the number of qubits. If we nested the execution of the gates, the costs would increase due to an increase in number of qubits, which in turn results in a fall in execution time.

The key takeaway from all this is that there is immense potential in this technology. At the same time, however, challenges remain. As highlighted in my interview with Sam McArdle, fault tolerance is an important problem to overcome. We will need to have a logical qubit with several error-correcting qubits.

The cost of scaling the solution to bigger molecules is not very viable at this stage. But the experiment referenced showed that quantum computers can be used to identify energy states through the Nitrogen fixation process. With more such experiments, the time taken to do it could come down to just a few days.

Another key breakthrough was achieved in July 2018, as researchers demonstrated that a qubit circuit made of quantized energy states of ions can be used to simulate simple molecules. Energy states of small molecules such as Hydrogen (H_2) can be calculated using just four trapped ions. The principle is that the ions in the array will exactly represent the interactions between the electrons of the molecule that is being studied.

There is a lot of hype within the quantum computing community about the superiority of trapped ion qubits over superconducting qubits. In the case of chemistry, the trapped ion qubits are perhaps simpler to calculate molecular interactions. But the advantage of superconducting qubits is that they are a lot easier to control using existing devices. As a result, we may find quantum devices take a "horses for courses" approach, that is, finding the right tool for the right job.

A healthy competition between researchers who fall under these two types of qubits is always good. It helps with the pace and quality of innovation. As soon as we are able to do several hundred gates on a fault-tolerant qubit circuitry, we should be in a position to model Nitrogen fixation within a few hours, as opposed to days or even months.

Despite these challenges, these experiments and breakthroughs give me hope that we will soon solve problems involving chemicals at scale. Chemistry's role in making the world greener, cleaner, and generally better can hardly be exaggerated. With an ability to simulate natural processes in laboratory conditions, we will not have to re-invent the wheel for chemical processes. We can draw inspiration from nature's behavior, and therefore create chemical processes that are as close to nature as possible. We've discussed how quantum computing can help us to achieve more accurate modeling of quantum systems, specifically in the case of Nitrogen fixation. One other key chemistry use case that could add immense value to the world is Carbon capture. Let's look at that in detail.

Carbon capture

We live in times where we are suffering consistent anomalies in weather patterns across the world. The impact of these weather anomalies is at the moment quite localized. In 2020 we have seen fires in Australia and rising temperatures across the continent, forest fires in California, floods like never before in Asia and Africa – all of which are everyday natural events that show us that we are in a state of climate emergency.

Scientists across the world have reached the consensus that climate change is happening. Thanks to the industrial revolution over the last three centuries, human action has helped increase the pace at which we are emitting Carbon dioxide (CO_2) into the atmosphere.

The surging world population of ~7.8 billion people has increased the demand for food and therefore agriculture. The pressure on agricultural produce due to the increase in population has resulted in the expansion of agricultural lands, which in turn has resulted in massive deforestation.

Industrialization and agriculture have contributed to the emission of CO_2 into the atmosphere. CO_2 and other greenhouse gases that we produce act as a blanket around the earth, preventing the heat from escaping. Forests could be a solution to this problem, but deforestation is starting to reduce the impact of forests on the earth's climate patterns.

Trees absorb CO_2 from the atmosphere, hence reducing the warming blanket effect. Trees also release water into the atmosphere. A large tree can release about 1,000 litres of water every day into the atmosphere. The Amazon rainforest for instance has roughly 600 billion trees and releases an average of 20 billion metric tonnes of water into the atmosphere every day (assuming it's sunny) and acts as our air conditioning.

However, in the Amazon rainforests, deforestation happens at a grand scale. We are losing 150 acres of forests every minute and 78 million acres of forests every year. We have already lost 20% of the Amazon rainforests. The Amazon rainforests' significance to climate patterns and rainfall across the world cannot be exaggerated. Therefore, we will need a plan B to ensure we mimic the role of forests and trees in at least reducing the CO_2 that is released into the atmosphere.

Carbon capture is the process of trapping Carbon in the atmosphere and isolating it in a storage unit. However, trapping Carbon that is in the air is not an easy process. How do we know what the best device and chemical is for the purpose of capturing Carbon? That's what quantum computing could help us with.

Carbon capture can be categorized into the areas of pre-combustion capture, post-combustion capture, and oxyfuel combustion. We are focused mainly on the post-combustion capture, where at the end of the industrial process, the CO_2 fumes emitted are captured, compressed, and stored.

To capture CO_2 from air at scale, we will need the right capturing technology devices equipped with the chemicals that can do the job efficiently. Currently, **carbon capture and sequestration (CCS)** methods use liquid amine/ammonia solvents to scrub the emitted CO_2. These solvents are energy-intensive in themselves to be produced, effectively making the process of carbon capture self-defeating.

The next generation of Carbon capture methods are focused on **activated carbons (ACs)**, zeolites, and molecular sieves. ACs are a form of Carbon with high porosity and surface area. They have been proven to be better at Carbon capture and are also less expensive than the CCS methods.

But we do not yet understand the interactions between functionalized ACs and CO_2. A research paper published by the American Chemical Society describes the analysis of this interaction using quantum theory (not quantum computing), available at `http://www.claudiocazorla.com/JPCC-Ca-CO2.pdf`.

The research explores the surface doping of the AC materials using calcium atoms and studying the interactions between the doped material and CO_2. They used the DFT method as we discussed previously in the case of fertilizers. They also identified that the calcium-doped Carbon materials have a high carbon-capture capacity.

In the same experiment, they identified that Nitrogen (N_2) bonded poorly with calcium-doped Carbon materials. The absorption capability of calcium-doped graphene was analyzed in the experiment and proven to be effective. The experiment also covered transition states in terms of the surface area of the material and how Carbon capture capabilities differed as the surface area of the material changed.

In summary, the study demonstrates a significant potential impact on the planet if we are able to perform Carbon capture at scale. While we have several options to perform Carbon capture, we will need to use the right technologies to help identify an optimal and sustainable solution for the purpose. Understanding reactions using quantum computers will help with identifying options and their efficacy with Carbon capture.

Despite all the efforts, there is still a lot of work to be done to understand the Carbon capture process. IBM and Exxon Mobil have come together in using quantum computing for a number of applications that benefit the environment. Predictive environment modeling, Carbon capture, and optimizing power grids are the three key outcomes expected from the initiative. Exxon is the first energy company to collaborate with IBM on such an initiative.

That brings us to the end of looking at applications of quantum computing within chemistry. You may recall that we also touched upon some interesting topics around molecular analysis in *Chapter 6, The Impact on Healthcare and Pharma*, too. Therefore, I have presented different potential applications of quantum computing in chemistry in this chapter that we haven't previously covered.

One of the interesting aspects of chemistry and quantum computing is the ability to tap into **Noisy Intermediate-Scale Quantum** (**NISQ**) devices. Let's look at why NISQ is a good fit for chemistry applications.

NISQ and chemistry

In my interview with Sam McArdle, we discussed NISQ as a method to make the most of "bad" qubits. In a typical logical qubit with error correction, you could have a small number of qubits doing the calculations, and a large army of qubits doing the error correction. For example, with surface code, you can have a thousand noisy qubits and one error-free qubit.

In NISQ though, we use the noisy qubits to do the calculations. As these qubits are noisy, the time taken to perform calculations must be short. If the calculations are not quick, we may end up with error-prone results. Typically, this setup would involve a shorter circuit and no error-correcting qubits. The system is re-initialized after every repetition to ensure errors do not build up.

As a result, we will need to use an approach that can accommodate lower coherence times. Coherence time just refers to the span that quantum states can survive for. Traditionally, an approach called **quantum phase estimation** (**QPE**) has been used to simulate the time evolution of a wave function. Using QPE to perform calculations on chemical reactions was first envisaged by Aspuru-Guzik and Seth Lloyd, but QPE requires an effective fault-tolerant device, as it has higher coherence times. With a fault-tolerant device, QPE is able to calculate the ground state energy of a chemical Hamiltonian.

The fault-tolerance needs of QPE and high-coherence circuit depth could be limiting factors for chemistry.

Another approach called **Variational Quantum Eigensolver** (**VQE**) has recently been employed to aid in the simulation of molecular interactions, and has given promising results. VQE needs shorter coherence times than QPE and can be used on noisy qubits with a low coherence time. As a result, VQE can be used on NISQ devices for the purpose of simulating chemical reactions. (Sources: `https://pdfs.` `semanticscholar.org/00ee/5a3cc1d14da2ec3e0ab15674dfb29b1d233c.pdf` and `https://pubs.rsc.org/en/content/articlepdf/2019/cp/c9cp02546d`).

But why is NISQ suitable for studying chemicals? We will need to understand "noise" in this context to answer that. Noise in a quantum computing context refers to the interaction of qubits (particles that make up the circuit) and their environment. In other applications of quantum computing, such as random number generation, this can result in errors in the calculations.

However, in chemistry, where we use the quantum computers to replicate nature and physics, the noise would represent the environment where the molecules exist and interact with each other. When noisy qubits are used to model molecular behaviour, it tells us how molecules will behave in nature. This is a property that we could potentially exploit, and noise in this case becomes a feature.

As a result, one of the biggest pain points of quantum computing becomes an invaluable feature for chemistry simulations. Harvard University's materials theory research space, called NarangLab, is focusing on using NISQ in the discovery of new electronic materials.

Traditional computers haven't really coped with simulating electronic materials. This would be better solved using quantum computers. Electronic materials are also largely composed of atoms that are organized in patterns. Therefore, we do not need to model all the atoms to study the behaviour of these materials. It is enough to pick a few representative atoms that will only need a few qubits to simulate their interactions.

Despite the complexities of chemical reactions, I believe that this could be a field that could start seeing commercial applications in quantum computing sooner than many other areas. The application of NISQ using VQEs to chemistry simulations will most certainly improve the "time to market" of these solutions.

As discussed in previously in this chapter, some of these solutions, like Nitrogen fixation and Carbon capture can have huge impact on the environment. Reducing Carbon emissions and the energy footprint of producing fertilizers are achievements that will have long-lasting implications. As we discussed in *Chapter 6, The Impact on Healthcare and Pharma*, understanding chemical reactions can also help us model drug efficacy better and faster.

Let's now move on to the other technology in focus – Blockchain, and how it can help in chemistry.

Blockchain in chemistry

We have seen the applications of Blockchain across different sectors so far, and in doing so, we have identified a few attributes of Blockchain that can be useful across different industries in similar patterns. For instance, Blockchain can be used in supply chains to reduce paperwork, make instant payments, and drive efficiencies. This is true for the pharmaceutical industry as it is for the chemical industry too.

Similarly, Blockchain smart contracts can be used as a data-driven approach to automate and honor contractual obligations across ecosystem players, suppliers, vendors, and supply chain participants. This is true in logistics and healthcare, and the same is true in the chemicals industry too. Therefore, I am not going back to those two examples, which we've covered in previous chapters, but rather I will reiterate these same uses for chemistry.

However, every industry has its own idiosyncrasies and it would be good to touch upon those while talking about how technology and innovation can help them achieve efficiencies, growth, or better revenue opportunities. Looking at the chemical industry, I can see Blockchain helping out with two key applications:

- Fostering the industry ecosystem
- Disaster recovery and post-disaster planning

Let's take a look at each of these applications in turn.

Fostering an industry ecosystem

I lived in Mumbai for about a year after I graduated from university and worked at a technology consulting firm called Patni Computers. I was based out of Navi Mumbai, which was also where Reliance Industries was based. Reliance is one of the biggest brands in India, founded by the legendary Dhirubhai Ambani. His sons, Mukesh and Anil, have taken over.

Mukesh has been phenomenal in driving the brand forward, while his brother Anil – whose fall from grace is well known in India and is covered in the likes of Forbes – has been rather less so. During my days at Navi Mumbai, I could see how Reliance were building their own little ecosystem. The ecosystem in this case would represent the suppliers, vendors, and other supply chain stakeholders. Even their physical presence in the city demonstrated ecosystem-wide engagement, spanning vendors, suppliers, and other stakeholders. Reliance Chemicals today is a major part of the Reliance empire, with $90 billion of reported revenue in 2019.

This ecosystem behaviour is still true, only that engagement and data sharing within an industry ecosystem happens digitally. Much like the food ecosystem, the chemicals industry will also need to take a marketplace approach (not the marketplace business model) in sharing data with different stakeholders.

This engagement can help build better standards around innovation and help the ecosystem come together to create specific chemicals for certain specific purposes. Going back to our fertilizer example, it would make it a lot easier to be highly innovative and differentiated if a company at the heart of the value chain could collaborate with suppliers to create a proprietary fertilizer composition that might need bespoke tweaks to their supply chain.

The German company BASF, the largest chemical producers in the world, are working with Quantoz, a Blockchain company. They have set up a platform for **Internet of Things (IoT)**-driven payments that a few other stakeholders are also part of. The use of Blockchain in an ecosystem context is still in its early days within the chemicals industry. However, there are genuine opportunities to scale once a few pilots have proven the efficacy.

We've covered how Blockchain can help us understand the production process of chemicals. It is essential to have end-to-end traceability and transparency of the supply chain that helps with the manufacturing, logistics, storage, and distribution of chemicals. Let's now look at the applications of Blockchain in disaster recovery of chemical plants.

Disaster recovery

On December 2nd 1984, the city of Bhopal in India faced a major disaster, which still haunts the local community. The Union Carbide pesticide plant released about 30 tonnes of toxic gas called methyl isocyanate. This gas mixed with the atmosphere and affected about 600,000 people living in neighboring towns and villages. Up to the present day, the death toll has been placed at 15,000 people, including both immediate fatalities and deaths over the years. Many people have lost their eyesight and those in the neighboring regions have faced health issues.

A comprehensive study of the links between deaths and sicknesses in the community, and the accident, is yet to be performed. Human rights organizations still claim that there are several tonnes of chemicals buried underground, and the government of India have declared the site as contaminated. The chemicals industry, like the energy sector, has done wonders in helping the world solve several problems. However, when things go wrong, they go wrong badly.

Disaster recovery becomes highly important in these scenarios. In undertaking disaster recovery, it is essential to understand the impact of the chemicals. In the case of the Bhopal gas tragedy, let's quickly look at how Blockchain could have helped the disaster recovery mechanism.

Data about the supply chain, the inventory, and the usage of raw materials on a Blockchain could be captured in a near-real-time registry. This would have allowed us to assess the quantity of chemicals that were being produced that could have been released into the air. Based on the quantity of chemicals tracked into the factory, and the amount left after the crisis, we would immediately be able to calculate the scale of the issue.

Once the amount of the chemicals released into the environment is assessed, immediate solutions can be devised in terms of the quantity and quality of medicines required for the affected. Due to the immutable nature of the register backed by Blockchain, we would also know what triggered the accident. Especially if we tracked the supply chain and the passage of raw materials and intermediate and final products through the manufacturing process, we would know where things went wrong.

Integrating IoT sensors into the process, where the temperatures and rate of supply of raw materials can be tracked at the micro level, can be useful. With all this data tracked, it can help the audit and insurance process post-disaster. Auditors can make informed decisions on supply chain changes, operational process changes, and chemical process tweaks, and add governance and controls accordingly to ensure business continuity.

All the data captured through the process can be invaluable to define best practices for future operational excellence. The chemical industry, much like the energy sector, can benefit a lot from such data-driven initiatives. An Accenture report in 2018 highlights the use of golden source of data using Blockchain for disaster recovery in the chemical industry. However, this use case is yet to be proven at scale.

As we have noted in previous chapters, Blockchain applications are gaining traction in supply chain management, trade finance and smart cities. Any value chain where there is a need to manage and maintain the integrity of goods being produced, transported, and distributed is an excellent use case for Blockchain. However, it is still early days for the technology. It is a 12-year-old technology that will most certainly go through its winters.

Conclusion

Deep technologies such as quantum computing and Blockchain can bring paradigm shifts in the way the chemical industry innovates and operates. Quantum computing use cases in chemistry are similar to those in healthcare, as they are largely about simulating and calculating chemical reactions using quantum algorithms and devices.

There are two other key acceleration factors for chemistry applications of quantum computing. One is the aspect that molecules can be modeled more naturally within qubits using different circuitry. We saw trapped ion qubits that were more suitable for chemistry than superconductor qubit circuits. The other interesting aspect is the ability to use NISQ devices for chemistry. NISQ devices can be perfect for chemistry as noise can be used as a feature in modeling behaviors of molecules.

This is not quite the case in quantum computing solutions for cryptography; therefore, in their ability to leverage noisy qubits, chemistry applications are special. We also touched upon the use of techniques like VQE that require lower coherence times. With all these aspects coming together, chemistry solutions can potentially be the first to be commercialized in the industry.

With Blockchain, however, the chemical industry hasn't really woken up to the potential. When the data tracking and sharing happens on an immutable record, the impact it could have from a risk management and disaster recovery perspective can add a lot of value. We also touched upon why Blockchain ecosystems can be relevant in the chemicals industry as they help with the creation of bespoke supply chains for specific chemicals more easily.

There are many opportunities in this industry, for those who can develop solutions to move beyond current limitations. There are technology barriers to be overcome for such solutions to be mainstream. But the key takeaway is that, with the chemicals industry, quantum computing applications might perhaps get ahead of Blockchain ones. In the subsequent chapters, we will explore the risks that quantum computing could pose to cryptography.

13

The Impact on Logistics

A few years ago, I was at a class on global business strategies at Saïd Business School, University of Oxford. The person addressing the class used to be the head of Volvo in China. He had taken over Volvo's China business when it was making only a few million and turned it into a multi-billion-dollar empire.

He was explaining the strategies that Volvo adopted to maintain its competitive advantage in the Chinese market. While we were discussing their China story, the discussion touched upon India. The Volvo executive said, "India is at least a decade behind China."

I just couldn't accept that comment. I asked him why he would say that when India had the GDP numbers, population, surging middle class, and a higher level of English proficiency. He mentioned that it was due to the broken supply chain and logistics infrastructure in the country. Each state in India has different tax rules and regulations, and when a firm was operating across multiple states, dealing with the supply chain efficiently is a major overhead.

This is not a challenge within India alone. This is a challenge across the world, where the logistics involved in running a global business can often be a drag for the business. One of the main reasons why Nokia couldn't respond fast enough to the rise of Apple in 2007-2008 was because of its supply chain, which wasn't nimble enough.

While supply chains are a key issue in several industries, the efficient use of road, train, and air transport can be a major factor too. All major economies in the world that are climbing up the GDP ladder have had to keep a sound manufacturing sector. Logistics is a fundamental element of a country's manufacturing capabilities.

In a sector that relies heavily on distribution, a small percentage improvement in the efficiencies of logistics could result in massive cost savings. These efficiencies, when scaled across a country, can lead to increased GDP.

During my discussion with Dave Snelling from Fujitsu, he mentioned that logistics was perhaps the hardest problem for classical computers to solve. This was not just because of the complexity of the problem space, but also because of the constraints that needed to be addressed in arriving at a solution. According to him, this was an industry where quantum computers could make a serious impact.

Apart from logistics, communication across the network in a safe and secure way is critical as well. Distribution networks that rely on efficient transport and the exchange of goods also rely on the safe, secure, and quick exchange of information. Quantum teleportation is an important use case that could compliment the logistics sector. This is especially true in military logistics, where information exchange often needs to go hand in hand with logistics.

Moving onto Blockchain, trade finance and supply chain management seem to be areas where the technology would be most useful. There are several initiatives across the world that are focusing on proving the use of Blockchain within logistics and trade finance.

In this chapter, I will be touching upon the challenges in logistics, transportation, and supply chain management, and how quantum computing and blockchain could be used to address some of the bottlenecks in the industry.

Let's begin by talking about one of the fundamentals of good infrastructure and effective logistics: an effective traffic management system.

Traffic management systems

Logistics and transport industries are fundamental to keep the engines on in an industrialized economy. We are in an age where cars are being connected to a network. The network server always has the intelligence of where every single car on that network is at any point in time. Self-driving cars are still a few years away from being mainstream, but connected cars are definitely here.

This is also true about other modes of transport. Public transport is also gradually starting to be driven digitally. China recently announced a driverless train traveling at 350 km per hour from Beijing to Zhangjiakou.

As a result of the digitization of this sector, we have the luxury of data, and the intelligence it can offer. This intelligence can be used to make the transport system more efficient. A simple example is how Tesla manages its network of cars. Tesla cars are essentially computers on wheels. They are connected to a server that knows where each car on the network is located at any point in time.

If I were a Tesla driver looking for a supercharger during my drive, I could look at the Tesla car dashboard while driving and it would tell me the nearest supercharger. More importantly, it would also tell me how free or busy the charging station is. It is able to do that because the server has information on where every car is, and if there are five cars charging at a station with six charging points, it can tell me that there is only one charging point free.

This is a simple implementation of intelligent traffic management. In November 2018, Volkswagen made an announcement that they were working on a quantum computing solution to project traffic volumes and transport demand. The solution will work like an air traffic control system. The system will know the location of cars through constant interaction and will be able to provide optimized routes for cars connected to the system.

We live in a world where the carbon footprint of transport is the second highest, only exceeded by industrial carbon outputs. A solution such as this will not only save time and costs but will also help us cut down carbon emissions at scale. However, these solutions can only help if a larger number of automobile makers come together.

Volkswagen is not alone in their quantum quest. Toyota, BMW, Ford, and a few others are also looking into traffic management systems. In my interview with Dave Snelling, he mentioned how Fujitsu's Digital Annealer is already helping BMW with their manufacturing processes.

In order to build a usable traffic management system, we will need all automobile providers to be equipped with sensors that continuously interact with the servers. We will also need these automobile providers to build standards around these data interactions. Let's examine why that is important.

Assume person A drives a Ford, and person B drives a Toyota. Both are on the road and start transmitting data to the server and receiving traffic information from the server. Now, this data can only be about Ford cars on the road for A, and Toyota cars on the road for B. That may not be very helpful unless 90% of the cars on the road are of the same make. Reference: `https://www.frontiersin.org/articles/10.3389/fict.2017.00029/full`

It is important to have all automobile makers come together and agree on data exchange standards and handshake mechanisms. Once that is enabled in our example, A driving the Ford will have information on B and vice versa. This will be because Ford and Toyota have now agreed to exchange information and their handshake mechanism is standardized.

Imagine this exchange of information happening across all automobile providers over the next 10 to 20 years. We will have a connected traffic management system in every car. The servers will receive millions of data points every second from vehicles on the road. They will need to have the ability to process that data in real time and return meaningful traffic insights and instructions to car drivers.

The solution of using connected cars is futuristic. However, traffic management systems can be developed using today's infrastructure and data sources. Another option to source traffic information is by using data from smartphones and cell towers. Automobile firms can collaborate with telecommunication providers and source geospatial data about people on the road. This may not be as accurate as data from connected cars, however, a traffic management system based on geo-spatial data sourced from telecom providers is possible today.

That is precisely the approach that the Volkswagen traffic management system has adopted. Traffic management is a combinatorial optimization problem and the D-Wave machines are good at solving them. In the Volkswagen experiment, D-Wave machines were used to identify optimized solutions for traffic management in a city with 4,000-5,000 taxis.

D-Wave's **quantum processing units (QPU)** are good at solving **quantum unconstrained binary optimization (QUBO)** problems by using two key inputs. One is a vector of binary variables in the form of qubit states. The second input is an N x N matrix that describes the relationships between these qubits. The idea is to find optimal routes for each taxi to ensure congestion is minimal.

For every taxi, we know the source, the destination, and the current routes of the taxi. We then identify a set of alternative routes for each of the taxis. These routes should be maximally dissimilar to the current route the taxi is taking. Therefore, for every taxi, **A**, "there will always need to be a route, **B**, that is true in the final solution." A variable per taxi per route T_{ab} is true in the minimum of the QUBO.

This data for all the taxis is coded into the D-Wave and the system goes through the adiabatic annealing process. This process identifies the solution that delivers the lowest number of congested routes. The low-energy state of the system that corresponds to the process should identify the low-congestion routes and the alternative routes that the cars would take in that scenario.

The system can be tested for efficacy by randomly assigning routes to certain taxis, which will result in the reassignment of new routes to the other taxis to arrive at a low-congestion state for the entire system. In the Volkswagen experiment, solutions were arrived at within 1-5 seconds of setting up the system. The same results could be obtained from existing industry software in 30 minutes.

The US Patent US20190164418A1 was granted in 2019 for Volkswagen's "System and method for predicting and maximizing traffic flow." In November 2019, Volkswagen's system was installed on buses in Lisbon to ensure their routes are optimized and enable smoother traffic flow through the city.

This quantum computing solution may not have provided a massive difference in solving these problems yet, but it opens up options for more real-time solutions to harder problems. In a world that is fast heading toward a climate emergency, any solution that will help save energy, emit less carbon dioxide, and lower per-capita carbon footprints is a step in the right direction. Let's now look at how the airline industry could benefit from quantum computing.

The Airbus quantum computing challenge

The first-ever commercial passenger flight took off on January 1, 1914, from St. Petersburg to Tampa. It's now more than a century since that happened, but innovation in aviation and airlines has largely plateaued, if not stagnated. Apart from the more recent initiatives from Elon Musk, Sir Richard Branson, and Jeff Bezos, that are focused on interstellar travel, we have hardly seen any major upgrades to air travel.

The airline industry has been mostly a loss-making endeavor, and just getting the business model right is hard enough for airline companies. Any research and development initiatives are few and far between in this industry.

This status quo might be changing, as Airbus is pioneering innovation efforts for the aviation industry. Their focus on quantum computing initiatives is especially interesting. They have set up a quantum computing application center in Newport, Wales. They have partnered with the Welsh government to set up Airbus Endeavor. The focus of this program is technology research and development for a digital and low-carbon economy.

Airbus' quantum computing efforts are not just focused on achieving logistical superiority through better air traffic management. They are also working on fluid dynamics, finite-element simulations, aerodynamics, and flight mechanics. Using quantum computing to model flight physics can lead to several benefits.

For example, currently, modeling the flow of air over the wings of a plane in flight can take 7 years. Source: `http://quantumbusiness.org/quantum-computing-future-flight-aviation/`

The innovation at Airbus is aimed at modeling every single atom of air that interacts with the flight wing within weeks. This can help them understand how their flight design will affect fuel consumption, reduce drag, and make flying more sustainable. Their study also involves using advanced materials in flights and how it would affect the efficiency of the aircraft.

Increasing the speed at which this modeling can be done (from several years to a few weeks), will most certainly speed up the design and manufacture of better aircraft in the future. Airbus has clearly understood the impact that the technology could have on its fortunes and has invested in a quantum computing firm called QC Ware.

QC Ware is building quantum computing capabilities across use cases ranging from chemical modelling, fluid mechanics, Monte Carlo simulations, machine learning, and optimization. As a result, it is able to help Airbus with their specific needs.

Airbus also recently launched a competition called the **Airbus Quantum Computing Challenge (AQCC)**. The competition was announced by Airbus CTO Grazia Vittadini at the DLD conference in Munich. This comes as a refreshing development to both the airline and the quantum computing industries.

AQCC is asking for the quantum computing ecosystem to work with Airbus to solve some of the hard problems that the industry is facing. The areas of focus for the competition are as follows:

- Aircraft climb optimization, which can help flights to achieve a low cost index
- Aircraft design optimization through **Computational Fluid Dynamics (CFD)**
- Quantum neural networks to solve partial differential equations
- Wingbox design and weight optimization to lower costs and environmental impact
- Aircraft payload optimization, to reduce fuel usage and costs

This is an interesting method to crowdsource solutions to some of the industry's major challenges and opportunities. Airbus has also said that the ownership of the solutions will remain with the teams submitting these solutions to the competition.

It is quite evident from Airbus' attempts that quantum computing is viewed as a technology that could solve problems that classical computers have struggled to achieve within feasible timeframes.

It is also clear that these are early days for the technology in the airline industry. But the industry is loss-making across the world and needs innovation to help it with operational efficiencies and cost reductions.

Airbus' defence business line is looking at data security and quantum resistant cryptography. Let's now look at quantum teleportation and data transfer in a quantum computing ecosystem.

Quantum networks

Logistics are dependent on the timely and secure transfer of data and information. In a military scenario, information about fighter jets needs to be transmitted in real time. In an autonomous car network, the location of cars needs to be transmitted and traffic control instructions need to be transmitted back to the cars. Another use case is in air traffic control, where information about flight locations and speeds are transmitted to optimize the traffic. In all these scenarios, we need the data to be safely transmitted between the sender and the receiver.

We live in an age where data security techniques are well behind where they need to be. For instance, the last decade has seen over a billion people in Asia join the internet. In India alone, 300 million people got mobile internet between 2015 and 2019. But most of these people do not have any awareness of connecting to the World Wide Web and performing financial transactions.

Data privacy and security have become increasingly significant to social media users and customers of large brands. The hashtag #FacebookIsDead has been trending for a long time because of their data privacy policies. Many are starting to feel that big technology companies like Amazon, Google, and Facebook have monopolized the use of the internet and have a clear monopoly over user data too.

While data privacy is one issue that needs addressing, data security is another major challenge that we need to resolve. The world is becoming increasingly connected through **Internet of Things (IoT)** devices. Data is shared across these devices, between consumers and businesses, like never before. Autonomous cars could be a normal thing in a few years' time, and with all this progress in technology, there needs to be a massive focus on cybersecurity.

Cybersecurity spending across the world is projected to hit $133 billion by 2022 according to Gartner. In the first half of 2019 alone, data breaches exposed 4.1 billion data records of people. We need to do better than that if we plan to live a safe and secure life when machines get more connected.

As the world gets filled with data, how can we ensure that we communicate in a secure fashion? Could we have a more secure and private internet? Can quantum computing help? There are a few answers to these questions. In a quantum network, information is transmitted as quantum information, using a qubit property called entanglement.

This property was described as "spooky action at a distance" by Einstein, which we highlighted in our first chapter. Two entangled particles can be described by the same quantum state, and therefore, observing the state of one of them will affect the state of the other particle. As "spooky" as it may sound, these entangled particles behave like a single quantum object and can be defined by one wave function.

In order to transmit quantum information between particles, they need to be entangled. Hence, the process starts with creating entangled particles and transmitting the particles safely to a distant location. Once this is successfully completed, we have a transmission channel for quantum information.

When one of the two entangled particles is assigned a state, it automatically affects the state of the other particle, which could be several miles away. When we perform an operation on one of the particles, that is instantly reflected on the other. This process is called quantum teleportation.

There are several pilots being run across the world to create a quantum internet that works on the principle of quantum teleportation. The European initiative is conducted by Europe's **Quantum Internet Alliance (QIA)**, which is working on creating a quantum network. A quantum network is where entangled quantum particles are transmitted between a network of nodes. Quantum information is transferred across these nodes through these entangled quantum particles.

China has made tremendous progress with its efforts to connect different transmission systems using photons. The University of Science and Technology of China have managed to distribute entangled particles to two earth stations, one based in South China and the other in the Tibetan Plateau. The efforts were led by Jian-Wei Pan in 2017, who used a satellite infrastructure for the experiment.

This solution may not be viable in everyday applications yet, due to the costs involved. There are experiments that use drones as part of the transmission network to make the process more commercially viable.

Therefore, in theory, once two entangled particles are set up, quantum information can be transmitted, with no possibility of anyone hacking into it. But, one of the key challenges in implementing quantum teleportation is creating the transmission channel using entangled particles. The current state of quantum networks in many ways mirrors the state of the early internet. However, things are developing quite quickly, with initiatives across the globe pushing research forward.

Europe's QIA, led by Ben Lanyon, is working on creating a transmission channel 100 kilometers long, with a station at the 50-kilometer mid-point. At each end of the channel, an entangled ion and a photon are created. The photons are then transmitted to the station in the middle through optical fiber, while also preserving entanglement with their corresponding ions.

The next step is to measure these photons, such that they are no longer entangled with their respective ions, and in doing so, the ions get entangled. This process is called entanglement swapping. This then allows a network of entangled particles to be spread far and wide, through which quantum information can be transmitted.

Although these experiments use one type of matter (in the preceeding case, calcium was used) to create the ions and photons, that doesn't have to be the case when quantum networks scale. Depending on the purpose of the qubit, a different type of material can be used to create entangled particles. For instance, calcium and strontium ions can be used to create Ca+/Sr+ crystals. Strontium ions are used to house qubits for computations and calcium ions are used to keep the strontium ions cool.

We may also need to create quantum memories (basically, storing data) in the network if we must store the qubits. Doing this, however, would require mutual standards that are agreed across the network.

It is early days for the industry as quantum network experiments are largely local. However, once quantum networks start to become more common across different regions, there will be a drive for standardization as we witnessed with the evolution of the internet. So, that's how a quantum network can be used to transmit quantum data. But how secure is the transmission of quantum information?

Data security

Entangled quantum particles are created and, if one of them is transmitted to a distant node, the setup can be used for secure quantum information exchange. As the state of one of the qubits changes, it automatically affects the state of its entangled pair. This process of using entanglement to transmit information in a quantum network is called quantum teleportation.

A key aspect to note with quantum teleportation is that states are never copied from one qubit to another. This is also why error handling in quantum computers is such a challenging task. The aspect of not being able to copy states of quantum particles is called no-cloning and is a fundamental axiom of quantum mechanics. Reference: https://www.nature.com/news/quantum-teleportation-is-even-weirder-than-you-think-1.22321#ref-link-6

The no-cloning property of quantum particles makes quantum cryptography robust. The state of quantum particles is disturbed when observed, and so it is theoretically not possible to eavesdrop on the transmission channel without raising the alarm. Therefore, establishing a transmission channel between entangled particles is an important step for quantum teleportation.

Another method for safely transmitting and using quantum information is called **Quantum Key Distribution (QKD)**. In this method, the quantum key is shared between the sender and the receiver as quantum data. If the key is intercepted, it will disturb the information and it might have to be resent. If the key is not intercepted, it can be used to encode messages that are shared through a classical mode of data transfer. `Bb84` is a QKD protocol that was developed in 1984 by Charles Bennett and Gilles Bassard that works on the same quantum property.

QKD relies on two key aspects of the communication. It needs:

- Quantum theory to be correct
- Devices used in the communication to be reliable

Until about 2010, QKD was considered to be impenetrable and completely reliable. However, in the 10 years since, scientists have been working on demonstrating that the devices that generate photons can be blinded by a strong light pulse. In doing so, the detectors can be remotely controlled by a hacker. This has led to research around "device-independent cryptography." Source: `https://www.sciencedaily.com/releases/2013/05/130528122435.htm`

We have so far discussed quantum computing use cases across transportation and flight physics. Those are areas where quantum technology can help solve problems that are hard for classical computers to cope with. However, the creation of a quantum network will not just be a safe and secure way to transmit confidential information in a military scenario, but could also become the internet of the future.

As a result, I felt that not only was it important to talk about the safe transfer of goods using an efficient logistics network, but it was equally important to touch upon the transmission of data in a network.

We've covered the use of quantum computing's role in assisting us with logistical problems, and how quantum networks could revolutionize communications and the internet. Let's now take a look at how Blockchain is being explored in the field of logistics and transport, all across the world. We'll see that the technologies of quantum computing and Blockchain have the potential to be highly complementary to one another when it comes to increasing the efficiency with which we track and transport our goods throughout the world.

Blockchain in logistics

Business across the world typically is done on trust. Historically, in many parts of the world, businesses often didn't have extensive documentation or contractual agreements in place. Most transactions were conducted based on trusted relationships. However, as businesses started to operate on a global scale, there had to be more processes and controls in place to protect all parties involved.

As businesses started to grow beyond borders, with several counterparties involved in a transaction, getting documentation completed often resulted in delays. The bureaucracy added costs and time to the transaction. When a multinational business relied on a supply chain that involved multiple hops across the world, it added inefficiencies to its manufacturing processes, for example. According to the World Economic Forum, reducing supply chain barriers could increase the world's GDP by 5% and global trade by 15%.

In the case of agriculture or food businesses, food products take several hops before hitting the shelves of the supermarkets. This not only results in operational overheads and delays but also, in the case of fresh food, in the loss of quality by the time it hits the shops. In many cases, there is extensive food wastage.

According to the **Food and Agriculture Organization (FAO)** of the United Nations, about one-third of food is wasted or lost, amounting to a loss of $680 billion in developed countries and $310 billion in developing parts of the world. There is so much inefficiency in the food supply chain that needs to be fixed.

With a warming world, we are going to see more fluctuations in food production due to either too much rain or drought conditions. This is disrupting trade routes across the world – one of the examples that we could look at is the shift in the balance of trade within Scandinavia.

In 2018, dry weather and a water shortage led to a fall in the production of crops in the region. As a result, some Scandinavian countries like Sweden became a net importer of crops like corn and wheat. Until then, they had been net exporters of the crop. The country's wheat production fell to a 25-year low. The total harvest of cereal crops in Sweden fell 43% from 3.2 million tonnes in 2017. However, the demand for these crops has always been high in European countries. Source: `https://www.ja.se/artikel/58675/swedish-cereal-production-on-lowest-level-since-1959.html`

Let's quickly examine the challenges of such shifts in trade and the implications for logistics. As a result of this sudden imbalance, Sweden had to import these crops. The shortage of crop harvesting was about 1.4 million tones.

So how do you suddenly create the logistics for importing volumes of that magnitude? How do you make sure the logistics are efficient and nimble?

Sweden had challenges in allocating port capacity for the crop imports and in the logistics to integrate the crop imports into their distribution channels. That is the infrastructure that is needed in the future if countries have to adapt to changes in weather patterns. However, that is only part of the puzzle; even if the infrastructure is in place in anticipation, the supply chain and logistics will need to be operationally efficient to reduce the cost burden.

Sweden is a small nation whose consumer base is relatively easily managed. However, imagine if this happens to bigger countries. Even if they are industrialized, they would struggle to cope with the changes in global trade landscapes driven by climate change. This could trigger inflation due to rises in crop prices across the world. This was observed on a smaller scale in Europe last year, due to a fall in cereal crop production.

The key takeaway is that we will need to start becoming extremely efficient with our logistics. Technology can help us get there.

Blockchain technology is perhaps most useful in logistics and supply chain management. The initial enthusiasm for the technology happened within financial services, and several stakeholders viewed it as a store of value. However, without a clear global regulatory framework, that is hard to achieve and scale. While the technology is going through its "AI-winter" moment within financial services, perhaps what will transpire is the emergence of more mature Blockchain applications within logistics.

Tracking goods

Blockchain technology offers the ability to track goods in near real time. In a value chain with multiple players and several different handshakes required to move the goods to the next step, this ability adds efficiency to the process. The handshake mechanism offered by the technology can cut operational costs for all parties in the supply chain.

IBM and Maersk started their journey together in June 2016, in setting up a Blockchain platform called TradeLens. TradeLens offers supply chain transparency and helps the logistics industry to resolve issues due to data silos. TradeLens today has over half of the data on ocean container cargo.

As this network of logistics providers scales across continents, TradeLens can act as the global trade platform with open standards. This will make the shipping industry across the world more efficient by bringing in transparency about the movement of goods across borders.

Accenture has built a Blockchain platform for logistics that acts as an immutable record of supply chain transactions. The bill of lading (a detailed list of a ship's cargo, which acts as a receipt upon delivery) can be replaced and the network can act as the single source of truth for trade documentation. Transparency and the efficient completion of paperwork is the key takeaway here as well. There are other players like ShipChain, Microsoft, and Oracle Corporation who are working on transparency within logistics.

The food supply chain

Let's briefly discuss the need for Blockchain technology in a supply chain context. Blockchain can be used in scenarios where there is a need for a network of participants to authorize a transaction. These participants store a copy of the transaction as they act as nodes on the network.

In a supply chain scenario, this framework can be extremely useful as the stakeholders involved will register their transactions on the Blockchain. For instance, in a food supply chain where a farmer, a logistics provider, a broker, and a supermarket are involved, each of them will be a node. As the farmer hands over the crops to the logistics provider, there is a handshake mechanism that authorizes the exchange of the crop. The handshake can also include the process of checking the quality of the crop.

In due course, such an infrastructure will create a rich and transparent data ecosystem for stakeholders to make data-driven decisions. However, in a distributed database, where there is centralized control of this data, it may not be as effective. Having said that, public Blockchain applications have had their fair share of technical limitations, as discussed in previous chapters.

I have seen a few companies in the supply chain space use permissioned Blockchain. It is still early days to say one is a better route compared to another. However, we have seen enough evidence that public Blockchain ecosystems are yet to gain mainstream trust, therefore permissioned Blockchain could be a bridge. With that, let's now look at Blockchain applications in the food supply chain.

The food supply chain is a special case within logistics because it deals with perishable goods. Inventory management in this case is a lot more sensitive, as goods have a limited lifetime. As a result, we need to have an infrastructure that can manage inventory at a more granular level. Blockchain technology can help inventory management at a micro level.

Firms like Walmart, Unilever, and Provenance are using Blockchain to manage the food supply chain. In the case of the food industry, Blockchain can be used to track the history of transactions involving the food, all the way back to its source.

When inventory management happens, if food stock goes bad, it can be selectively destroyed. When the history of the food item is known, it can be tracked to the source to ensure essential controls are in place to ensure better quality in the future.

Food supply chains are also special because most of them involve smallholding farmers, who are currently being squeezed for margins by the logistics providers or other middlemen in the value chain. There are over 570 million smallholding farmers in the world who take up 75% of the world's agricultural land. The ideal scenario for these farmers would be to use technology and track the ownership of the food products and create selective transparency along the way about the pricing of the food item.

In today's world, farmers often don't have the data to assess the supply and demand for their crops. This cripples their ability to suitably price their crops and puts them at the mercy of the middlemen in the supply chain. However, this can change with the transparency created through Blockchain. The data on pricing can be provided to the farmer to ensure they are not being exploited.

Ownership is another aspect of the food supply chain that needs to be fixed. This can be categorized as blue-sky thinking, but in the food value chain, it is essentially a farmer selling his goods to the end customer. The supply chains of the future should respect and reflect that in the commercial constructs as well. The logistics providers, inventory providers, food quality auditors, and even the supermarkets, are just providing a service to the farmer to carry out that sale efficiently.

Therefore, if I am buying a box of oranges from Tesco, I am purchasing it from a farmer in Kenya. As a result, the money I pay to buy those oranges should mostly reach the farmer's pocket. There could be a pre-agreed commission distributed to the logistics provider for offering their service, and the supermarket for offering shelf space.

There are two fundamental differences between the way this model would work and the current model. One, the ownership of the food product is with the farmer until the consumer buys it off them. Two, payment for the food is almost instantaneous through the value chain. Both of these are technically possible using Blockchain technology and its smart contracts feature.

The benefit to the consumer is that they know the quality they are getting as soon as they know the provenance of the food product. Remember, this is how farmers used to sell their crops in the good old days in a farmer's market; the reputation of their produce would be a key aspect of their success or failure.

The new global food supply chain should be no different. Trust and brand should be as applicable to the Kenyan farmer selling their oranges in London as it is to the independent local seller in a small-town marketplace.

However, this model will need to be imposed on the food supply chain by the governments of countries. As there are several middlemen who will lose out, this is not easy to do for a private sector firm. A public-private sector partnership could deliver this model over a period of time. AgriLedger, a Blockchain-based company, is working with the World Bank and the government of Haiti to solve this exact problem.

The ownership model may be hard to change as the aforementioned middlemen will be unhappy with that. It will, therefore, be a slow transition to extend a new ownership model. Also, keeping the farmer as the owner of the food item until it reaches the customer, is more of a business model, process, and an operations question rather than a technological one.

But the immediate payment to the farmer should be possible straight away with the implementation of a Blockchain solution. In existing food supply chains, the farmer gets paid months after delivering the crops to the middlemen. Often, they can't afford the delay, and take cash from the middleman at a massive discount. This is because farmers cannot afford to run out of working capital. With immediate payments enabled, farmers should get their money within days, if not hours, of delivering the crop. This can only make it a healthier ecosystem, not just for the farmer, but for all of us.

Several other firms are looking at improving the food supply chain, but they are approaching the problem from a consumer's perspective. Walmart's Blockchain initiative provides consumers with information on the history of their food, from source to shopping basket. That is indeed a step forward, but the food supply chain needs a complete revamp and "from the ground up" thinking, not just transparency for the consumer.

Sustainable supply chains

In December 2019, I attended a conference on sustainable finance in London, hosted by Finextra. One of the topics that was in focus on the day was sustainable supply chains. Although it was a brief 20-minute speech, it got me thinking about both the necessity to make supply chains sustainable, and the outcomes it would have on our environment.

Let's take a food supply chain as an example. There are several key criteria we will need to look at to make sure that it is sustainable:

- Was the crop produced in a sustainable fashion? This raises more granular questions such as:
  - Was there any deforestation involved in procuring agricultural land for the crop?
  - Was the crop produced with sustainable irrigation techniques?
  - Were fertilizers used in producing the crop?
  - If fertilizers were used, what was the carbon footprint in producing them?
  - Were children employed to produce the crop?
- Was the crop transported in a sustainable fashion?
  - Was the crop packaged in a sustainable fashion? Were plastics used?
  - What was the carbon footprint of the logistics used to get the crop to the supermarket?

Some of these sustainable criteria for the food supply chain are already being audited, reported, and managed efficiently; however, they are all documented on paper. We will need a supply chain marketplace that sources data about all these aspects and uses them to create a sustainability score for every food item sold in a supermarket.

Therefore, when a customer looks at pack *A* and pack *B* of apples, they will have the ability to rank them not just on price, but also on the quality of the supply chain. Blockchain can help with filling a lot of the gaps in creating such a marketplace for retail customers to benefit from.

This can also be used for consumer goods. Unilever has been piloting Blockchain to add transparency and efficiencies to its supply chain. They are focusing on the account payables for their American supply chain, which is currently quite manual and inefficient.

A solution for that from Provenance, another Blockchain company, has been piloted to tag and track tuna from Indonesia. They have gone one step further to also capture and verify the sustainability claims of the supply chain stakeholders. This effort needs to be scaled across other food items, and even outside of food supply chains.

All of this information can then be provided to the consumer through a QR code, which, when scanned, will provide an end-to-end view of the supply chain and the sustainability score.

These methods have all been trialed by Unilever, Walmart, and Provenance, but the limitations of Blockchain technology are perhaps the reason why these solutions haven't scaled. As Blockchain emerges out of its winter hibernation, we should see more practical applications at scale.

Transport

The trucking industry is an example of where Blockchain can add value within transportation. Over $140 billion is tied up in disputes within the transportation industry. Payments take on average 42 days after an invoice is received. This is all due to the inefficiencies of the paperwork involved in the truck industry.

Moreover, about 90% of truck companies across the world own less than six trucks. This means the allocation of goods and trucks is another major overhead and results in half-filled trucks and operational cost leaks. When the truck industry is managed on a Blockchain, most of the contractual obligations can be laid out on a smart contract, and the payments can be triggered as soon as the criteria are satisfied.

A handshake mechanism to identify the end of a journey of the truck can be agreed, and when the smart contract receives that, it can trigger the payment. This will also help with the working capital requirements of these small truck owners. The **Blockchain in Transport Alliance (BiTA)** is an initiative that has members who cover over 85% of truck-related transactions in the world.

With the world moving toward same-day delivery models, it is imperative that the truck industry becomes extremely efficient. IoT sensors can be used in trucks to measure the volumes of freight and make the most of truck capacities. IoT can also help when the goods being transported are sensitive to temperatures.

A combination of IoT sensors and Blockchain technology can keep track of temperatures when pharmaceutical goods are being transported. If the sensors detect a change in temperature, Blockchain can trigger an alert, or charge any agreed punitive damages arising from that change in temperature. This will also reduce dispute scenarios as it will all be backed up by immutable data on the Blockchain network.

The performance of a fleet of vehicles can also be registered on a Blockchain. There are companies like CarFax, who act as intermediaries holding this data. However, when a buyer wants to know an immutable record of a vehicle's performance information, they should be presented with a verified set of data that will decide the price of the vehicle.

Much like several other industries we have touched upon, Blockchain has a $500 billion opportunity within the transportation vertical, according to Morgan Stanley. The challenge, however, is in the technology itself – both logistics and transportation can generate a lot of data.

If we used IoT to support logistics monitoring and measurement, that would add to the data volumes too. There haven't been promising implementations of Blockchain at scale that can handle such data volumes in real time. Until the throughput problem is solved, these use cases may stay in the pilot stages.

Vehicle manufacturing

Another key use case for Blockchain is acting as a register of vehicle parts. The entire manufacturing process can be registered on Blockchain, including the source of raw materials, suppliers, procurement, and manufacturing steps. The manufacturing steps involved could be monitored with machine-level data tracking using IoT devices. According to a Gartner report, the manufacturing industry could see a cost-saving of $176 billion by 2025 using Blockchain technology.

All this data should be able to provide a traceability mechanism for the production line of vehicles. Sensors can keep track of the quality of the vehicle parts once they hit the road. The performance of the vehicles can be measured and managed, as discussed in previous sections, using IoT devices too. Therefore, when there is a faulty part reported, the Blockchain system will know how and where to source it immediately.

As a new part is provided as a replacement, a handshake mechanism using tags can ensure that the replacement part was sourced from the right vendor. In doing so, the health sheet of the vehicle is built from a very early stage and through its lifetime. The average cost of a product recall in manufacturing is $8 million. This cost can be massively reduced using Blockchain for the end-to-end traceability of parts.

A study by Capgemini interviewed 447 manufacturing firms using Blockchain and identified that over 60% of them had already changed the way they were interacting with their suppliers. Despite all the benefits, there are initial barriers that the technology needs to overcome to see mainstream adoption.

The **Return on Investment (ROI)** for the technology and operational overhauls needed is unclear and often can be a major roadblock in big organizations. Identifying sponsors within an organization without a clear ROI narrative can be challenging. The other key challenge for adoption as per the Capgemini report is the interoperability (or the lack of it) of Blockchain with legacy systems and processes within these big manufacturing firms.

Apart from the technology limitations that we see with Blockchain, organizational challenges still remain. Mainstream adoption can only happen once these two roadblocks have been cleared.

We have now covered the transportation and logistics use cases of both quantum computing and Blockchain. As you can see, these two technologies have the potential to lead us into a far more efficient, transparent, safer, and better-connected world.

Conclusion

In this chapter, we have covered the use cases that quantum computing and Blockchain could deliver within logistics. This is an industry where there are several inefficiencies due to a lack of digitization. As a result, it could be a green field for technology to create value in.

In the case of quantum computing, the major use cases we touched upon are efficient traffic management systems. We discussed the use of quantum computing when connected cars become more common. With today's infrastructure, traffic management can be achieved using telecoms data/geospatial data.

We also touched upon Airbus' attempts to add efficiencies to the aerospace industry. Flight physics can be modelled more accurately using quantum computing than with classical machines. As a result, aerodynamics around the wings of the aircraft can be modeled and fuel efficiencies can be achieved by optimizing flight take-off and landing. In a world being badly hit by climate change, every single bit of saving on carbon emissions can help us.

Moving onto Blockchain, we saw how it could be used within supply chain management and traceability. The food supply chain use case is especially interesting as it can be both beneficial to the consumer and the farmer in many ways. We saw innovation that caters to both ends of the supply chain.

Finally, we also touched upon how Blockchain can help with transportation, manufacturing, and the truck industry.

The applications of these two technologies are huge, and the potential value addition can't be exaggerated either. However, both these technologies have some major challenges to overcome before they see mainstream adoption. They should be able to co-exist in a business environment, as the use cases are rather complementary. In the next chapter, we will look at how quantum computing and NISQ can be used in the field of chemistry.

14

Interview with Dinesh Nagarajan, Partner, IBM

The last century saw two world wars and several other wars of invasion and retaliation. Nations waged war upon one another for access to resources that would make them more powerful. During World War II, Hitler's invasion of the Caucasus was one such instance, with him going after the rich oil resources there. Winston Churchill's strategic push in North Africa was to hold key port cities in the region so that he could have access to India, which was then a British colony.

Access to oil was a fundamental reason for the wars fought in the Middle East in the second half of the century. However, geopolitical issues are slowly starting to move away from depleting resources such as oil or iron ore, to a resource that keeps growing despite consumption – data. By 2025, the world is expected to be 175 zettabytes rich, of which about 90 ZB will be from the **Internet of Things (IoT)**.

 1 zettabyte = 1 trillion terabytes

Nations are gearing up to monopolize data mines, which will include defense data, financial data, healthcare data, and the personal data of citizens. Therefore, it is important to understand how they intend to leverage technology to gain data supremacy. There was a time during the Cold War when there was an arms race between the superpowers as to who had more nuclear warheads.

Today, that trend is being seen in the number of patents in technologies such as quantum computing, Blockchain, and AI. Therefore, when we discuss these technologies, it is important to understand the role they would play in cyber wars that nations would want to dominate. Therefore, when I was looking at thought leaders to interview for the book, I knew I needed to get an expert in this space. Dinesh Nagarajan, Executive Partner and Global Competency Leader at IBM, was certainly one of them.

Dinesh and I worked together at PwC in 2014, where he was focusing on cyber security propositions for banks and I was focused on Chief Data Officer advisory propositions. He joined IBM in 2016 and has gone from strength to strength. Dinesh shares his insights on cyber risks and how technology and the explosion of data has made us vulnerable. He stresses that it is not just technology that can help us with cyber risks. We will also need to ensure there is awareness around cyber risks and the controls available to protect ourselves at all levels of society.

Dinesh's technology background combined with his involvement with clients who are trying to combat cyber risks gives him the ability to understand the impact of technology innovation on data security and privacy. He is able to understand and stay on top of technology capabilities that exist with different stakeholders in the cyber landscape. However, he is also able to apply that understanding to the context of cyber wars and cyber risk management. Both Dinesh and I enjoyed the process of this interview, and I hope you find it useful too.

Arun: Dinesh, thanks for joining me today. Let's start with a brief introduction. Tell us a little bit about your career in cyber security. How did you get into IBM? What has your journey been like so far?

Dinesh: Arun, thanks for having me. I'm Dinesh Nagarajan, my role at IBM is Partner and Global Competency Leader. I lead the data and application security competency globally for IBM security services. I have over 20 years of experience, and in the last 15 years I've worked primarily in the cyber security industry. In my roles within the cyber security space, I've been lucky enough to work with several leading organizations. I've also been fortunate enough to be involved on both sides of the coin. As in, I have worked on the technology side, as well as in the services industry.

I've had the opportunity to work in the industry and within consulting in cyber security. My work has largely been about helping large-scale financial firms with cyber security transformation projects in the UK and Europe. In the last year or so my role has broadened and so has my outlook. I now have a global role with a global focus on cyber security transformation.

I am now working with clients in North America, Asia Pacific, and the Middle East. I've been with IBM for the past 3 years. Therefore, I travel a lot, meeting firms across the world and helping them address cyber risks. That has definitely helped me get a global view of the cyber security world. I get to see how clients approach this space, not just from a technical lens, but from a process, awareness, and sometimes even a cultural lens. I find that aspect quite interesting, as cyber security is as much a people issue as it is a technical issue.

Arun: That's a brilliant point, Dinesh. To help set the context of this conversation, let's briefly talk about the data explosion that we've seen over the last 20 years. The dot-com boom has helped internet-based business models and applications go mainstream. We have seen many social media apps that initially led the data explosion, but now we are seeing a trend that is led by the IoT world. We are going to have terabytes of data in a day being generated by self-driving cars.

Data creation is going to increase 60% year on year and hit numbers like 175 ZB by 2025. About 70% of that is going to be from the internet of machines. I am not sure if we are ready to manage that data explosion from a cyber security perspective. Are we innovating at such a rate that we can no longer effectively manage the outcomes of that innovation? How is this going to affect cyber security?

Dinesh: That's a very good question. In a typical scenario, with innovative solutions and business models, security is always lagging behind. In some cases, there is a good appreciation of the security mechanisms that need to be deployed with all of these changes. However, in most cases, there is a lack of understanding and a lack of appreciation of the criticality of cyber security.

The last two to three decades have brought about some fascinating growth in technological advancements across most industries. This is the fifth wave of industrial revolution. I think the speed and the pace of change has been phenomenal. Most industries in this period have gone through digitization that transformed previously manual processes and services into digital equivalents. This is often accompanied by data exchange and interactions digitally.

Therefore, organizations today are interconnecting legacy systems that previously have never been exposed outside the data center. These systems can be mobile applications, web applications, or social media. There is a fundamental change in the way organizations want to service their clients. There is a demand and a change in the way customers consume services these days. There is a demand to deliver services quicker. There is an "always-on" requirement that customers would like to leverage at any point of time, all the time, 24/7.

Customers also expect instant gratification and instant feedback. This forces organizations to be very agile and to be able to respond to these asks. Therefore, the most important interface to the client today is digital. Be it financial services, logistics, healthcare, or any other critical service we need, we have started to rely on and trust digital means more than legacy ways of doing things.

Most of these interactions are often on the web frontend, mobile apps, or on social media. The next wave of interactions will not just be between customers and these interfaces, but also between machines. There is a prediction that there will be more than 50 billion devices on the IoT in the next 5 years. The other interesting prediction on the data side is that even the smallest organization will produce 20 times more data in the next 3 years than what they're producing today. These numbers are staggering.

In the midst of all this, there is a massive push with regard to moving to the cloud. A move to the cloud shouldn't be viewed as just technology transformation. There is also business transformation involved. Let's take FinTech for instance. FinTech is driving traditional banks to adapt to new business models and ways of servicing. As data is being hosted on cloud infrastructure, and shared using open banking, we see new business opportunities for third-party solutions that can leverage this data. Oftentimes, banks can themselves create these solutions.

The move to the cloud is also changing the typical traditional IT ecosystem. Previously, most critical applications and services were hosted in a secure data center. Now they are deployed on a public cloud, interconnected with third-party services. Therefore, as these transitions and transformations are in progress, the prediction is that cyber-attacks are going to increase in the next 3 years. It is not just the number of cyber-attacks, but the intensity and the sophistication of the attacks will also increase. We will need to be prepared for that.

We see that cyber threat actors have industrialized the whole cyber-attack scenario. They have automated and orchestrated methods for breaking into a client's infrastructure. Once they have broken into the infrastructure, they are able to very quickly get to the target system. This is the kind of level of sophistication that threat actors have developed. But unfortunately, not all organizations have been able to match up in detecting and responding to cyber-attacks with the same level of sophistication.

There's a lot of work being done to improve cyber security processes and systems. But there is still a lot more to be done. You must have heard about the ransomware attack on a global shipping liner, one of the biggest shipping companies in the world. One morning, the company's laptops had messages with red and black lettering. Employees were asked to pay in bitcoins to recover their files. Restarting laptops took them back to that screen.

The attack hit the entire network and employees were asked to shut down their laptops and disconnect from the network. About 49,000 laptops and 3,500 of the 6,200 servers were affected. The attack caused so much disruption that even their IT teams were helpless at the time. It brought the entire firm to a standstill for about 9 days, when the recovery of 2,000 laptops got them back into business. This is a firm whose ship hits a port in the world every 15 minutes, with most ships being able to carry 20,000 containers. If such a large company can be a victim of cyber-attacks, it is hard to fathom how smaller organizations can cope.

Now, that's how cyber criminals can inflict near financial destruction on even the biggest of organizations. Therefore, it's no longer a case of just installing antivirus software and assuming you are safe from virus attacks; cyber security is much bigger than that. Many of the organizations I talk to understand that a sophisticated attack could cripple them for days and weeks and plan around that. However, there are several organizations that are perhaps in denial about the dangers of this threat.

Arun: We are still discussing the problem statement here. Unlike my other interviews, where the problems discussed were known widely, cyber risks are often not known widely. We can look at cyber risks from various different perspectives. One is the corporate angle that you've already mentioned. The other angle is from a consumer perspective. We see the increase in the risks not just in the developed world but also in the developing world.

For instance, both of us know that Reliance Jio has brought about 200 million people in India on to mobile internet over the last 2 to 3 years. I was in India in August 2019. I visited a temple with my family. When I walked out of the temple, there was a woman selling flowers, and she had a QR code printout hanging on her little mobile stall, which we used to pay. It is unlikely that this lady understood cyber security. She understood that money was reaching her bank account digitally, but with no concept of what the threats are.

 QR codes are Quick Response codes that are used for digital payments.

We also heard recently that India's Kudankulam nuclear plant got hacked by nation state hackers. Therefore, the country's growth from a consumer side has opened it up to new vulnerabilities. Public sector officials are going on to the internet with no clue about these cyber risks. Therefore, there is a massive awareness problem, especially in emerging markets. What are your thoughts around this?

Dinesh: I think awareness is very important. Awareness is one thing, but regulatory bodies should also step in here. They need to enforce basic safeguards that service providers should be able to provide, to protect the rural population; a liability model that could be established between the customers and the service providers, which will force them to provide cyber safeguards. I think there is a definite role for regulatory bodies and governments across these growth markets. While you're creating new avenues of services and new ways of delivering business value to consumers, you also need to provide the necessary guardrails.

Without such controls, those services and businesses will not thrive. Without safeguarding mechanisms for the end consumer, trust in the digital space will very quickly evaporate. Losing customer trust can be detrimental to the whole industry. As a result, consumers can stop buying things from a particular service provider because they are more vulnerable to cyber threats. Consumers could even stop transacting from their mobile phones if they completely lose trust for their internet providers.

That would impact companies who offer their products and services digitally. The entire digital economy and financial inclusion story may end up being a house of cards. In India especially, the government has done an excellent job of leading innovative trends. I do not see any reason why they cannot do more to create guardrails to protect the vulnerable consumer.

Arun: We've touched upon enterprise security; we've gone through the role of retail consumer-level security and then how regulators can provide some solutions. We've set the context, so I'm now moving on to the potential solutions to this challenge.

Both of us are engineers by background, so let's talk technology for a few minutes. What are the technology solutions that are out there, and beyond technology, what are the process, policy, and behavioral measures we can have in place?

Dinesh: We both know that technology is not the silver bullet. There is no single technology (today) that we can rely on to solve this problem. The other key point to think about is that technology keeps changing very fast. 10 years back, as long as you had a secure username and password you considered yourself secure. It is no longer the case and things have moved on quite a bit from that. Security has moved on from there to focusing on protecting infrastructure, the operating system, and the application. It has moved up the stack starting from the infrastructure. However, now the focus is on data.

In the new world, organizations don't even own their infrastructure anymore. If you are planning to host your data or your applications in the cloud, you don't own the infrastructure, and you don't own the platforms or the operating systems. Therefore, you just need to focus on protecting your data and your clients' data. As a result of this spotlight on data protection, there is more of a focus on, and investments are moving toward, data protection. Consequently, there is more of a focus on data encryption, and there are various ways of doing data encryption.

There is encryption, tokenization, data masking, and several new realms of identity and access management. Biometric identity and access management is a key aspect for data security. Having your security control literally where the data resides rather than on the infrastructure or the operating system layer is considered critical. In doing so, you are basically protecting data as it moves around these different tiers.

There are stronger and more adaptive ways of controlling users' access to data. We will need to build in authentication and authorization capabilities to protect data using clear data security models.

We also have "shift left" security practices that are becoming more mainstream now, where security controls are built into applications at an early stage of the development cycle. Therefore, the application is secured by design. While these measures are largely there to prevent an attack or unauthorized access to data, you are still going to expect a certain small percentage of attacks to get through these controls.

If a data breach happens for whatever reasons, you still need the capability to detect, respond, and mitigate very quickly. The ability to act quickly against an attack and keep servicing your customers is called resilience. This has now matured into a space where it is no longer just a technical problem but is also a business problem. It is not just about how much data has been breached, and how you can fix it technically. It is also about how many clients have been affected by the data breach, whether they still have access to your services, and whether you can continue services for those clients. Therefore, beyond technology, business resilience takes center stage in the new world we live in.

Let's go back to the example of the shipping company, which had tens of thousands of desktops, and its network, affected by ransomware. For Maersk, resilience would mean having the ability to continue getting their ships to hit the target ports on time and delivering containers despite the attack. The technical team in the background will perform forensics around the attack, fix the vulnerability in their system, and try to bring their computers, servers, and their networks up. However, the critical thing is being able to operate in the absence of all of this digital support.

Coming back to your question, in the shipping company example, technology may have prevented the attack. But it is changing at such a pace that organizations will often need to resort to operational resilience in the face of such attacks. One other thing I find lacking in the industry is a collaborative mechanism of sharing intelligence about a coordinated attack.

I think that is an effective way of preventing cyber-attacks at scale, because, once there is intelligence about the modus operandi of the attackers, they are forced to rethink. They will have to go back to the drawing board to launch another attack. There are initiatives in the UK and in Europe in some industries to share intelligence about cyber-attacks. But there needs to be more intelligence-sharing as the risks are not just limited to these developed parts of the world.

Arun: Thank you. Let's now address the elephant in the room. There is a lot of hype around cutting edge technologies like quantum [computing] and its repercussions for data security. Blockchain applications could be obsolete because of the encryption methods (RSA and ECC) they use. The internet could be in serious trouble once quantum computers become mainstream.

How are we positioning ourselves for the threat, and could that threat also be an opportunity? Can we also use quantum computing to protect ourselves and our data?

Dinesh: That's another interesting question. There is a general awareness about the risks and opportunities of some emerging technologies, but not to the extent that I would ideally like to see. There is interest in understanding the risk for asymmetric cryptography from emerging technologies. In the last year, we have done some work with clients in this space. Most of the organizations who are most interested are in the financial services industry. We have also spoken to a few automobile companies about security mechanisms as some of these emerging technologies go mainstream.

Organizations are interested because the rate of change of technology is usually once in 7 to 8 years, typically. Every time they have to make changes to their technology or infrastructure stack, the cycle of change lasts about 7 to 8 years' time. That timeframe is what is concerning them, because they think that in 7 to 8 years' time some of these emerging technologies could become a reality. Therefore, even if they identified a solution to help with readiness on cyber security, it may not happen in time to face the threat.

Therefore, all of their systems, be it a financial market's infrastructure or a self-driving automobile system, will be exposed. Many of these firms have started to think, plan, and also socialize this risk with their boards. Now from an IBM standpoint, we feel that in order for you to protect yourself from these new technology paradigms, you need to go through a maturity journey. You can't start planning for it today and fix it tomorrow, because these technologies are still evolving, and by the time you think you have a fix, it is perhaps already outdated.

The mitigation against cyber risks that these technologies will pose will come from increased awareness and agility. We use the term crypto agility to refer to how easily you can migrate from one cryptographic technique to another. Therefore, you need to keep your technology stack agile enough to adopt different cryptographic techniques that can help you defend your systems against a cyber-attack.

Theoretically, we can use new ways of transmitting information supported by some of these emerging technologies. Theoretically, we could keep our information safe from external attacks. However, it is too early to say if that would be a viable solution as the technology is still evolving. I think firms planning to combat the threats from emerging technologies will need to go through a maturity journey.

Everyone should understand what technology innovation means to them and what the risks are. Once the risks to their systems and infrastructure are understood, they will need to go through a planning phase. The planning phase will involve how the cryptographic landscape can be improved. There needs to be a detailed assessment of how their infrastructure, applications, and processes can become crypto-agile.

Once this is understood, then it is just about transforming the stack to be prepared for the new wave in computing. In the next few years, it will become increasingly clear as to what part of your crypto landscape is secure and what isn't. A crypto-agile architecture should then help swap and change areas that are assessed as being vulnerable in the new era.

So, our role in IBM is to bring that awareness, plan and execute the assessment, and take clients through a maturity cycle to future-proof their data.

Arun: That was quite a lot of insights on technology measures to combat this threat. Any other points you want to talk about before moving on to other aspects of cyber risks?

Dinesh: Yes. I am particularly concerned about data security as IoT-based applications become more and more commonplace. A large number of IoT devices are exposed to cyber risks because IoT manufacturers often do not address security issues. They don't build security into their devices. If they had thought about security during the design phase, the output of the product would be far better than what it is today.

Other key progress I would like to see is within DevOps. Organizations need to consider data security when they are adopting DevOps. There needs to be security design principles mandated when developers start building applications. They think about how their application will behave for the users when it goes into production. However, they often fail to think about how secure their application will be when it is rolled out into production.

Some of these risks need to be mitigated in the grand scheme of things if we want to address data security holistically. Organizations are starting to understand security risks better and are trying to mitigate them. In order to do that, some of them have tried to do risk assessment and, more importantly, risk quantification. One of the often-repeated challenges in cyber security is risk quantification. It is quite hard for organizations to quantify their cyber risks.

As a result, there are very few organizations today who can quantify the risks effectively. Where organizations adopt cyber risk frameworks to drive better maturity and therefore quantify these risks, they are better prepared. As cyber security experts within organizations are able to quantify the risks, they are able to speak the language the board of the firm will understand. They are therefore able to have a discussion at the highest level, where the impact is well understood and therefore well addressed.

Arun: At least within financial services, I understand that cyber risks can be quantified through operational risk capital allocation methods. However, I haven't seen that level of sophisticated risk management techniques within other industries.

Let's now move on to another interesting topic that I would like your input on. You mentioned that you now work with clients across the world. At the start of this decade, we had a geopolitical scenario between Iran and the US. While the US used traditional defense and military mechanisms, Iran basically indicated that they might resort to a cyber-attack. Since then, the US has been ramping up its activities to protect the country from cyber-attacks. There are also reports that there is a possibility for the electricity grid in the US to be attacked and they're looking at ways to protect it. So that is a new-age war technique – cyber war. So, what are your thoughts on that?

Dinesh: This is an unfortunate development and such cyber-attacks have been going on for a while now across industries, across the world. Every time there is a sanction from the United Nations, folks in cyberspace would expect a wave of attacks that they need to be prepared for. I don't see that trend changing. You can call this some sort of a cyber-arms race that's going on in the background, which is not very visible to the public. The race is based on who's got the technology, data, and information advantage and who's going to continuously stay ahead of the new technology paradigms that are coming in.

It's a continuous "intelligence gaining," "information gathering" type of exercise too. For instance, if you are in the IoT space, the person with the advantage will know the vulnerabilities and the weaknesses in the IoT ecosystem, and this information is not disclosed. They'll retain that information so that they can leverage it as and when they want. Therefore, nation states that have developed sophisticated cyber capabilities do not suddenly become active or plan for an attack. In any sense, they are always active in the background.

They keep performing research and reconnaissance and find information on the target. It's like spies as we knew them in the previous century. Except that this is largely digital. Everyone's gathering intelligence about security vulnerabilities or security shortcomings of a particular platform or country. In some cases, interestingly, some nation states proactively orchestrate weaknesses in enemy territory. They will deliberately introduce backdoor weaknesses of a certain type that they can always leverage and use when the time is right. So, they've been constantly active, and I think this is going to be the unfortunate case in the future, and a case that we should be able to deal with.

Nation states are not only looking to attack critical national infrastructure that may be targets, but they can also pull off an attack or breach private companies. We may also need to look at this risk through a different lens. How many such nation states would be bold enough to attack another country's critical infrastructure, resulting in a large loss of life or massive public disruption? I'm not sure that will happen.

Sporadic destabilizing activities like attacking vulnerable organizations is what they may typically target. I do not believe that a large-scale attack to destabilize an entire country and bring it to its knees is something on the cards.

Having said that, it could happen in the future. Most organizations that are capable of such attacks operate under the radar and it is not easily possible to see and track them. I think their biggest concern is to be identified as someone behind a cyber-attack that cripples an enemy nation. Nobody wants to be there. So, I think that's one of the driving factors in them operating completely in the dark and under the radar.

Arun: I think we'll just close this with one further question. Just the possibility that someone with a technological breakthrough could take on the entire world sounds like when the race to invent the atom bomb was on around World War II. Any comments on that?

Dinesh: True – the race for information dominance is on. There are several stakeholders investing billions in this space to get ahead. For some, it is the data security advantage that the technology is going to give. For others, it is the ability to process information better and faster. There are several use cases of these emerging technologies that are not just focused on breaking traditional cryptography.

That's one side of the coin, but investments by top nation states into this technology are being made with a view to playing a dominant role in cyber wars. A breakthrough in this technology could lead to a new global balance of power.

Another aspect to think about is that, when the breakthrough happens, we don't even know if these countries will publicize it. While all indicators are that a breakthrough is still a few years away, it might have happened already. Nobody really knows how the landscape is going to change tomorrow. It's a very fascinating space. I also feel that more organizations could get involved in the R&D efforts of this technology. I think it is important to create a community that is moving toward a common good through their efforts to innovate.

Arun: As we talk about R&D budgets, it is worth noting that China are ahead of the crowd there. They have invested several billion dollars into quantum science. The US is just catching up. In the last 10 years or so, about 70% of successful patents within the quantum space have been from China, and second in that list is the US with just 12%.

Dinesh: Yes, we need a wider group of countries and organizations investing in this technology. Let's take the way Linux was developed, for instance. It was a community-driven effort, and it has democratized the operating system space. On a similar note, I hope we have wider participation in the innovation around emerging technologies that will make them more viable for mainstream users. We may soon have an internet that leverages these emerging technologies.

If we created all that as a community, rather than centralizing achievements around the technology, it would de-risk the whole world. Decentralized research and development efforts coming from across the world will definitely help reduce cyber risks. Hopefully, we won't end up having a superpower due to their emerging technology and information advantage.

Arun: Yes, let's keep our fingers crossed on that. Let's close the interview on that note. Thank you so much for your insights around cyber security, and how technology advancements are affecting this space. It was such an insightful conversation.

Dinesh: Thank you for inviting me to do this, I enjoyed it thoroughly.

Conclusion

There have been times over the last few years when I have felt that it is almost unfair that technological supremacy could result in a superpower nation or organization. That is especially true when it comes to quantum computing. However, there are several aspects of quantum computing that are being researched across the world. Therefore, I genuinely hope we will have several superpowers, each taking the lead on one aspect of quantum technology.

Dominating one aspect of quantum technology such as quantum communication may be an enviable position. China has definitely taken the lead when it comes to quantum communication. Their quantum satellite experiments have put them ahead of the pack. However, there is still much to be achieved in quantum computing. There are challenges when quantum particles are used to transmit information or model problems. Some of these roadblocks need to be addressed to gain complete dominance through quantum technology breakthroughs.

The conversation with Dinesh has offered several key insights into the field of cyber security in a world that is innovating in a massive hurry. Despite the threat from quantum computers, there are ways to mitigate the risks by increasing the maturity around cyber risks. By going on that maturity journey, organizations are able to systematically identify weaknesses in their landscape.

Through careful planning with cyber security experts, organizations can prepare themselves to be *crypto-agile*. As quantum computers get closer, we should be able to see the evolution of their capabilities. In the meanwhile, if organizations can understand their cryptographic strengths and weaknesses better, they should be able to address areas of weakness by upgrading to a better cryptographic methodology.

Dinesh also briefly mentioned that there are organizations that are still in denial about the threat, and they are putting themselves and their customers in a risky situation. Even where organizations have identified and understood the threat, their change cycle of 7 to 8 years could be a major hurdle in effecting firm-wide transformation to be quantum-proof.

Finally, one critical point that Dinesh made was about business resilience. As always, it is the *so what's* that matter. We may look at all this as a technology issue. However, when systems are breached and data is lost, businesses struggle to continue servicing their customers. Therefore, it is critical for businesses to get to a position where they are operationally resilient. It is the customers that matter when all is said and done. Technology is just a means to an end.

15

Quantum-Safe Blockchain

The thesis of this book revolves around exploring two technologies: quantum computing and Blockchain. I have touched upon the key concepts and the history of these two technologies. There were a few interviews and industry-focused chapters where I brought to light the practical applications of these technologies. This was to establish that, despite several challenges, these technologies have fundamental use cases.

We have established that these two technologies are here to stay. They may go through winters, where their relevance may be challenged. Yet, the most impactful technologies weather such storms and resurface as soon as they become relevant. Technologies could see low points due to limitations or a lack of ecosystem maturity. In the case of Blockchain, we touched upon the trilemma that highlighted that the technology is yet to scale. For instance, a completely decentralized ledger often struggles to demonstrate the throughput that today's payments infrastructure can accommodate easily.

In the case of quantum computing, there are challenges such as decoherence, where data is lost due to interactions between the qubits and their environment. It is early days for both these technologies and more needs to be done for mainstream adoption. However, the capability that lies beyond the limitations is what we highlighted earlier.

The "*so whats's?*" of both these technologies can't be disputed. They have use cases across different industries that could potentially create leapfrog moments. Technologies creating leapfrog effects impact the lives of millions of people in their target market. The invention of the PC, the internet, and smartphones to applications such as PayPal, M-Pesa, and Alipay have all affected lives of billions of people across the developed and the developing world.

We also discussed how the use cases between these two technologies are complementary. Quantum computing is mostly focused on the computing infrastructure and can also provide intelligence capabilities that are beyond today's classical computers. Blockchain on the other hand is a data integrity layer.

In a largely data-driven world, we need an infrastructure that can offer intelligence and simulation capabilities that can tap into the richness of the data. However, without a framework to ensure that the data being stored and used by these machines is of high data quality and integrity, all the intelligence would be of little use. Without the intelligence, high-integrity data can sit on a computer without being of much use too.

Therefore, we need both technologies to go mainstream to deal with the data challenges in the future. However, there is a catch. The two technologies are on a collision course. Cryptography is an integral part of both quantum computing and Blockchain. There is a potential scenario where the Blockchain solutions we have today will be obsolete as soon as quantum computers scale and become mainstream.

Therefore, despite the business case for these technologies, we may only see one of the two technologies being relevant in the future. That is a scenario that we could overcome though. Blockchain can still be relevant if it can overcome another technology barrier. This chapter is all about discussing the collision course between the technologies and exploring the solution to this scenario.

A race against time

The internet, despite its challenges, has largely worked well for us. It has been a major building block in helping economies across the world prosper. The cost of accessing the internet has fallen drastically across the world. For instance, in India alone, the number of people accessing mobile internet has grown from about 242 million in 2015 to 451 million at the end of 2019. Source: `https://www.statista.com/statistics/558610/number-of-mobile-internet-user-in-india/`

Mobile penetration has created leapfrog moments across the world in the past. Mobile internet penetration has taken it one step further. For instance, Africa was able to see mobile payments scale like never before through M-Pesa. This wouldn't have happened without mobile penetration. China took it one step further as mobile internet penetration led to a payments boom with Alipay and WeChat. These two firms contributed over 90% of the $40 trillion worth of mobile transactions in China.

In India, on the other hand, several new business models are being launched due to the spread of mobile internet. There are innovative apps that allow users in rural areas to perform day-to-day transactions using their regional language in a voice-based interface. These models are unheard of, especially in emerging markets. However, this growth comes at a cost. The explosion of the internet brings with it risks to cyber security.

Many parts of the world where the internet has managed to penetrate in the past few years have a massive lack of understanding and awareness of data privacy and data security. As a result, the growth we are seeing today might actually be a fertile land for the cyber wars of tomorrow. Most data on the internet that sits on servers and is locked down by today's security mechanisms is vulnerable to cyber-attacks.

This threat becomes a ticking time bomb when we introduce quantum computers into the mix. Quantum computers could spell disaster for data stored on the internet. Information exchange on the internet as we know today uses the **Rivest– Shamir–Adleman** (**RSA**) algorithm and **Elliptic-Curve Cryptography** (**ECC**). These algorithms are used to encode and decode information transmitted on the internet. These algorithms are public-key cryptographic techniques where the encryption key used to encode data is public, and the encryption key used to decode data is private.

Let's take a brief look at what each of these cryptography techniques involve, and touch upon the vulnerabilities they have in the quantum world.

The RSA algorithm

In a scenario where a message needs to be sent from Party A to Party B, A could just write the message on a piece of paper, and send it over to Party B. If the information is confidential and needs to be protected, Party A could jumble the message using an encryption key. As long as Party A and Party B have exchanged the keys beforehand, Party B can use the key to decrypt the message and read it. The method of encrypting and decrypting a message using the same private key is called symmetric key encryption.

But what if Party A and Party B haven't exchanged the key to decrypt the message beforehand? That is a scenario where asymmetric key encryption techniques like the RSA algorithm are quite relevant. In the RSA technique, A and B will have a key-pair each constituting a public and private key. The public keys are exchanged between A and B. Party A will use B's public key to encrypt their message and send it over to B. This encrypted message that's sent to the Party B can be decrypted only by using Party B's private key.

This has allowed RSA to be used in scenarios where the private key couldn't be shared between A and B beforehand. The RSA algorithm has been used in emails and **Virtual Private Networks (VPNs)** and can be seen in many browsers too. Despite several use cases on the internet, the RSA algorithm has been in the spotlight only recently.

The RSA algorithm was first developed by Ron Rivest, Adi Shamir, and Leonard Adleman in 1977 and is even named after them (Rivest, Shamir, Adleman). However, it was shelved then, as it was hard to understand the real-world applications at that time. In 1997, as the dot-com boom was taking shape, the RSA algorithm suddenly became relevant as internet-based businesses, emails, social media, and micro messages became commonplace.

The RSA algorithm fundamentally relies on the principle where an operation is relatively easy to compute in one direction, but the reverse is extremely resource-intensive. One of the key examples of such calculations is prime factoring. If I took two prime numbers, 997 and 667, we can easily arrive at 997*667 equals 674,969. However, the reverse is extremely hard. If we were asked to find the prime factors of 674,969, we would struggle to do it within reasonable time bounds due to the difficulty involved in the calculation and the amount of trial and error involved.

Algorithms that exhibit this property are called trapdoor functions. Identifying such algorithms is fundamental to creating a secure public key cryptography technique.

In the preceding example, if you were given one of the two factors and the result of 674,969, it would again make the operation simpler. In real-world RSA implementations, prime numbers are extremely long. For instance, RSA 1024 has 1,024 bits and could have numbers with up to 309 digits.

In a public-key cryptography technique, the difference between the ease of solving the problem in one direction to solving the problem in the other direction is important. For instance, with RSA the challenge has been that as prime factors have increased in size, the difficulty difference between computing the multiple on one end, and the difficulty in identifying the factors at the other end, has reduced. Due to the explosion of mobile internet, security mechanisms have had to get more resource-intensive too.

As a result, RSA is not viewed as a scalable solution, as it becomes more resource intensive as the prime factors become bigger. Apart from that, algorithms such as the quadratic sieve and general number field sieve have made it relatively easier to crack the prime number factoring challenge. We need other alternatives to RSA to have a scalable security solution. Let's now look at one of those, in the form of ECC.
Source: `https://www.comparitech.com/blog/information-security/rsa-encryption/`

ECC

ECC is an alternative that is starting to gain popularity recently. It is based on discrete logarithms in groups of points on an elliptic curve. The elliptic-curve algorithm can be explained using the following equation:

$$Y^2 = X^3 + aX + b$$

When we map the elliptic curve using the preceding equation, we get a chart that looks like a variant of the following curve:

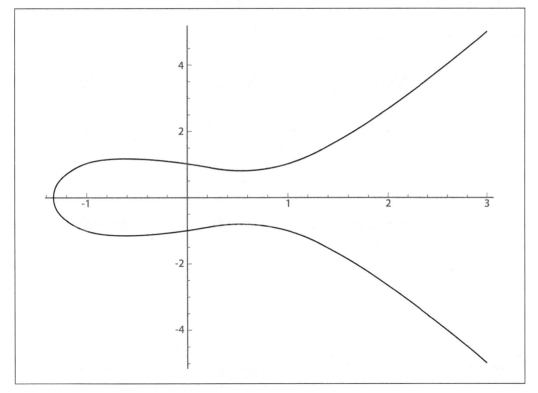

Figure 1: A plotted elliptic curve

The curve has a few special features, one of them being its horizontal symmetricity. The half of the curve that lies below the x axis can be described as the mirror image of the half that lies above the x axis. However, there is another property that is more relevant from a trapdoor function perspective.

The property can be explained by imagining a game of billiards played on a board with this curve on. If we were to shoot the ball between two points on the curve, it will necessarily strike the curve at a third point. The third point can be visually predicted using the shape of the curve.

However, if after a few (n) such shots from starting point A, the ball arrives at point B, for a new person who hasn't seen the game, it is hard to understand the number of shots even if point B and the starting point of the ball are known. Therefore, it would easy to get from point A to B if we knew n. However, it is hard to find n even if we knew A and B. This is a unique property of the elliptic-curve algorithm that makes it a good trapdoor function.

In a real-world representation of ECC, the general idea is to assign messages as values of X in the preceding equation to find Y. That would give us (X, Y) as the points on the curve. Therefore, a security mechanism using ECC will need a curve equation, a public point in the curve, and a prime number. The public point can be visualized in the billiards example as being shot to itself n times, where n becomes the private key.

According to a recent paper published done by European researchers, ECC provides better security compared to RSA. The paper considers the energy needed to break cryptographic algorithms and compares it with the energy required to boil water. In the comparison between RSA and ECC, to break the RSA 228-bit algorithm, we would need an amount of energy equivalent to that needed to boil a spoon of water. On the other hand, to break the 228-bit ECC key, we will need enough energy needed to boil all the water on earth. Source: `https://eprint.iacr.org/2013/635.pdf`

ECC is seen as a more energy-efficient alternative to RSA even for the encoders. The CPU and memory usage is more optimal too. However, RSA is more widely adopted. This is primarily due to the complexity involved in understanding ECC. ECC, when not understood well enough, can be implemented wrongly, which in effect could become a security vulnerability.

The potential applications of ECC are many. The US government has started deploying this security mechanism for internal communications. Apple iMessage, the WhatsApp messenger, and the Tor anonymity network use the **Elliptic-Curve Digital Signature Algorithm** (**ECDSA**) for secure interactions. The more relevant usage of elliptic curves in the context of this book is found in Bitcoin and Ethereum.

Now that we have briefly touched upon the RSA and ECC techniques to protect our data, let's examine why they become insecure when quantum computers become viable and mainstream.

Does quantum computing mean chaos?

So why is internet security, as it stands today, a ticking time bomb? Would there be chaos if quantum computing became mainstream, and what are the chances of that happening? These are the questions that have largely been troubling nation states worried about cyber warfare. CEOs of top banks and healthcare firms dealing with sensitive client data are also worried about data security.

Let's quickly look at where the quantum computing world is and why it might be a threat to global data security. In 1994, Peter Shor presented two quantum algorithms. One that could factor large prime numbers and another that could compute discrete logarithms in a finite field of prime order. The former could be a threat to the RSA method, and the latter would address elliptic curves.

Shor essentially showed that almost all public key encryption techniques we use today can be cracked using a quantum Fourier attack. He used quantum Fourier sampling to find the periodicity of the mathematical object. This in turn allowed him to solve the factorization problem.

The threat of quantum computers has been there for the past 25 years. Therefore, theoretically, quantum computing algorithms could indeed cause havoc to the world of data security as we know it today.

However, in 2015 researchers identified that it would take a billion qubits to crack the RSA 2,048-bit signatures. This number (1 billion qubits) was revised to 20 million in 2019. The number of qubits was attributed to the disproportionate number of qubits that were needed for error correction in a quantum computer. The noise in a quantum computer is a difficult problem that must be overcome before we can start thinking of it going mainstream. Source: `https://cacm.acm.org/news/237303-how-quantum-computer-could-break-2048-bit-rsa-encryption-in-8-hours/fulltext`

Despite that, in 2012 a 4-qubit quantum computer was used to factor the number 143, and two years later a similar-sized quantum computer was able to factor the number 56,153. Therefore, the capabilities of quantum computers are getting better at a very fast pace. In December 2019, Craig Gidney from Google and Martin Ekera from the KTH Royal Institute of Technology published a paper titled *How to factor 2,048-bit RSA integers in 8 hours using 20 million qubits*.

Suddenly, the problem of cracking the RSA 2,048-bit numbers became 5 times easier. The previous estimated requirement to solve the problem using quantum computers was 1 billion qubits. Gidney and Ekera used a mathematical technique called modular exponentiation and demonstrated that it was a more efficient way to perform factorization. They show in their research paper that when factoring 2,048-bit RSA integers, their construction's space-time volume is a hundredfold less than previous implementations. Source: `https://arxiv.org/abs/1905.09749`

Some of Google's quantum supremacy claims may have to be taken with a pinch of salt. Google's paper on quantum supremacy was leaked by NASA in 2019 and was later followed by an official Google press release. During that release, Google claimed that their 53 qubit Sycamore chip can perform calculations that would take 10,000 years for the most powerful classical computer to compute.

IBM refuted this with a scientific response. They calculated that the entire quantum state vector of Google's Sycamore chip can be stored within Summit – the world's largest supercomputer, which has 250 petabytes of storage. The fact that classical computers have to resort to disk storage to come close to the abilities of basic quantum computers is illustrative of the gulf between the two technologies.

IBM also showed that the classical supercomputer could simulate the Sycamore chip in approximately 2.5 days and not 10,000 years as Google claimed. The resource efficiency that Google had managed to achieve was indeed great, but perhaps quantum computers are yet to become as great as they are hyped to be.

Another recent publication by Microsoft's Quantum team claimed that implementing Shor's algorithm with the right mix of algorithmic tricks could break RSS and ECC more efficiently. They implemented their algorithms for ECC standards set by the **National Institute of Standards and Technology (NIST)**, a unit of the US Commerce Department. Source: `https://www.microsoft.com/en-us/research/wp-content/uploads/2017/09/1706.06752.pdf`

The publication revealed that their algorithms could use 2,330 logical qubits and Toffoli gates to break the NIST standardized curve P-256. Similarly, they were able to show that Shor's factoring algorithm needed 6,146 qubits to break the 3,072-bit RSA keys.

Toffoli gates are ideal for building up large-scale reversible circuits that have thousands of qubits and billions of gates, as they work in both classical and quantum environments. The gates sit between the high-level, abstract algorithm and the low-level, assembler-like instruction set that will ultimately drive the quantum computer. You can find out more at `https://cloudblogs.microsoft.com/quantum/2018/05/02/the-quantum-computing-effect-on-public-key-encryption/`.

As a result of efforts from Google, IBM, and Microsoft, there is a good possibility that quantum computers will become more practical in the near future. Error correction could become more efficient, and we will need fewer qubits for computation. With the advent of better algorithms making quantum computers more real, there is a genuine threat to RSA and ECC-based security. Both these cryptography techniques are the fundamental security mechanisms that the internet, governments, and many financial services firms currently rely on.

I hope that addresses the point that the security mechanisms we currently use with the internet, bank accounts, credit cards, governments' confidential data, and messaging could all be put under great threat with the emergence of quantum computing. A hacker could record message today, and in 10 years or so, when quantum computers could decrypt the message, read it. It may not be a major risk for credit card information, but government and defense secrets are more sensitive to such issues.

The threat is amplified by the fact that many key nation states that are hoping to use quantum breakthroughs for cyber wars and wouldn't necessarily want to reveal their advances in quantum technology. Therefore, they may be ahead of our benchmark information from IBM, Google or Microsoft. Let's now look at the different quantum-safe cryptography techniques that could potentially go mainstream to make our data quantum-proof.

Quantum-Safe Cryptography

Every problem is an opportunity to innovate. Shor's algorithm was based on quantum Fourier sampling to crack asymmetric cryptography algorithms. Therefore, cryptographic systems that would be quantum-safe need to be immune to quantum Fourier sampling as well as other classical and quantum attacks. In April 2016, NIST launched the **Post-Quantum Cryptography (PQC)** Standardization challenge. The mission is to find a PQC technique that could potentially protect our data from the threat of quantum computers.

Out of 69 applications accepted to the challenge, 26 were chosen as semi-finalists in Jan 2019. The objective of NIST's efforts is not just to find a PQC technique that works on paper. They also want to make sure that the technique is practical in the world of mobile and tablet devices and **Internet of Things (IoT)** networks. In the world where machines transmit data to one another, securing them with low resource consumption is essential.

Let's look at the different categories of cryptographic techniques that have been submitted to NIST. It is important to ensure that these techniques are not just theoretically immune to quantum computing but are also practically feasible at scale. As discussed, these protocols have to be capable of dealing with Shor's algorithms. Let's look at lattice-based cryptography and code-based cryptography techniques.

Lattice-Based Cryptography

Lattice-Based Cryptography (LBC) is perhaps the most researched type of PQC. A lattice is nothing but a grid of points that stretches out to infinity. It is not possible to represent a lattice using a computer due to its finite resources. Therefore, we use something called a basis that is a collection of points or vectors that help represent a lattice.

LBC relies on the difficulty in solving a geometric problem in a multi-dimensional lattice. For instance, the geometric problem to solve could be the **Shortest Vector Problem (SVP)** where we need to identify a good basis with short vectors. This unfortunately is not easy in lattices where we could have thousands of dimensions.

The other common LBC problem to solve is the **Closest Vector Problem (CVP)** where a point P is given and the closest point needs to be identified. LBC techniques seem to be the most popular PQC techniques for several reasons.

Lattices have been researched for over 200 years. As a result, their mathematical properties are well understood. The mathematicians who were instrumental in developing the understanding of lattices had no idea about quantum computers. Despite that, their work offers insights that can help with LBC.

Lattices offer a versatile method of developing cryptography protocols like never before. As a result, they are the most studied and researched cryptographic field. Of the 82 applications that the NIST received for the PQC standardization challenge, 28 of them were lattice-based.

Unlike RSA encryption, which can be categorized as a worst-case reduction technique, LBC has average case reduction. This means that on average the LBC techniques are secure unless every instance of the lattice problem is easily solvable. In an RSA encryption technique, if the numbers used have certain number-theoretical properties, they are easy to crack. Therefore, we need to ensure that is not the case during key generation.

In the case of LBC, we only need to choose the parameter size and generate the keys. On top of being more secure, they are less resource hungry. For instance, the encryption process of an LBC-based technique (R-LWE) on an 8-bit IoT device finishes in 2 million cycles. RSA 1024 takes 23 million cycles more to run the encryption. Source: `https://arxiv.org/pdf/1805.04880.pdf`

This makes LBC quite relevant for the IoT world we live in. It can also be useful for mobile and tablet devices that need resource-efficient encryption techniques that are quantum-proof. While the LBC algorithms can run faster than RSA encryption, they are still slower than **Code-Based Cryptography (CBC)**. Let's review this category of post-quantum cryptography.

Code-Based Cryptography

CBC relies on the difficulty of decoding a general linear block code. The code could belong to families such as Goppa codes or quasi-cyclic codes. The McEliece algorithm, which is an asymmetric encryption scheme, was shown to be insolvable using quantum Fourier sampling. No polynomial-time quantum algorithm has been known to decode a linear block code.

The McEliece algorithm was first developed over 40 years ago but wasn't as popular as RSA or ECC. This was largely due to the key size being huge (0.5 MB vs 0.1 for RSA and 0.02 for ECC typically). However, it has come to spotlight now due to the need to make cryptography quantum-proof.

The advantage of CBC is that it is typically more performant than the LBC method from a computational efficiency perspective. However, when choosing the right cryptographic technique for a platform or an application, it is important to look at factors such as key size, resource consumption, computational efficiency, signature length, and confidence of security.

Both these techniques (CBC and LBC) have their pros and cons. Their applications will vary based on the context of usage. For instance, in an IoT environment, where we will need to have smaller keys and relatively better resource efficiencies, lattice-based cryptography may be a better solution. Therefore, a "horses for courses" approach (the right tool for the right job) needs to be adopted, rather than viewing one technique as a silver bullet to keep our data safe in a post-quantum world.

Much like the NIST challenge, the European Commission has funded a research consortium of eleven universities and firms with 3.9 million euros. The initiative is called PQCrypto. The ambition is to identify PQC techniques over three years. Out of the 69 submissions to NIST, 22 were designed or co-designed by members of PQCrypto. Source: `https://pqcrypto.eu.org/nist.html`

Despite all these hopeful efforts, there is also the realization that any new cryptosystem takes 15 to 20 years to be ready for scalable industrial application. Therefore, the scientific community is up against this challenge to ensure all our data is protected. While there is a wider problem around data security on the internet in a post-quantum world, we also have a specific security concern with Blockchain applications.

Blockchain Cryptography

Many Blockchain use public key cryptography. They are asymmetric in nature as the sender and the receiver each have a public and a private key. As discussed earlier, in an asymmetric encryption scheme the message encrypted with the receiver's public key can be decrypted with their private key. For someone without the private key, it is extremely hard to decrypt the message, therefore creating a trapdoor encryption mechanism.

The Blockchain security mechanism depends on the hardness of this trapdoor mathematical function. Many cryptocurrencies and Blockchain use ECC. This includes the Ethereum and Bitcoin blockchains, as the 256-bit elliptic-curve key is as secure as a 3,072-bit RSA key. Smaller keys of the elliptic curves are more resource efficient as they need less storage.

We discussed how Blockchain cryptography works in detail in *Chapter 1, Introduction to Quantum Computing and Blockchain*. Therefore, I will just briefly touch upon this topic to refresh your memory. The trapdoor functions, otherwise called **One-Way Functions (OWF)**, are fundamental to Blockchain security. Users of the Blockchain create digital signatures using these functions that can be easily checked with the right key.

A cryptocurrency could be viewed as a chain of digital signatures. Every digital signature has a backward and a forward link, in that it signs the hash of the previous block and the public key of the new block. This can be treated as a handshake mechanism as ownership of a coin is transferred from one person to another all using digital signatures.

The transaction history on the Bitcoin network, for instance, is represented in blocks. Every block can hold multiple transactions. To add a block to the ledger, a mathematical condition needs to be met. The entire network keeps calculating to arrive at the solution for the mathematical condition (as per ECC), and once that is met, the block is added to the network.

Therefore, when someone wants to hack the Blockchain, it is not just a single transaction that they need to hack, but a whole chain of signatures. The brute force methods to hack these signatures would just not be a viable solution due to the resources needed to do so.

There are various methods that have been tried to hack a Blockchain, and some have been successful too. We discussed this in *Chapter 1, Introduction to Quantum Computing and Blockchain*. Some of the key types of Blockchain attacks are as follows:

- Smart contract attacks
- Transaction verification attacks
- Mining pool attacks
- Network attacks
- Wallet attacks

All of these types of attacks on Blockchains are well-documented. More types of attacks are being identified and understood. As per GitHub, there are over 30 different types of smart contract vulnerabilities that can be exploited by hackers of Blockchain.

Sybil attacks and Finney attacks are types of transaction verification attacks. Sybil attacks occur when an entire network is hacked by the attacker. In a Finney attack, the attacker mines a block, send the coins to someone willing to buy unconfirmed transactions for some goods, and then goes back to the network to confirm the transaction and gets the money back.

Network attacks involves a standard **Distributed Denial of Service (DDoS)**, where a server is brought down by multiple requests taking its resources. A wallet attack involves using social engineering against the victim to attack their wallet. Blockchain hackers have already identified several ways to tap into the vulnerabilities of the framework.

However, most of them do not involve solving the encryption with the ease that the receiver of the transaction would. This is where quantum computing could prove to be lethal to Blockchain networks that rely on encryption techniques like ECC. Cracking ECC in Blockchains using quantum technologies could result in broken keys that keep assets safe. Therefore, hackers have higher incentives to target Blockchain networks, as they have economic value stored digitally.

There are Blockchains such as **QRL (Quantum-Resistant Ledger)** and IOTA that were developed using PQC. However, the majority of Blockchain applications still use ECC, which is not quantum-safe. Very much like the efforts of NIST to identify a quantum-proof cryptographic technique for the internet, we will need an industry-wide upgrade of Blockchains to keep the quantum threat at bay.

Let's now look at some of the techniques that can make Blockchains more secure in the post-quantum world. Some of the techniques being used or explored by Blockchain are as follows:

- **eXtended Merkle Signature Scheme (XMSS)**
- **Blockchain Post-Quantum Signatures (BPQS)**
- **Winternitz One-Time Signatures (W-OTA)**, as used by IOTA

As I explain these three methods, it may become obvious that these are all interrelated techniques and have a lot in common. However, each of these techniques have their own applications they are more suitable for.

Security in a post-quantum world

Cryptographic schemes are more secure as the hardness of the problem to be solved increases. In a post-quantum world, the ECC method becomes easily solvable for reasons we saw earlier. One of the alternatives that can be used to make encryption quantum-proof is using hash-based signature schemes. Let's look at XMSS, which uses hash functions.

eXtended Merkle Signature Scheme (XMSS)

XMSS is one of the hash-based signature schemes that is being explored by QRL. There are two key aspects of XMSS that makes it a good candidate for post-quantum encryption. It uses a hash function, and it follows a **One-Time Signature (OTS)** system. It is also based on the Merkle signature scheme. The Merkle signature scheme was developed by Relph Merkle in 1970s and is quantum-resistant. As the Merkle signature scheme relies on secure hash functions, they can be categorized as PQC.

The public key in the Merkle signature scheme can only be used to sign a limited number of messages. In the case of the OTS methodology, it will typically be used to sign only one message. Therefore, on a Blockchain that follows OTS using the Merkle signature scheme, a public and a private key-pair needs to be generated for every signature. The public key in XMSS is generated by a **Pseudo Random Function (PRF)**.

The following diagram of a Merkle tree should be able to bring its workings to life. In a Merkle tree there are typically n key-pairs generated, where n is a power of two. The top node compresses all the public keys through a concatenation of hash functions applied on to its child nodes.

In this scheme, when a sender sends a signature, it would contain the signature, the public key at the leaf node of the tree, the index of the leaf node sent, and an authentication path. This detail will prove that the key-pair sent is part of the Merkle tree. For instance, in the following tree diagram, if we were to use the key-pair with the leaf node pk_2, the sender will publish the following:

- The signature
- The leaf node (public key) – pk_2
- The index of the published key-pair – 2
- An authentication path of hash functions – h_3, h_8, and h_{13} in this case

The receiver will use this information to then compute the path from pk_2 to h_{14}.

Source: https://pdfs.semanticscholar.org/f38c/562c21fa1a94871e5f577669f7c4b9520632.pdf

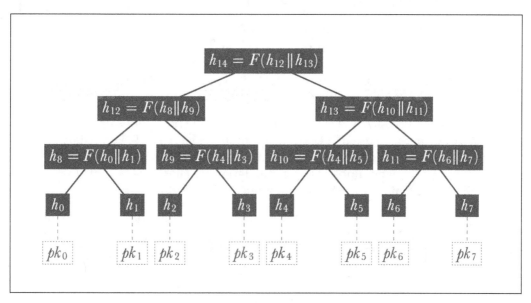

Figure 2: A Merkle tree with 2^3 OTS key pairs

The OTS scheme combined with the hashing function makes the Blockchain more secure. Even if the hacker finds the private key, they are not able to break into the Blockchain as the previous transactions can't be forged. This is because the previous transactions would have used a different key-pair.

The private key in XMSS holds an index that is updated every time a signature is generated. In effect it holds information about the next unused OTS key-pair. A signature in this scheme holds the index of the OTS key-pair and the path on the Merkle tree. By holding the position of the nodes in the tree, the verifier can identify the root node. From the root node, the verifier can then compute the public key. If the public key matches, then signature is valid.

Despite the secure hash function and using the OTS to make it even more secure, XMSS has its downsides. The keys are large, and if the trees grow in size, it can be resource intensive for small devices to use this technique. Source: `https://eprint.iacr.org/2018/658.pdf`

Let's now take a look at the BPQS technique, which is being explored as an alternative for XMSS.

Blockchain Post Quantum Signatures (BPQS)

BPQS has been specifically designed to make it resource efficient while generating the key and signature and performing verification. These were all pain points in XMSS. BPQS is a variant of XMSS and it uses one authentication path instead of a tree. Therefore, it can be visualized as a chain of hash functions instead of a tree.

The BPQS can behave like an OTS scheme but can easily scale to multiple signatures too. Although the OTS scheme is viewed as secure, the applications of Blockchain can often necessitate the use of a key-pair for multiple signatures. For instance, if a charity is publishing its public key to receive funds, it may want to keep it for at least as long as a given fund-raising campaign runs. Therefore, despite the fact that BPQS is a variant of XMSS, it can theoretically support few time signatures.

However, BPQS is seen as subset of XMSS that focuses on fast signatures. It still uses an OTS methodology (W-OTS) like XMSS. Therefore, instead of visualizing it as a full-fledged Merkle tree like in XMSS, we can perhaps visualize it as a chain of 2-leaf Merkle trees. The following diagram helps to visualize the XMSS tree chain:

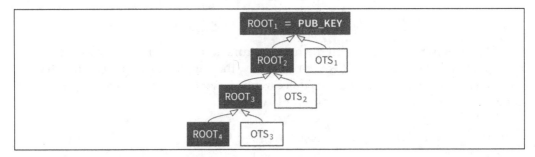

Figure 3: Visualization of the XMSS tree chain Source: `https://eprint.iacr.org/2018/658.pdf`

Due to its properties, the BPQS method can be used in applications that sit at the convergence of Blockchain and the IoT. Let's now look at the W-OTS scheme that is being used by IOTA.

Winternitz One-Time Signatures (W-OTS)

We discussed that the XMSS uses an OTS scheme that is a variant of the W-OTS scheme. BPQS on the other hand uses W-OTS. The W-OTS is being used in one of the better known Blockchain applications, IOTA. IOTA is a distributed ledger technology developed by the IOTA foundation that uses the W-OTS methodology to make itself quantum-robust.

IOTA bundles up its transactions that are related or linked. The bundle hash is normalized to create a private key and a part of the key is revealed. Therefore, a key can be used only once to withdraw a given value. The private key goes through several operations to break it down into several fragments and is then processed through a hash function. A hash function called the kerl hash function is used to create the signature.

At the other end, validation of the signature of a transaction is performed by using the bundle hash and the signature that is sent. The signature is processed in the reverse order to arrive at the fragments of the private key. This is then put through the hash function to arrive at the address. Source: `https://docs.iota.org/docs/getting-started/0.1/clients/signatures?q=QUantum&highlights=quantum`

IOTA claim that their method is quantum-proof, and the complexity involved in the creation of the signature and validating it perhaps reflects this. To me, however, all this highlights the fact that we need real sophistication to combat the quantum threat.

We have now looked at three different types of quantum-proof cryptography that are used by Blockchain applications. However, these are the exceptions. The typical Blockchain developer creating an application using the Ethereum developer's framework wouldn't really have any idea of the quantum threat.

This needs to change. Every Blockchain developer needs to understand the impact that quantum computers could have on the value network they are creating for the world to use. Unlike the internet, which is more of an information network, a Blockchain can be used to hold assets and valuables. If it gets hacked, there is more at stake. Therefore, an understanding of network security is a basic aspect that every person designing and developing a Blockchain application must have.

It also goes to show that, much like the internet, where data security will need to be upgraded for post-quantum period, we will need Blockchains to be quantum-proof. This is especially true for ecosystems like Ethereum, which are used to build Blockchain applications across the world.

Every organization that is evaluating a Blockchain suite to create applications for their customers will need to ensure that they are quantum-proof. All these efforts will ensure that only the quantum-proof Blockchain platforms gain traction for industrial purposes. This will cause some attrition initially, but platforms that quickly adapt would soon be winners as a result of the course correction.

Conclusion

It is not just Blockchain that is on a collision course with quantum computing. It is almost the entire internet that is at risk. Quantum computing is a serious threat, not just to Blockchain platforms, but to all platforms using techniques like RSA and ECC. However, there are solutions in the form of quantum-proof cryptography for both the internet and the Blockchain industry. Adopting these techniques would necessitate careful consideration of the application and context in which these techniques will be deployed.

I must admit that this chapter has been quite a technical one. However, I have tried to simplify the narrative around cryptography as much as possible. I have covered the key cryptographic techniques, RSA and ECC, and their applications across the internet and Blockchain solutions.

I then touched upon how and why they are at risk once quantum computers go mainstream. There is still a lot of hype around when that will be. Some say it is 2027, some argue it could be 2031. Google, IBM, and Microsoft have their own takes on how soon quantum supremacy could happen. Google is also known to be experimenting with LBC in their Chrome browser in preparation for the quantum era.

I have discussed the various techniques including LBC and CBC that can offer quantum-proofing for the internet. It is essential that the outcomes from the NIST challenge are not taken lightly and that there is a top-down global initiative to move to a quantum-proof internet.

We discussed the Blockchain vulnerabilities in a post-quantum world, and why it is imperative for Blockchain applications to be quantum-proof. The Blockchain industry is going through a winter at the moment. I believe the industry needs to move toward quantum-proofing before it can re-emerge and start being relevant again. There are solutions such as XMSS and BPQS that Blockchain platforms can leverage to become more secure.

In summary, despite the threat from quantum computers, there are solutions that the Blockchain industry can and should adopt to stay relevant. Despite the possibility of a collision between the two technologies, there are genuine opportunities for them to co-exist. The Blockchain industry needs to adapt to stay relevant in the post-quantum era.

In this chapter, we delved into the details of how information and value networks need to adapt to the post-quantum era. In the next chapter, we will look at how nation states are positioning themselves to tap into the informational advantage that quantum technologies could give them.

16
Nation States and Cyberwars

We live in an age where data can be a more powerful weapon than an atom bomb. Data is being used to win elections in the biggest economies of the world. Nation states are looking at deploying cyberwars to attack each other tactically and strategically. As a result, data protection of national intelligence and defense secrets is becoming extremely important.

According to a report released by the **International Data Corporation (IDC)**, the data that we are creating is expected to reach 175 zettabytes by 2025. A zettabyte is a billion terabytes, or 10^{21} bytes. Much of this data is expected to be on cloud infrastructure. Therefore, we will need to ensure that this entire infrastructure is cyber secure.

We saw in *Chapter 3*, *The Data Economy*, how the rise of data creation has led to several technology paradigms. For instance, AI finally became relevant and viable after going through several winters. Thanks to the success of the internet, the network of data, we have Blockchain, the internet of value. The rise of machines interacting with one another couldn't have happened without the internet.

The Internet of Things paradigm is perhaps one of the biggest challenges for cyber specialists. Of the 175 zettabytes that we are likely to have created by 2025, 90 zettabytes can be attributed to the interaction between machines. Cyber security sophistication across the internet of machines is still in its infancy.

In this chapter, we will discuss how various technology paradigms have created vulnerabilities for cyber criminals to exploit. We will look at how quantum technologies can be a threat as well as a savior in this context. In doing so, we will understand how the superpowers of the world turn to technology superiority to ensure that they dominate the cyberwars.

Let's begin by exploring how growth over the last decade, aided by the mobile internet, has created vulnerabilities for cyber criminals to exploit.

When growth can be dangerous

Data does not get to the cloud all by itself. We need telecoms providers to act as the plumbing between points where data is created and where it is stored. Telecoms infrastructure as a whole also has to be protected from cybercrime. Several parts of the world are embracing the mobile internet on account of the telecoms infrastructure.

For instance, in India alone, between 2015 and 2019, over 275 million people gained access to the mobile internet. While the internet infrastructure was mostly created in the last three decades, telecoms has evolved itself into what it is today, and that too at a rapid pace. The infrastructure to keep telecoms networks cyber proof is lacking in most parts of the world.

An explosion in internet users across Africa and Asia has created leapfrog moments like never before. 2.8 billion people across these two continents were connected to the web as of Q2 2019. This will create numerous opportunities in financial services, healthcare, lifestyle, e-commerce, education, and several other aspects of life.

Research carried out by Ericsson revealed that just a doubling of internet speeds can add 0.3% to GDP growth. However, all this growth comes at a cost. Most of these rural areas lack awareness of cyber security and the social engineering techniques that exist in the world of cybercrime.

For instance, in early 2020, it was revealed that North Korean hackers had managed to breach the Kudankulam nuclear power plant in India. This plant is less than 80 miles away from my hometown in India. Many parts of the country only acquired mobile internet access within the last 5 years, and an awareness of cyber security is low, if not non-existent.

Recently, Amazon's CEO, Jeff Bezos, was hacked through the WhatsApp account of the Crown Prince of Saudi Arabia. Therefore, even the most cyber-aware citizens of the world are not immune. If cyber criminals can successfully target the world's richest man who is running one of the largest technology firms, then a farmer in a rural part of Africa wouldn't stand a chance. If the farmer is on a Blockchain that tracks his transactions, that Blockchain is vulnerable, too.

We live in a world where geo-political wars are now fought on cyber grounds. When an Iranian official was recently killed by American drones, the retaliation was expected to be through cyber attacks.

Apart from the penetration of mobile internet and the Internet of Things, which constitute potential routes for hackers, edge computing could be another technology paradigm that needs to be well supported in terms of cyber security frameworks. In the edge computing world, we have more data and business logic sitting on the client. In a mobile internet-first world, this could mean that mobiles would be more intelligent, and the interaction with the cloud would be more selective.

Therefore, mobile users will need to ensure that they are very aware of the apps that they download and use on their phone. As edge computing becomes more of a norm than it is today, it could become the wild west for cyber criminals. Just imagine if IoT devices started interacting on the edge. There is a lot of data flow in the network of devices, without the central cloud infrastructure.

This opens up the cyber security world to a plethora of new issues. With all these technology paradigms evolving almost on a daily basis, it offers new opportunities for cyber criminals to take control. Leading countries across the world are investing billions in technology R&D to ensure that they stay ahead in the war game. A technology breakthrough that can result in a data advantage is better than a breakthrough in nuclear technology these days.

Having provided a brief overview of contemporary and future cyber security issues, let's focus on talking about the growth in emerging markets and how that could be a major blind spot for cyber security.

Fertile grounds

In order to understand the criticality of cyber security across the world, it is important to set the context of the discussion. The last three decades have most certainly been an incredible period for the world of data innovation. During this period, perhaps, we have innovated ways to create and exchange data and value, but perhaps have failed to innovate sufficiently to protect the data.

We saw how the evolution of the ARPANET led to the rise of the internet in *Chapter 3, The Data Economy*. The internet most certainly laid the foundations for a flurry of internet-based applications and business models that were largely data driven. Search engines, social media, and messaging apps became commonplace:

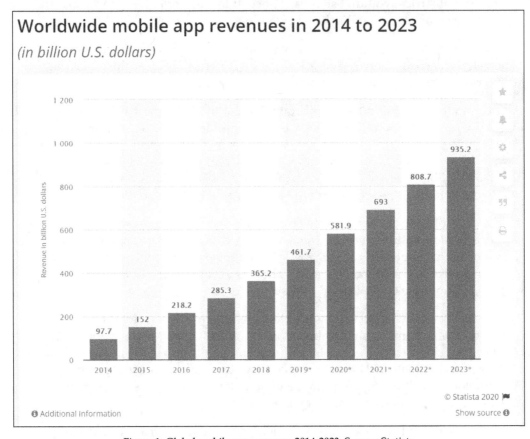

Figure 1: Global mobile app revenue, 2014-2023. Source: Statista

We also saw a rise in ecosystems led by Apple and Google. Mobile phones became the personal computers we would carry in our pockets and replaced devices such as music players and gaming consoles. The mobile apps market as of 2019 was $461 billion and is expected to be just short of a trillion dollars by 2023. The preceding chart shows the extent of this growth.

Until about 2010, most of these developments were mostly noticeable in the developed economies of the world. Thanks to mobile penetration, it was perhaps in the past 10 years when mobile-based businesses reached the rural population of the emerging world.

M-Pesa in Africa was perhaps the first model to emerge across the emerging world, where telecoms providers and mobile phones came together to create a scalable business. Little did we know then how impactful mobile phones could be across different walks of life in the developed world.

However, M-Pesa was a perfect case study for several organizations across the world to take note of. That was the beginning of a massive wave of inclusion across Africa, Asia, and Latin America that followed, powered by the mobile internet. In all these cases, the first step was mobile penetration, followed by internet penetration.

M-Pesa's leapfrog moment in Africa inspired a wave of innovation in China. Alibaba and Tencent unleashed businesses that were leveraging the sudden rise in internet penetration in the country. Alibaba's payment arm, Alipay, took over from PayPal in 2013 as the world's largest mobile payment platform.

In the following 5 years, it would record growth the likes of which had never been seen before. Alipay grew to 608 million monthly active users by 2019. In 2019, the size of mobile payments in China was $40 trillion, over 90% of which was on either Alipay or Tencent's WeChat platforms. Alibaba's Singles' Day in 2019 saw $38 billion in sales in comparison to US Black Friday and Cyber Monday sales of $16 billion. The growth in China due to mobile internet penetration has resulted in consumerism never before seen. This has inspired growth measures in other parts of Asia.

We have been seeing new trends in India and South-East Asia in the past 2 to 3 years. In India, growth was catalyzed by three key factors.

Mukesh Ambani, the richest man in Asia, kick-started a mobile internet revolution in the country through Reliance Jio. Within 3 years of launching Jio, 200 million people across rural parts of the country obtained internet access. As per a McKinsey report on Digital India, by 2018, there were 560 million mobile internet users in the country. Source: `https://www.mckinsey.com/~/media/McKinsey/Business%20Functions/ McKinsey%20Digital/Our%20Insights/Digital%20India%20Technology%20 to%20transform%20a%20connected%20nation/MGI-Digital-India-Report- April-2019.ashx`

The second reason behind the growth in India is the policy and government-driven infrastructure surrounding identities, digital banking, and payments. The digital economy in the country was boosted by the demonetization efforts in December 2016, when the government banned currency notes of certain denominations. This happened in conjunction with the launch of a biometric card known as "Aadhaar."

Over 1.1 billion Indians have an Aadhaar card. Getting an identity solution in place has led to digital financial inclusion like never before. This also coincided with the government-backed payment infrastructure called **Unified Payments Infrastructure (UPI)**. The following chart highlights the rise of internet users in India:

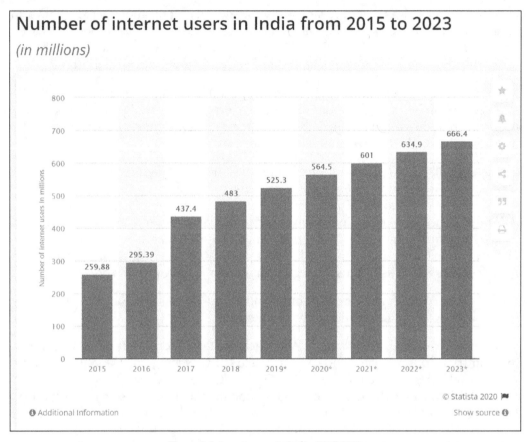

Figure 2: Internet users in India, 2015-2023

The third, and perhaps most interesting, reason for this growth is the fact that technology giants across the world are viewing India as the final frontier. For instance, Amazon and Walmart have taken over India's e-commerce market to keep China's Alibaba in check. Alibaba, however, owns more than 50% of India's payments market through Paytm, while Walmart's acquisition of PhonePe in 2018 has seen its share of the payments market rise to 42% in under 2 years.

Recently, I was having a debate with the CEO of my portfolio company on data security and privacy in India. He was of the opinion that people in regions such as India, South-East Asia, and Africa are very conscious of data privacy and security. I argued that the lady selling flowers on a cart, outside a temple in India using a QR code and a Paytm application, doesn't care or think about data security. She only cares about money reaching her bank account and assumes that the payment technology is safe and wouldn't let her down.

Why are these developments relevant in the discussion of cyber security? The mobile internet across the world has given rise to new business models that make the common man vulnerable to cybercrime like never before. People who never had any prior knowledge of technology devices have moved to smartphones, mobile internet, payment wallets, QR codes, and mobile transactions, and all within a 5-10 year period.

There is a serious lack of awareness of cyber risks accompanying this furious rate of growth across the globe. The internet is no longer just an information network. With e-commerce and payment apps becoming ubiquitous, the internet has evolved into a wealth network. We therefore need a framework supported by technology to protect these people who have embraced innovation in the last decade.

We have discussed how growth around human-led communication and transactions on the mobile internet can create new cyber risks. Let's now look at how the internet of machines can create vulnerabilities.

Age of the machine

We have discussed different technology paradigms that are potentially making the world open for cyber criminals. However, more than 70% of the data that is going to be created in the next 5 years is going to come from machines and communication between them. This can create major challenges for data security as the Internet of Things ecosystem is at a nascent stage in its understanding of cyber risks.

The growth of AI and the Internet of Things has given rise to a new theme in the field of robotics. Machines powered by intelligence like never before are starting to take over monotonous jobs that were previously performed by human beings. Social media often comes to life when a statistic on how soon humans will lose their jobs to machines is released.

Machines certainly have a genuine place in the future of work: technology really does make it easier for us humans when the task at hand involves something like going through thousands of pages of text. During my days at PwC, we were exploring the use of AI to help us review thousands of pages of regulatory and legal text and provide insights in relation to key strategic questions.

Amazon and Alibaba have deployed robots in their warehouses to make their logistics more efficient. We also understood from Dave Snelling from Fujitsu that their quantum annealers were powering the robots at BMW. Therefore, there are use cases where machines can definitely perform better than humans. However, I often refute hyped social media claims about machines taking over because I believe we can beat the machines by simply being more human.

Despite all these technological developments, we are still quite some distance away from general AI. For machines to be empathetic, and to employ discretion in making decisions in fields such as healthcare or financial services, this scenario is still several years away. That is where humans will remain relevant in the future of work for the foreseeable future.

The rise of machines in our day-to-day lives has increased our reliance on them. Just a couple of days back, I had an issue with my life insurance premium because my Apple Watch had failed to sync with my phone. The syncing process was important for my insurance provider to receive details of my fitness regime and price my insurance premium for the month.

This is more noticeable at scale in manufacturing economies. In the US, there are 2 robots for 100 human workers in manufacturing. This ratio is highest in South Korea, where there are 7.1 robots for 100 human workers in manufacturing. This ratio is expected to skyrocket through this decade. Therefore, machines are here to stay. The following chart from Statista shows the rise of machines across the industrialized economies of the world:

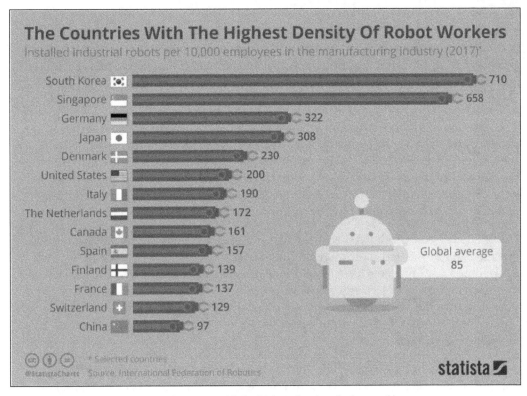

The Countries With The Highest Density Of Robot Workers

Installed industrial robots per 10,000 employees in the manufacturing industry (2017)*

South Korea	710
Singapore	658
Germany	322
Japan	308
Denmark	230
United States	200
Italy	190
The Netherlands	172
Canada	161
Spain	157
Finland	139
France	137
Switzerland	129
China	97

Global average
85

* Selected countries
@StatistaCharts Source: International Federation of Robotics

statista

Figure 3: Countries with the highest density of robot workers

The rise of machines and the Internet of Things have opened up new possibilities. I am able to track the consumption of electricity per device in my home. Every device emits signals in terms of usage, which is then captured by an intelligent machine. This machine learns from the patterns in these signals to warn me if my washing machine is wearing out, or if my dishwasher needs servicing.

Even the printers we use these days have a mechanism to order their own ink. We are reliant on our mobile phones sending the correct data to the correct service providers to ensure that our lives continue without any disruptions. I recently came across an AI application that powers smart speakers to fill my supermarket basket and order it. Self-driving cars are another important use case at the convergence of Internet of Things and AI.

The data age has come to a point where the Internet of Things' infrastructure produces data across all walks of life. The data captured using this technology is then stored in a cloud. Blockchain can bring integrity to this data infrastructure and has the ability to ensure it is shared with the right stakeholders. AI can exploit this data and provide insights to make all our lives easier. We are reliant on all these technologies to keep going. However, they also have their dark sides.

In 2019, Facebook announced that they had shut down their AI initiative after the machines had invented their own language to communicate with each other. We are perhaps getting into a territory that we have so far only known and seen in movies. The Internet of Things network is notorious for the lack of cyber security infrastructure. The **Bitcoin Gold (BTG)** Blockchain was hit by a 51% attack in January 2019. $70k worth of double spending were reported on Blockchain as a result of this attack.

Another key technology paradigm that has emerged in the last 5 years is edge computing. Computer engineers would agree that architecture is cyclical, like fashion. In the 1990s and early 2000, we had a lot of applications that were installed on a pc or laptop. They were using client server interactions, where there was a thick client (Pc-installed) communicating with a centralized server.

Over the last 15 years, with the advent of cloud computing, we have seen most of these thick clients disappear. Most of our apps are cloud-based, and have most of the data and intelligence on the server. The rise of the Chrome operating system, and storage solutions such as Dropbox and Google Drive, are examples of the same trend. We have started using Google Docs more frequently than the traditional word processing apps that are installed on our PCs and Macs.

However, this mode of working assumes a continuous internet connection. I do find it very inconvenient that my music app or YouTube stops playing when I am on the London Underground. This was the reason for edge computing, where some data and a lot of the business logic can sit at the client end. A cloud connection will take place only when necessary, thereby making the user experience more seamless.

This can be a particularly useful feature, when machines have to send micro messages to each other, without having to rely on a cloud infrastructure. If there is no cloud infrastructure, the machines rely on the integrity of the network they are part of. In a world where such networks are starting to become increasingly common, we can be exposed to cybercrime on a large scale.

An example of this would be self-driving cars. One of the key use cases of edge computing is said to be the self-driving car industry, where several terabytes of data is expected to be produced on a daily basis. However, most of this data doesn't have to be sent to the cloud in real time. Most of this data is needed by the vehicle and its network of other vehicles to regulate traffic on the road.

A San Francisco-based start-up, Renovo, is working on an edge infrastructure, where self-driving vehicles can interact on the edge among themselves. When the cars go to their recharging points, they can connect to the cloud infrastructure and send the data required at that point. This makes the process a lot more efficient and user friendly, as only the necessary data is being sent to the cloud in real time.

This is a good example of machines capturing and using data in real time through edge computing. However, imagine this network of cars being hacked due to vulnerabilities in the network. Not only can the hacker exploit the data within this network, but they can also create havoc on the road if they wanted to. This is another instance of how innovation is giving rise to new ways of data creation, but there is very little action in terms of how this data is going to be protected.

We discussed in the previous chapter the fact that the internet and the Blockchain industry using RSA- and ECC-based encryption are at risk of attacks in the post-quantum world. This is true for most of the innovation discussed in this chapter so far. However, many of these technology and innovation developments have failed to take into account even some of the basic cyber security defenses.

Therefore, the first step to addressing this problem is to create awareness regarding cybercrime globally. Financial inclusion, healthcare, data access, and payment transactions can all be reasons why a farmer in Africa wants the internet. However, they need to know that their data is vulnerable, and so is their money, once they connect to a network. Much like retail investors in financial products are made aware of the risks associated with using the product, internet users must also understand the risks of doing so.

Major developed and emerging economies have taken note of these vulnerabilities that exist. They understand that being able to tap into these vulnerabilities gives them a major advantage in tapping into the sentiments of the citizens of an enemy country. Using these data loopholes to make subtle changes to the mindsets and behaviors of citizens of another country is seen as a major weapon in cyber wars.

Let's now examine how some of the largest economies of the world are getting into a technological arms race in order to exploit the data that the world is mindlessly creating.

The cyber arms race

The new decade had just dawned, and before we had even got into our stride in the New Year, geopolitical tensions had risen as the US launched a drone attack and killed an Iranian military official, Qasem Soleimani. Iran was expected to retaliate, and they did. However, the military retaliation was expected to be only a small part of their action plan. Washington DC has been preparing for a widespread cyber attack to create chaos in the country.

CNN reported that government officials in the US have been working with cyber security firms such as Dragos, CrowdStrike, and Cloudflare. Several scenarios were created that were designed to understand the vulnerabilities and the potential scale of the threat. Some of those scenarios included attacks on the US power grid, targeting oil and gas firms relying on electricity.

The US elections are planned to take place this year, and cyber attacks could have serious implications on the future of the country. Several companies, including Microsoft and Cloudflare, have offered to provide cyber security to key stakeholders involved in the elections. However, just the amount of attention that this new trend is receiving at the highest levels goes to show how much damage a cyber attack can do to a country as powerful as the United States. It is therefore essential that countries across the world are prepared to combat this new threat.

Thanks to technological innovation, there is no lack of start-ups that are finding solutions to stay on top of cyber attacks. 2019 saw a record high in investments going into cyber security firms. The following chart shows the growth of venture capital investments in this area:

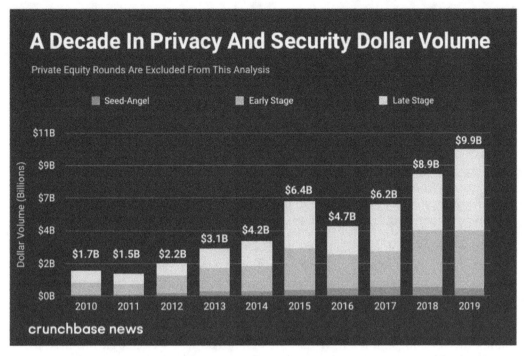

Figure 4: Venture capital investments in the area of cyber security. Source: `https://news.crunchbase.com/news/almost-10b-invested-in-privacy-and-security-companies-in-2019/`

Venture capital investment in cyber security companies reached $10 billion in 2019, up from $1.7 billion in 2010. The global market for cyber security stood at $120 billion in 2019 and is expected to grow to $143 billion by 2021. While cyber security is one side of the coin, investment in technologies such as AI, Blockchain, quantum computing, and IoT afford a nation a competitive advantage over its economic and geopolitical competitors and rivals.

Countries that can use these technologies to capture data better using IoT, store that data safer using Blockchain and a quantum infrastructure, communicate safely using secure networks, and make intelligent decisions using analytics, have an advantage over others. A sign of an innovative economy is the percentage of GDP that it is willing to allocate to research and development.

The higher the R&D investment as a percentage of GDP, the higher the country's commitment toward improving its innovation ecosystem. Let's quickly review the innovation ecosystem across the top countries and compare how they fare on the innovation graph that follows.

United States

The United States has, without a doubt, been the global headquarters of technology innovation. R&D investment as a percentage of GDP may not be as high as some of the Scandinavian countries, but the Silicon Valley ecosystem has been the hub of technology innovation and investment. The sheer magnitude of US GDP sees far more money flow into tech than almost anywhere else in the world. It has become a case study that other countries have wanted to emulate over the years.

Silicon Valley was at the forefront of the dot com boom and bust, and the survivors of that crisis have supported the next generation of entrepreneurs. Venture capital investment in the US hit $105 billion in 2019 across 4,633 deals. Despite the fall in the flow of capital from China due to the trade war, 2019 venture capital investments were higher than in 2018 ($103 billion).

Investment in technologies such as AI, Blockchain, and quantum computing needs to be taken into account to assess how competitive the US is across these deep technologies. Let's look specifically at the quantum computing ecosystem in the US, as that is more relevant for us.

Quite a bit of quantum computing investment has emanated from the large tech giants such as Google, Intel, IBM, and Microsoft. For instance, Google has invested in D-Wave, whose quantum computers are being used quite extensively by the quantum computing community. Similarly, Intel has invested in QuTech and has begun a 10-year collaboration to develop a fault-tolerant quantum computer.

Microsoft and IBM have mostly kept their quantum computing research in-house. IBM has been quite active in this area, and has published its progress on a regular basis. At CES 2020, it announced that it had doubled its quantum volume on its 28-qubit machine from 16 last year to 32 in 2020.

Even academic institutions in the US have been quite involved in R&D within quantum computing. The University of Waterloo set up the **Institute of Quantum Computing** (**IQC**) in 2002 with funding from Mike Lazaridis, the founder of Blackberry. Based on the number of publications in quantum computing, the University of Maryland is another US-based academic institution that scores high.

In an attempt to take the lead in quantum technology, the US President Donald Trump signed the National Quantum Initiative Act in August 2019. This allocates $1.2 billion for quantum computing research. With all this intent, you would think that the US must be leading the initiative in the quantum computing industry, but this is not the case, as the scales of innovation across the globe are now tilting toward the East. China has a massive advantage when it comes to quantum communication.

China leading the world

China has historically been considered the copycat by the technology world. However, the last decade has seen China blindside the rest of the world as its businesses became global. This brought capital into the country like never seen before and they have done well in terms of allocating some of that to technology innovation:

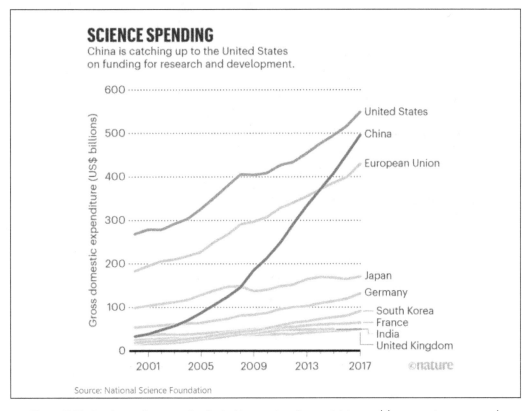

Figure 5: National spending on technological innovation. Source: `https://www.nature.com/articles/d41586-020-00084-7`

Venture investments in China were on the rise through the last decade. In 2018, China saw $107 billion invested across 5,356 deals, but thanks to the trade war, this number fell to $49 billion across 3,348 deals in 2019. However, this hasn't really stopped China's progress in closing the R&D investment gap between them and the United States.

The preceding chart shows how close China has got to the United States as regards technology innovation. But, when it comes to quantum computing, they are most certainly the world leaders. In 2017, China filed twice as many patents as the United States in quantum computing. 70% of patents in quantum technologies were awarded to Chinese universities. The US occupies second place, with 12% of the patents.

China's President Xi has committed several billion dollars' worth of investment in quantum computing with a view to achieving global dominance in the technology. Alibaba's CEO, Jack Ma, has allocated $15 billion across multiple technologies that also includes quantum computing. At this rate, by 2030, China will leave the rest of the world behind in its quest for quantum computing, both based on investment and outcomes.

Let's now take a brief look at what China has achieved so far in this field. Chinese Universities are contributing in a big way to research and development efforts. The following chart brings to life how much Chinese universities and companies are contributing to the field of quantum computing:

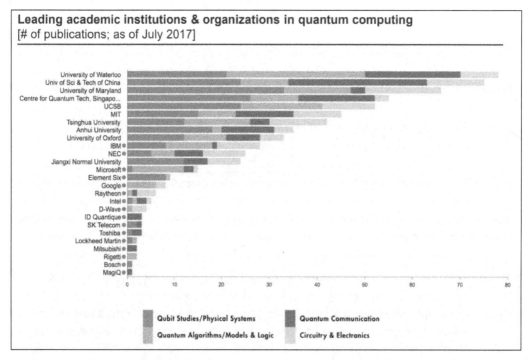

Figure 6: Leading academic institutions and organizations in quantum computing, based on the number of publications. Source: https://quid.com/feed/the-three-leading-academic-institutions-in-quantum-computing

The **University of Science and Technology of China (USTC)**, under the leadership of Jian Wei Pan, has been making rapid strides in quantum computing research. Pan, who is hailed as the "father of quantum," pioneered USTC's efforts in the field of quantum communication. USTC's quantum communication network connects eight cities, including Beijing and Shanghai, using satellites.

In 2016, Pan led China's efforts in launching Micius, the world's first quantum satellite. Using this satellite, video calls were made between Beijing and Vienna using quantum encryption. Clearly, China is the leader when it comes to quantum communication. However, they are still catching up with the US and Europe in the field of quantum computing.

Let's now look at the efforts of Europe and the UK in relation to quantum technologies.

Europe and the United Kingdom

As China and the US are striving for global dominance, throwing several billions into quantum science, Europe and the United Kingdom are steadily making progress with relatively modest research efforts.

UKRI (UK Research and Innovation) is at the forefront of quantum computing R&D and ecosystem development in the UK. UKRI's **National Quantum Technologies Programme (NQTP)** has just surpassed a total investment of £1 billion in the technology. The programme will cover the following aspects across the quantum industry:

- A focus on products and services using quantum technologies.
- Funding for industry-led research activities.
- Ensuring a rich supply chain for quantum projects.
- Venture capital and early-stage investment.

The NQTP programme has made a £120 million investment in four hubs, focusing on different clusters within quantum computing:

- Sensors and Metrology led by Birmingham University will work on quantum sensors and measurement technologies.
- Quantum-enhanced imaging by the QuantIC hub was set up with the involvement of the universities of Glasgow, Bristol, Edinburgh, Oxford, Heriot-Watt, and Strathclyde.

- The **NQIT** (**National Quantum Information Technologies**) hub is led by the University of Oxford. It is focusing on applications such as drug discovery, random number generation, and quantum communications.

- The quantum communications hub, led by the University of York, with the involvement of Bristol University, is focusing on **Quantum Key Distribution** (**QKD**). As a result of their efforts, we may be able to perform a banking transaction on our mobiles secured by quantum technologies.

Following the UK's push toward quantum research and development, Europe didn't want to be left behind. The European Commission, in October 2018, committed €1 billion toward quantum computing, calling it the "Quantum Technology Flagship." The European Research Council is working closely with the University of Bristol to tackle real-life challenges using quantum computing.

The first phase of the Flagship project that runs until 2021 has an allocation of €132 million. This capital will be deployed across 20 projects across four areas:

- Quantum communication
- Quantum simulation
- Quantum computing
- Quantum metrology and sensing

Source: `https://ec.europa.eu/digital-single-market/en/quantum-technologies`

The funding for the technology post 2021 will be part of Europe's Horizon 2020 programme.

Apart from these ecosystem building efforts, Europe has been a key center as regards quantum computing innovation. For instance, the Netherlands has been an important hub for quantum technology. Recognizing that, even Microsoft has set up its quantum labs in the country.

So far, we have looked at the risks that the pace of innovation and rate of data creation are posing in a digital world. We have looked at how nation states are investing billions of dollars in taking a lead with the technology that can give them pole position in the data race. Something that would also be worthy of discussion is the role that quantum networks could play in this context.

The hype surrounding quantum networks

In the section discussing China's focus on quantum communication, we saw that they were able to pioneer quantum-encrypted communication channels that are secure from hackers. Quantum encryption is a good step forward. However, information flow on quantum networks is being hailed as the holy grail of secure communication.

Imagine an internet where nobody can eavesdrop on your messages. Imagine an internet where you can communicate and transact freely without having to worry about data security. That could be possible as qubits lose their states as soon as observed. Therefore, when there is a hacking attempt, the sender and the receiver of the message can identify it. The implications of this technology paradigm for communications in military and defense can hardly be underestimated.

A quantum network could be visualized as a network of three quantum devices that are 50 to 100 kilometers apart. China created the first quantum satellite in Micius, and Europe is trying to stay a close second. The Delft University of Technology in the Netherlands is working on creating a quantum network that could become the future of the internet.

Quantum entanglement can be used to create a quantum network. The first step is to create what are called "entangled nodes." This is achieved by a process whereby entangled protons are exchanged between these nodes. Once these nodes are entangled, entire qubits can be transmitted between them, without physically sending the qubits across the network.

This is precisely what Micius, the first quantum satellite, did in order to communicate across several ground stations. Entangled photon pairs were created using crystals and lasers. These entangled photon pairs were split and transmitted to different ground stations. Therefore, quantum information could be transmitted between these stations, which were located in the cities of Delingha and Lijiang, 1,203 kilometers away.

This has been hailed as an achievement that is a trillion times more efficient than using the best fiber technologies. However, the Micius experiment transmitted 6 million entangled pairs per second, of which only one pair reached the ground. Therefore, there is still a lot of work to be done.

Despite these challenges, using the property of entanglement is the safest way to communicate. The Institute of Quantum Optics and Quantum Information in Austria, and the Delft University of Technology in the Netherlands, have collaborated to prototype a quantum network.

The teams worked on manipulating calcium ions using lasers to create a qubit with the superposition of two energy states. The ion also emitted a photon with a qubit encoded in its polarization states. As the qubits are entangled, they can be transmitted to two quantum stations that are separated by a distance and can be used for communication.

During the experiment, the teams tested a process called entanglement swapping. In this process, the two nodes would transmit an entangled photon to a station in the middle. The photons will be measured at the station in the middle, which will result in them losing entanglement with their ions. However, this process caused the two ions to become entangled with one another.

The teams are now looking at building a network across three cities in the Netherlands that will use entanglement swapping to transmit quantum information. There is clearly a long way to go for quantum networks to be mainstream. It is still early days and it is hard to say that quantum networks would be the future of the internet. However, scientists across the world are now making progress on a regular basis that shows signs of promise.

If the promises come true, then we may be able to build a safe infrastructure for the internet. We could also build a secure internet of machines such as self-driving cars that can exist on the edge without having to rely on a cloud infrastructure to make decisions.

Conclusion

In the last 30 years, human beings have become a cyber race, entirely reliant on the internet for their livelihoods. I can imagine a day without electricity, food, or even water. But a day without the internet feels unimaginable. We live in a day and age where children see switching off the Wi-Fi as punishment. A fused light bulb that has stopped working is seen as a light bulb that doesn't have internet access anymore.

We talk to smart speakers to remind us and to play our favorite songs, thereby leaving a piece of us online. We have our fitness data stored on cloud infrastructure, hoping that it would reduce our insurance premiums, or help us win a step count competition. Thanks to payments and remittance technologies, we are able to send money to our friends and family across the world at will.

With so much of our data sitting online, what we often forget is how secure it is. The idea of losing our data to a hacker as an individual can be scary. However, imagine a scenario where a country loses its data to hackers. If hackers can take control of citizens' identities, defense information, national power grids, and nuclear power sites (the list is endless), it could spell disaster.

Countries no longer require sophisticated machine guns or drones or atom bombs to hurt their enemies. Cyber attacks, planned and orchestrated at scale, can bring a nation to its knees even better than sporadic drone attacks. In this chapter, I have discussed why innovation has made us all vulnerable to such cyber threats.

However, with widespread awareness efforts, and some technological breakthroughs, we may be able to move to a secure state for all our data. The first challenge is, who will get there first? And the second challenge is, can quantum technologies live up to the hype?

It is still early days to say with any degree of confidence that quantum networks will be the future of the internet. There are sporadic small-scale successes that we see with scientific experiments across the world. However, broader achievements are needed across several parties involved in the quantum space in order to make a meaningful impact within a reasonable time frame.

There is a lot of hype, but somewhere amid all the hype, there is still hope. Let's now have a quick recap of the key discussion points raised thus far in the following chapter.

17
Conclusion – Blue Skies

Life is like a box of chocolates, you never know what you're going get.

– Forrest Gump

Considering the wise words of Forrest Gump, the opportunity to write this book has definitely been "like a box of chocolates". Now that I am in the last chapter of this book, I can say that it has been a rewarding, humbling, and an amazing learning experience.

After two years of delivering a weekly blog post at Daily Fintech, the second most read FinTech blog in the world, I knew I could write. I had planned to begin a writing career in 2020. But the opportunity to write a book arrived a year earlier than I anticipated. I knew life had thrown me a curve ball, that I was well positioned to hit out of the park.

Many of my friends have been working on books in AI, Blockchain, and quantum computing over the last couple of years. When I looked at authors of books in quantum technologies, I saw physicists and computer scientists. I was definitely not one of those. I had to carve out a thesis for the book that focused on what I was a specialist in.

In one of my earliest conversations on quantum computing with a Silicon Valley entrepreneur, she had mentioned that one needs to have a PhD in Physics, Math, and Computer Science to get quantum technologies completely. I knew it was a lighthearted comment, but there was some truth in it. Therefore, when I was developing the thesis of the book, I knew I had to stick to my strengths.

My strengths came from my journey as a **Venture Capital** (**VC**) investor over the past 5 to 6 years. My experience as a VC had taught me two key lessons over the years. The first one was that technology was just a means to an end, and it is essential to focus on the "*So What?*" The second lesson was that a technologist should be able to keep the narrative simple.

Before I started my VC career, I was working in banks as a data and technology specialist. It often involved working with Managing Directors and C-Suite executives. Many of these highly accomplished individuals looked at technology as a silver bullet. They felt there was a special technology out there that could solve their business model and process inefficiencies. I had to keep stressing to them that technology was just a means to an end.

Therefore, as a VC, one of the key focus areas for me was to look beyond the hype. I had to focus on the business applications and viability of technologies I was evaluating. In 2019 alone, I had the pleasure of looking at over 400 technology start-ups. This number would go past 2,000 if we took the last five years into account. This is pretty typical for most people in the VC industry.

This experience had placed me in a unique position to look beyond the hype that I was witnessing around quantum technologies. Every time I heard about a concept in this space, the first question I would ask is, "so what problem is it going to solve?" My approach to this book has been exactly that.

I didn't want to cover the Math or the Physics behind quantum computing extensively, because I wasn't equipped to talk about that. However, I knew how to look past the hype of a technology and focus on what it brought to the table, and the potential business applications.

The other key attribute that I have developed as a VC is keeping the narrative simple. Often times, I see entrepreneurs with strong technology backgrounds struggling to move away from their jargon. The scientific field has people who will be able to cope with such language and explanation, but when a technology is in the process of going mainstream, it is essential to create a connection with the wider ecosystem. That connection can only happen by simplifying the narrative around the technology.

Beneficiaries of these technologies, be it businesses or consumers, should be able to relate to the applications of the technology. For instance, as a consumer of a bank, you only care about what mortgage rates, credit limits, and deposit rates you get from them. You don't care about if they used Monte Carlo methods or Historical Simulation to assess their credit risk.

This book essentially is a culmination of all these thought processes. It has been extremely difficult to simplify something as complex as quantum computing. At the same time, it was a delightful experience to explore quantum computing from an application perspective. In this chapter, I will bring together the different dimensions of quantum technologies that I have tried to cover in this book.

Let's first pay attention to the elephant in the room. How hyped is quantum computing? Every technology goes through ups and downs, and quantum computing is no exception. Let's consider where we are with quantum computing, based on what we have discussed in this book.

Is there hype?

The principles of quantum mechanics that quantum computing relies on have been around for more than a century. The idea of quantum computers, as we discussed in the early chapters of this book, was introduced in the 1980s by Richard Feynman. Since then, every time there was a groundbreaking algorithm like Shor's or Grover's algorithms, it has added to the hype.

On a similar note, where there has been a proof of concept conducted successfully like China's quantum satellite initiative (Micius), optimism goes through the roof. That's just the way human beings are wired to react due to the increased dopamine levels arising from the newness of these inventions. That is also what keeps the ecosystem optimistic and in the hunt for new breakthroughs, despite the odds.

Recall my interview with Dave Snelling, and the picture he drew for me:

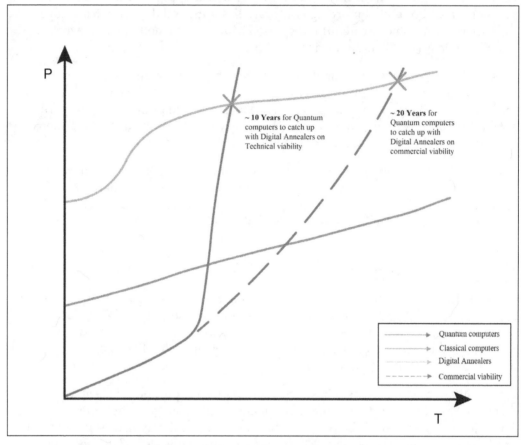

Figure 1: A rough drawing by Dave Snelling, explaining the trends in annealing

Very much like the field of artificial intelligence, quantum computing has gone through several ebbs and flows since the 1930s. During my discussions with Dave Snelling from Fujitsu, he mentioned that quantum computers are between 15-20 years away from mainstream adoption. We discussed how some specific capabilities of quantum annealers could happen quicker than gate-based quantum computers.

Therefore, we may be able to see solutions for optimization problems a little sooner than Dave's timelines. Please see the preceding figure for an illustration. Organizations like Fujitsu are also working toward bridging the gap between classical and quantum computers through digital annealers. There are several applications that we have highlighted throughout this book that are made possible by digital annealers, and many of them are already in a commercial environment.

However, one consistent aspect of this technology that several players have tried to leverage is "quantum supermacy". Quantum supremacy has been used even by the likes of Google to create PR about their initiatives around the technology. Even Gartner are not immune to chipping into this hype. Their following chart plots expectations for AI over time:

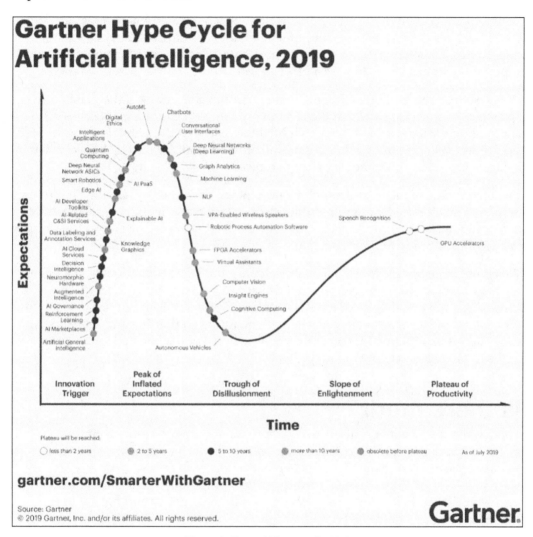

Figure 2: Garter AI hype cycle, 2019

The preceding "hype chart" shows Gartner's view of how far machine learning powered by quantum computers is from reaching peak hype. I personally don't believe this field will peak within the next ten years. We are going to see a couple of more peaks and troughs in the next ten to fifteen years before the technology goes mainstream.

Dave Snelling and many others whom I interviewed for this book provided their thoughts on quantum supremacy. For instance, according to Dave, quantum supremacy cannot be just about processing speed. It has to be about the ability of quantum computers to solve problems that haven't been possible by classical computers within reasonable time.

Google's claims about performing a calculation in a few days, where it would take 10,000 years for a classical computer, may not necessarily satisfy the scientific community. Therefore, when there is a claim from a firm about achieving quantum supremacy, it must be taken with a pinch of salt.

One desirable outcome of the hype around quantum computing is that it helps raise awareness around the risks that the technology can pose. During my discussion with Dinesh Nagarajan from IBM, he highlighted the risks that the technology could pose to existing cryptographic techniques used by the internet. He also highlighted that, in large corporations, technology change typically takes 7-8 years.

Therefore, some of the hype around the technology could help quantum computing to receive much-needed attention from the boards of these firms that are vulnerable in a post-quantum world. As the technology evolves, these organizations can prepare to be agile and ready to face the threat.

This is not to justify the irrational exuberance around some of the cool technologies we have in today's data-driven world. It is hard to not have that excitement, considering the possibilities of the technology. However, it is important to understand the reality of where we are with quantum computing and set realistic expectations based upon that. Let's now look at some of the interesting use cases of the technologies we covered in the book.

Is there merit?

There was a recent conversation on Twitter that I got dragged into about the merits of quantum technology. The question posed was if I saw merit and real-world applications from quantum technologies. The answer is yes, because, at least in the last year, I have seen a few quantum computing startups moving into commercializing their solution. However, I would be cautious and not get too excited about these solutions just yet.

Most of these companies have solutions that can have groundbreaking impacts on various aspects of our lives. But they are yet to prove themselves in a live environment, at scale. Solutions I have come across just in the last 12 months are spread across diverse fields including healthcare, climate technology, financial services, and even oil and gas. Most of these are problems that are hard for classical computers to solve.

Despite the state of maturity of the technology, there is no denying that there is potential. Health and wealth have been two key areas where innovation can have massive impact on the ground. This is especially true in emerging markets where there are billions of people without good access to healthcare or financial services. Let's briefly touch upon the use cases that we discussed in the book both in the chapters covering interviews and others.

Healthcare

We touched upon use cases where quantum computing could be used to improve the process of drug discovery. There are two angles to this. One is where the technology can shrink the time to market for drugs as it can simulate scenarios where the drug can be effective or otherwise. This process hasn't been as efficient with classical computers.

The second aspect of this use case is the quality of the fit of a drug to a specific health condition can be assessed with a greater degree of confidence than using classical computers. Putting these two aspects together, we can start seeing better drugs delivered faster to market.

Quantum computers can also help with diagnostics and treatment of complex health issues such as cancer. There are several variables that a doctor would need to take into account while prescribing the right course of action for a cancer patient. Using quantum computers could give us a solution that takes into account the correlations between the different variables.

Today, this process is mostly manual, where doctors assess the criticality of the condition, the body part affected, and the potential impact of the cancer cells on the healthy ones before deciding on the treatment method. Having looked at health, let's briefly touch upon the wealth use cases.

Financial services

This is an industry in which I have spent most of my career. As a result, I have had first-hand experience of the data challenges that the financial services industry has. Going back to Fujitsu's Digital Annealer, we are already seeing live applications inspired by quantum methodologies.

The Annealer has already proven to be much faster than classical computers for problems such as portfolio rebalancing and risk management for instance. While the financial viability of performing a portfolio rebalancing on an instantaneous basis is still unclear, the ability to do so would certainly be useful. Especially in times of market stress conditions, if a portfolio manager wants to quickly reshuffle their portfolio and reduce risks, the ability to do it instantaneously would be a great boon.

I have worked in a regulated environment where the need to perform some of the risk analytics in real time was vital. Most hedging decisions rely upon risk reporting capabilities that are computed overnight. Being able to make these decisions and corresponding changes to the portfolio instantaneously or intraday as a crisis unfolds in the market would result in a massive advantage within the financial sector.

Financial services are also a field where there are many correlated variables that need to be taken into account to compute an efficient risk-return profile. This correlated variables problem is also true in understanding the possibility of a recession, for instance. Modeling these possibilities with a high degree of confidence is something that is also being worked on by quantum experts across the world.

Having looked at financial services, let's briefly consider quantum computing's implications for logistics.

Logistics

Logistics is a field that has some of the hardest problems for classical computers to solve. We discussed the shortest flight path problem and the travelling salesman problem. These are optimization problems that could be solved using digital and quantum annealers.

We touched upon the experiments that Airbus is undertaking with the quantum computing community. They are trying to model the interaction of air with the wings of their planes. Understanding the aerodynamics of a flight better can add fuel efficiencies during take-off and landing. This can be a huge win for a world that is in a climate emergency, and of course lead to higher profits for the companies achieving greater efficiency.

Climate

That leads us nicely into climate-related use cases for quantum computers. Let's take the fertilizer industry, for instance. Nitrogen-based fertilizers are the most widely used and are the most in demand from the agriculture industry. However, the current manufacturing process is energy-intensive and has a high carbon footprint.

Ironically, nature deals with nitrogen fixation in a much simpler and energy-efficient way. The inability to model nitrogen fixation in lab conditions has crippled our attempts to emulate this more efficient manufacturing process. There are several ongoing research projects attempting to model nitrogen fixation using quantum computers. This will be a huge win for humanity, as we have a pressing need to move to more sustainable industrial processes.

We also discussed other innovative use cases like climate modeling. Today, climate modeling is a far cry from being able to model the vast complexity of our world. There are AI startups that are looking to solve this problem. We must account for a great number of interrelated variables, from carbon emissions, to ocean currents. We must also account for feedback loops such as melting glaciers; this phenomenon leads to less global ice coverage. Ice reflects the sun's rays. Therefore, less ice means more heat being absorbed by the Earth, which in turn melts more ice and so on. If we wish to model our changing climate effectively, we will need more powerful technologies process this complexity, ideally in real-time.

A quantum computer can take into account the correlation between these variables and provide us a clearer view of where we are, with a higher degree of confidence. We also discussed other potential use cases such as modeling carbon capture using quantum computers. Let's now touch upon the use of quantum computers for election modeling.

Moving on from global climate, let's briefly consider how quantum computing will impact our political climates.

Elections

The past 5 years have seen a major shift in global democratic processes where social media has played a significant role in governments being elected. This may not come across as great as an issue as healthcare, financial markets, or climate change, but policy makers coming to power in major economies like the US, Europe, India, or China have the ability to change the lives of billions of people.

Max Henderson kindly offered his insights from his work at QxBranch, where he has been using quantum annealing for election modeling. I would be keen to follow up with him later this year as the American elections unfold in 2020.

That should give you a view of the potential of the technology. Yes, it is early days. Yes, there are challenges. But the possibilities are simply mind-boggling, and I am glad that humanity will be moving toward a brighter future with such breakthrough innovation. Let's now look at the roadblocks ahead that must be overcome before we see this innovation really take root.

A bumpy road ahead

That section title is a give-away in some sense. There is sometimes skepticism and cynicism about the possibilities of quantum technologies, because there are major roadblocks that we need to clear. We can't talk about the rosy future with all of the cool applications that entails, without acknowledging the "if"s and the "but"s involved.

We had an interview with Sam McArdle dedicated to error correction, because this is a major blocker for quantum computers to go mainstream. The error correction occurs because quantum particles storing information interact with the external environment and therefore lose the information that they hold over time.

Unlike traditional computers, quantum computers rely on qubits. Information held in qubits cannot be copied into other qubits for fault tolerance. This is a limitation and a feature of quantum particles that makes this field both challenging and exciting. However, without finding ways to keep quantum particles like photons that carry information, it is hard to see quantum computers going mainstream.

In today's quantum computers, there can be a thousand noisy qubits for every error-free logical qubit. There is a high level of redundancy required in order to handle errors in these machines. However, this needs to change for better adoption of quantum computers. In our discussion with Sam, we touched upon NISQ techniques where these noisy qubits can be used for computing for certain business applications.

This is currently being explored in fields like chemical research, where noise can be a feature and not a disruption. Chemical reactions can be modelled using noisy qubits that represent the noisy environment that they would occur in reality.

These challenges need to be addressed before we can dream of a world where quantum computers can play a major role. One of the key themes of the book has been how quantum computers can pose a threat to existing cryptography that most of data and digital value interactions rely on. Let's take a brief look at that.

The collision course

The first time I learned about the potential scenario where quantum computers can get through cryptographic techniques that we use today, I was quite astounded. Quantum computing at that point became a major technology paradigm for me, which has the potential to be as big as the PC or the internet.

The possibility of quantum technology putting the internet at risk is one challenge, but the lack of awareness that the common person has about this possibility is a greater issue in my view. We live in a day and age where data and money transactions have become frictionless, invisible, and therefore mindless.

We are also entering the age of machines where 70% of the potential 175 zettabytes of data that will be created by 2030 will be from machines. Self-driving cars, wearables, and home appliances that transmit information are all creating huge volumes of highly sensitive and personal information. It is indeed a scary proposition that most of these machines will be at the risk of being hacked the moment quantum computers are able to scale.

On another note, Blockchain, which is a very recent invention, has resulted in a flurry of applications across the world. Many of these applications store value, data, and some even store legally binding information. Most Blockchain solutions today use RSA or ECC algorithms to protect data interactions. Some of them even claim these security mechanisms as their differentiation.

However, unless these Blockchain applications move to quantum-proof cryptography, they could be obsolete very soon. We discussed lattice-b cryptography and code-based cryptography that can be categorized as post-quantum cryptography. The potential risk of quantum computing will make users move away from these solutions even if quantum technologies aren't mainstream.

This, when combined with the Blockchain winter we are seeing now, could mean that the entire ecosystem needs to introspect. There are some Blockchain or Distributed Ledger technology platforms like IOTA and QRL that claim they are quantum-proof. However, they represent the minority of the Blockchain community; those who are better prepared to address the risk.

There needs to be a coordinated effort across regulators, governments, and large corporations to make key applications on the internet quantum-proof. The **National Institute of Standards and Technology (NIST)** are conducting a search for post quantum cryptographic techniques that can protect the internet.

During my discussion with Dinesh Nagarajan, he mentioned that it is critical for organizations to be "crypto-agile". The dot com boom brought about the agile software development methodology. The quantum era will necessitate solutions to have crypto-agility. This would mean that their infrastructure, platform, and application layers will need to have the ability to swap and change the cryptography that they use. This ability will ensure that they can upgrade the cryptography in a short time and be prepared for any potential cyber risks.

We discussed the challenge that organizations have in preparing for the quantum threat. Organizations need to go through a maturity cycle that results in state of crypto agility. However, most of these large organizations are used to taking 7 to 8 years to upgrade their technology platforms. Therefore, there is some nervousness that if there are any major quantum computing breakthroughs during that time, these organizations are not yet prepared.

In essence, it is not just the Blockchain ecosystem that is on a collision course with quantum technologies. The world that is on the internet is on this collision course too. Therefore, it is imperative that a sustainable cyber solution for data and value exchanges are identified and deployed.

We will also need leadership and governance across continents to stay on track in terms of evolving technology innovation and how that could create new cyber threats to a data driven world. As and when threats are detected within a technology or a platform, controls need to be identified to ensure they are safe for businesses and consumers to use.

We are entering an age where we will not have decades to protect our data. We must be able to do it within a few years, if not months, if we are to keep pace with the power of quantum computing. On that note, let's now touch upon how nations across the world are gearing up for quantum computing.

Nation states and ecosystems

When you have a technological advantage to get hold of the defense secrets of an enemy nation, would you hold back? If the technology allowed you to take control of internet, healthcare information, and information of big financial transactions, wouldn't that tempt you to invest in the technology?

That is precisely why China have invested several billions of dollars into AI and quantum computing. They are clearly leaders within the field of quantum communication with their Micius initiative. This has spurred action across the world as the US, Europe, the UK, Canada, and even India jumping onto the quantum computing band wagon. They have all each allocated about $1 billion for quantum computing research.

It is good that governments are getting involved in the evolution of their regional quantum computing ecosystems. That would help ensure best practices are generally shared, and certain standards are followed across the ecosystem. In the UK, for instance, there are four quantum computing hubs led by different academic institutions. Startups, corporates, and investors collaborate with these hubs to make the most of the research capability.

Despite these efforts, the risk that one of these nations getting ahead in the quantum race cannot be ignored. Even today, we are not sure if any of these nations have actually cracked the quantum puzzle. If one of them have managed to achieve quantum supremacy, there are chances that they are going to be quiet about it. Having a technology advantage in this day and age is similar to having an advantage with nuclear weapons in the post-war era.

Geopolitical wars in future could be fought in a more subtle way, where data is the oil and technology is the weapon. When you have the cyber advantage over an enemy nation, you can disrupt critical infrastructure such as power grids, traffic networks, banking services, hospitals, and all other systems that rely on the internet.

That could cause large scale disruption, bring the capital markets down for days, and lead to billions in losses to the affected nation.

Let's hope that countries build suitable defenses and controls before their adversaries figure out how to cause such damage.

The sky is blue

I am an optimist at heart, despite my VC job where I must make realistic assessments of technology startups. I still have to make optimistic predictions that they will break through their technological, operational, and market barriers. In doing so, they would help achieve high returns for my fund and my investors.

The best part of being a VC is that the job acts like a window into the future. This is because we get early access to innovative companies across industries. Even if a fraction of them succeed at disrupting value chains and ecosystems at scale, the world could be a different place in a few years. By investing in such innovation, we can watch that transition from a nascent state.

With quantum technology companies, I have the opportunity of doing just that. 2019 was perhaps the first time we had several quantum technology companies knock on our doors for funding. They are first movers, but they also have the unenviable job of penetrating or creating a market for their solutions. I am sure that in 2020, the space will start looking different.

In 2020, many of these early movers will be closer to identifying market fits for their products and services. Some of them may even have pilots and live deployments in a commercial environment. It is going to be an exciting few years where we will see excitement, frustration, breakthroughs, roadblocks, and crazy growth.

In this roller coaster ride that quantum computing promises to offer, one attribute of humanity will persist – hope. A hope that we are all working toward a better future for the world. A hope that despite all odds, we will arrive at our destination and achieve our vision for ourselves, our organizations, our countries, our world, and for humanity itself.

Other Books You May Enjoy

If you enjoyed this book, you may be interested in these other books by Packt:

Dancing with Qubits

Robert S. Sutor

ISBN: 978-1-83882-736-6

- See how quantum computing works, delve into the math behind it, what makes it different, and why it is so powerful with this quantum computing textbook

- Discover the complex, mind-bending mechanics that underpin quantum systems

- Understand the necessary concepts behind classical and quantum computing

- Refresh and extend your grasp of essential mathematics, computing, and quantum theory

- Explore the main applications of quantum computing to the fields of scientific computing, AI, and elsewhere

- Examine a detailed overview of qubits, quantum circuits, and quantum algorithm

Advanced Deep Learning with TensorFlow 2 and Keras

Rowel Atienza

ISBN: 978-1-83882-165-4

- Use mutual information maximization techniques to perform unsupervised learning
- Use segmentation to identify the pixel-wise class of each object in an image
- Identify both the bounding box and class of objects in an image using object detection
- Learn the building blocks for advanced techniques - MLPs, CNN, and RNNs
- Understand deep neural networks - including ResNet and DenseNet
- Understand and build autoregressive models – autoencoders, VAEs, and GANs
- Discover and implement deep reinforcement learning methods

Leave a review - let other readers know what you think

Please share your thoughts on this book with others by leaving a review on the site that you bought it from. If you purchased the book from Amazon, please leave us an honest review on this book's Amazon page. This is vital so that other potential readers can see and use your unbiased opinion to make purchasing decisions, we can understand what our customers think about our products, and our authors can see your feedback on the title that they have worked with Packt to create. It will only take a few minutes of your time, but is valuable to other potential customers, our authors, and Packt. Thank you!

Index

www.ingramcontent.com/pod-product-compliance
Lightning Source LLC
LaVergne TN
LVHW081515050326
832903LV00025B/1500

* 9 7 8 1 8 3 8 6 4 7 7 6 6 *